HUNTINGTON LIBRARY
PUBLICATIONS

JOHN BALE'S

King Johan

EDITED WITH AN INTRODUCTION

AND NOTES

BY BARRY B. ADAMS

THE HUNTINGTON LIBRARY

SAN MARINO, CALIFORNIA

1969

Copyright 1969

By the Henry E. Huntington Library and Art Gallery
Library of Congress Catalog Card Number 67-12048

Printed and designed by
Princeton University Press, Princeton, New Jersey

CONTENTS

ABBREVIATED REFERENCES

Ann. mon.: Annales monastici, ed. Henry Richards Luard, Rolls Series 36. 5 vols. London, 1864-69.

Apology: The Apology of Iohan Bale agaynste a Ranke Papyst. . . . London, [1550?].

Brut, English prose, ed. Brie: *The Brut, or The Chronicles of England*, ed. Friedrich W. D. Brie, Early English Text Society, OS, 131, 136. 2 pts. in 1. London, 1906-08.

Catalogus: John Bale, *Scriptorum illustrium majoris Brytanniae . . . catalogus*. 2 vols. Basle, 1557-59.

Collier: *Kynge Johan: A Play in Two Parts by John Bale*, ed. J. Payne Collier, Camden Society. London, 1838.

Craik: Thomas Wallace Craik, *The Tudor Interlude: Stage, Costume, and Acting*. London, 1958.

Creeth: John Bale, *King Johan*, in *Tudor Plays: An Anthology of Early English Drama*, ed. Edmund Creeth, Anchor Octavo. Garden City, New York, 1966.

Davies: W. T. Davies, "A Bibliography of John Bale," *Oxford Bibliographical Society Proceedings and Papers*, V, iv (1939), 201-279.

Elson: John Elson, "Studies in the King John Plays," in *Joseph Quincy Adams Memorial Studies*, ed. James G. McManaway et al. Washington, D.C., 1948.

Eulogium: Eulogium (historiarum sive temporis): chronicon ab condito usque ad annum Domini M.CCC.LXVI., a monacho quodam Malmesburiensi exaratum, ed. Frank Scott Haydon, Rolls Series 9. 3 vols. London, 1858-63.

Fabyan: *The New Chronicles of England and France, in Two Parts, by Robert Fabyan*, ed. Henry Ellis. London, 1811.

Farmer: *The Dramatic Writings of John Bale*, ed. John S. Farmer, Early English Dramatists. London, 1907.

Foxe (1563): John Foxe, *Actes and Monuments of These Latter and Perillous Dayes. . . .* London, 1563.

Foxe (1570): *Actes and Monumentes*, 2nd ed. 2 vols. London, 1570.

Foxe (1576): *Actes and Monumentes*, 3rd ed. 2 vols. London, 1576.

Grafton: Richard Grafton, *A Chronicle at Large and Meere History of the Affayres of Englande and Kinges of the Same. . . .* 2 vols. London, 1569.

Higden: *Polychronicon Ranulphi Higden, monachi Cestrensis*, ed. Joseph Rawson Lumby, Rolls Series 41. 9 vols. London, 1865-86.

Holinshed: Raphael Holinshed, *Chronicles of England, Scotland and Ireland*. 6 vols. London, 1807-08.

Index: John Bale, *Index Britanniae scriptorum, . . . Index of British and Other Writers*, ed. Reginald Lane Poole with the help of Mary Bateson. Oxford, 1902.

Manly: John Bale, *King Johan*, in Vol. I of *Specimens of the Pre-Shaksperean Drama*, ed. John Matthews Manly, Athenæum Press Series. Boston, 1897.

Meaux Abbey chronicle: Thomas de Burton, *Chronica monasterii de Melsa*, ed. Edward A. Bond, Rolls Series 43. 3 vols. London, 1866-68.

Miller: Edwin Shepard Miller, "The Roman Rite in Bale's *King John*," *PMLA*, LXIV (1949), 802-822.

Moser: Otto Moser, *Untersuchungen über die Sprache John Bale's*. Berlin, 1902.

Norgate: Kate Norgate, *John Lackland*. London, 1902.

Pafford and Greg: *King Johan by John Bale*, ed. John Henry Pyle Pafford and Walter Wilson Greg, Malone Society Reprints. [London], 1931.

Painter: Sidney Painter, *The Reign of King John*. Baltimore, 1949.

Pammachius: Thomas Kirchmeyer [Naogeorgus], *Pammachivs*, ed. Johannes Bolte and Erich Schmidt. Berlin, 1891.

Matthew Paris, *Chronica: Chronica majora*, ed. Henry Richards Luard, Rolls Series 57. 7 vols. London, 1872-83.

Matthew Paris, *Historia: Matthaei Parisiensis, monachi Sancti Albani, historia Anglorum*, ed. Frederic Madden, Rolls Series 44. 3 vols. London, 1866-69.

Obedience: William Tyndale, *The Obedience of a Christen Man and How Christen Rulers Ought to Governe. . . .* [Antwerp], 1528.

Pollard: John Bale, *King Johan* [selections], in *English Miracle Plays, Moralities and Interludes*, ed. Alfred W. Pollard. 8th ed. revised. Oxford, 1927.

Ralph of Coggeshall: *Radulphi de Coggeshall chronicon Anglicanum*, ed. Joseph Stevenson, Rolls Series 66. London, 1875.

Robert of Gloucester: *The Metrical Chronicle of Robert of Gloucester*, ed. William Aldis Wright, Rolls Series 86. 2 vols. London, 1887.

Roger of Wendover: *Rogeri de Wendover liber qui dicitur flores historiarum*, ed. Henry G. Hewlett, Rolls Series 84. 3 vols. London, 1886-89.

Spivack: Bernard Spivack, *Shakespeare and the Allegory of Evil: The History of a Metaphor in Relation to His Major Villains*. New York, 1958.

Summarium: John Bale, *Illustrium maioris Britanniae scriptorum . . . summarium*. Wesel, 1549 [i.e., 1548].

Three Laws: A Comedy Concernynge Thre Lawes von Johan Bale, ed. Arnold Schroeer in *Anglia*, V (1882), 137-264.

Tilley: Morris Palmer Tilley, *A Dictionary of the Proverbs in England in the Sixteenth and Seventeenth Centuries*. Ann Arbor, 1950.

Tr. Reign: The Troublesome Raigne of John, King of England, ed. Charles Praetorius. 2 vols. London, 1888.

Walter of Coventry: *The Historical Collections of Walter of Coventry*, ed. William Stubbs, Rolls Series 58. 2 vols. London, 1872-73.

DNB	*Dictionary of National Biography*
EDD	*English Dialect Dictionary*
EETS	Early English Text Society
EHR	*English Historical Review*
JEGP	*Journal of English and Germanic Philology*
MLN	*Modern Language Notes*
MLR	*Modern Language Review*
N&Q	*Notes & Queries*
OED	*Oxford English Dictionary*

INTRODUCTION

TEXT

THE MANUSCRIPT

JOHN BALE's most ambitious dramatic work, the historical morality *King Johan*, is preserved in a unique manuscript copy, MS. HM 3, at the Huntington Library in San Marino, California. The play was not printed until 1838, when the Camden Society published an edition prepared by John Payne Collier. It is in the introduction to this edition that we find the earliest account of the manuscript. Collier claimed that it was unknown to him when the first edition of his *History of English Dramatic Poetry* was published (1831) and that it had only recently been acquired by the Duke of Devonshire from among some papers probably belonging to the Corporation of Ipswich.[1] The only other evidence touching on the early history of the manuscript is contained in a small blue folder, also at the Huntington and labeled "from HM 3." At one time two leaves detached from the manuscript and unavailable to Collier in 1838 had been sewn into this folder, which Collier has inscribed as follows:

> The M.S. Copy of the Play which I bought for the Duke of Devonshire many years ago was deficient of these ensuing leaves which I have recently obtained from a Mr Pulman who was a friend of W Fitch. In fact they ought to have formed part of the Dukes MS, from which they had been abstracted before I bought it. I. P. C.
>
> I have copied them for my "King Johan" printed by the Camden Society.[2]

Fitch is mentioned in another notation on the same folder, this in a hand and ink different from those of Collier's note:

---

[1] *Kynge Johan*, pp. v-vi.

[2] Collier's transcript of these two leaves is still at the Huntington. For some reason he never published it, even though the Duke of Devonshire, in a letter dated December 4, 1847, granted him permission to do so. The Duke's letter to Collier is no longer extant; its contents were reported by Willy Bang in the introduction to *Bales Kynge Johan, nach der Handschrift in der Chatsworth Collection* (a photographic facsimile of the manuscript), in *Materialien zur Kunde des älteren englischen Dramas*, XXV (Louvain, 1909).

[1]

These two Manuscript Leaves were stitched in a printed Copy of the play of "King Johan"—belonging to M^r. Wm Stevenson Fitch of Ipswich; and the following memorandum was in the book in the hand writing of Mr Fitch—

"2 leaves of the manuscript play from which this was printed, with Marginal Notes by Bale, and differing from the printed part."

Apparently this is Pulman's note, but nothing that is known of him or of Fitch throws any additional light on the manuscript's provenance or history.[3] It seems to have remained in the collection of the Duke of Devonshire until 1914, when it was acquired by Mr. Huntington as part of the Kemble-Devonshire collection.[4]

The manuscript is a composite one, written in two distinct hands at different times. The part written first, consisting of a single gathering of eleven sheets in folio, was designed as an independent production and later expanded by a second scribe, who inserted two leaves of an irregular size within the folio manuscript and added a number of quarto leaves to the end. The final four leaves of the folio manuscript had been detached and mislaid by 1838; the text of the first two of these—those eventually recovered and copied by Collier—has been completely canceled with large X's, except that the initial thirty-four lines of the first leaf have been left intact. Since the text in the added quarto leaves carries on without interruption from the point of cancellation, it is clear that the quarto leaves were intended to replace all of the last four folio leaves except for these thirty-four lines. There can be no doubt of this, even though the final two leaves of the folio manuscript are still missing.

At a time when all four detached folio leaves were missing, the

[3] Fitch has been identified as postmaster at Ipswich and a collector of manuscripts who died in 1859. See Pafford and Greg, p. vi.

[4] There is no notice of the manuscript in the *Catalogue of the Library at Chatsworth*, 4 vols. (London, 1879), or in Sotheby, Wilkinson & Hodge's *Chatsworth Library: Kemble-Devonshire Collection of English Plays & Play-bills* (London, [1914]). Neither Collier's *Bibliographical and Critical Account of the Rarest Books in the English Language*, 4 vols. (New York, 1866), nor the second edition of his *History of English Dramatic Poetry*, 3 vols. (London, 1879), contains any new facts about its history. The sale of a portion of the Devonshire collection to Mr. Huntington is described in the *New York Times*, March 19, 1914, p. 6; although the Bale manuscript is not mentioned, it no doubt was included among the four thousand items which changed hands at this time. See George Sherburn, "Huntington Library Collections," *Huntington Library Bulletin*, I, No. 1 (May 1931), 42-43.

pages of the composite manuscript were numbered in ink from 1 to 63. According to this pagination, the original manuscript of eleven sheets fills pages 1-22, 24-25, and 27-38; the two leaves recovered subsequent to pagination (arbitrarily designated pp. *1-*4) bear numbers that have no relevance to any arrangement of the manuscript.[5] The two leaves inserted by the second scribe are paged 23 and 26 (versos blank and unnumbered); the quarto leaves added at the end are paged 39-63. There is also an inclusive pencil foliation, added at a time when the composite manuscript was substantially in its present state.

From this summary description of the physical makeup of the manuscript it is clear that we have not just a composite manuscript but two separate versions of the play. The version which the first scribe has preserved in the eleven sheets of the folio manuscript will be called the "A-text"; the expanded version, which adopts unchanged much of the A-text but adds a considerable amount of fresh material, is the "B-text." This distinction, however, is only a rough one and must be refined in the light of some facts not yet discussed.

The text as originally copied into the folio manuscript underwent some minor alteration at the hand of the first scribe even before the second scribe began his expansion. Some of these changes were evidently made during the initial writing process, while others were introduced by the scribe returning to his finished draft. Furthermore, although the B-text is primarily an expansion of the A-text as described above, this expansion was not limited to the insertion and addition of separate leaves, for the second scribe has added some fresh material in the margins of pages 11, 29, 32, 35, and 37. He has also made a great number of alterations in spelling and punctuation, corrected many obvious errors, inserted a number of words between the lines, and otherwise altered the wording and appearance of the A-text. Finally, the second writer has made some few changes in his own as well as his predecessor's work, most of them manifestly done in the process of transcribing. The end result—the B-text—is thus a

---

[5] All four page numbers have been lined through and are difficult to decipher, but they seem to read "69," "68," "69," and "69," presumably with reference to Collier's edition, where the manuscript lacuna is noted on pp. 68 and 69.

thorough revision as well as an expansion of the A-text, but one which adopts unchanged a large portion of the A-text.

Since it has been established conclusively that the hand of the second scribe is that of John Bale (see below, n. 17), it is possible to draw a distinction between the "scribal" and "holograph" portions of the composite manuscript. This distinction, of course, does not correspond to that between the A- and B-texts since an appreciable amount of the scribal portion was incorporated (either revised or untouched) into the B-text. Only those pages written entirely in Bale's hand (pp. 23, 26, 39-63) may be properly termed "holograph"; the remaining pages of the composite manuscript are properly "scribal," even though they contain corrections and, occasionally, fresh material in the author's hand.

With these facts in mind, it is now possible to offer a more detailed description and analysis of the physical features of the manuscript and of the two versions of the play which it contains.

THE A-TEXT

The twenty leaves of the scribal text measure about 8⅜" x 12⅜" and have been mounted individually on thin strips of paper which measure about 12" x ⅝".[6] The marks for sewing which are preserved in some leaves reveal that this section of the manuscript was once bound; and the unusual system of signatures, with facing pages paired by matching letters in the bottom margins, indicates something about the original format, since these signatures, which run from "a" to "k" (omitting "j"), would be just sufficient to fix the arrangement of a single gathering of eleven sheets. Watermarks appear in folios 3, 5, 6, 7, 13, 15, 16, 17, and 21, but not on what the signatures indicate to be the conjugates of these leaves. The lost conjugates of folios 1 and 2 presumably had this watermark, and except for the irregularity resulting from their absence, this distribution is perfectly normal for a single gathering of eleven sheets with folio folding. Although the details of some of these watermarks are obscure,

---

[6] The mounting seems to have been done shortly after the manuscript was acquired by the Duke of Devonshire; only the two temporarily lost leaves have escaped this treatment. Although these paper strips have occasionally been attached in such a way as to cover some of the text, they are sufficiently transparent to permit the underlying script to be read when the leaf is held up to the light.

it appears that we have in fact two slightly different marks. That on folios 13, 15, 16, and 17—which together with their conjugates, folios 11, 10, 9, and 8, must have constituted the four innermost sheets of our gathering—closely resembles Briquet's Nos. 11375, 11376, and 11385: a hand or glove with flower above, but with the thumb extended to the observer's left when the mark is viewed from the recto of the leaf.[7] The remaining watermarks show what seems to be the same hand or glove in a different position: in folios 3, 21, 5, 6, and 7 the thumb is extended to the observer's *right* when examined from the recto of the leaf.[8] Thus there is no way of matching all nine of the surviving sheets by watermarks; and since the system of signatures proves that no half sheets were used in this section of the manuscript, we must conclude that we do not have precisely the same make of paper throughout.

Although the A-text, as noted above, survives in a fragmentary state, there is no reason to doubt that it was once a complete play. Of the 2,831 lines of the present edition (including Appendix A), 1,814 lines existed (not always in their present form) before the author undertook the preparation of what we know as the B-text. Since the A-text scribe averaged slightly more than 45 lines of writing per page, we may estimate that the complete A-text ran to not more than 2,000 lines, even if both missing leaves were filled with text. This represents a maximum loss of 186 lines, and, as we shall see, it is probable that these lines are preserved, at least in a modified form, in the B-text.

Since the extant A-text ends in midsentence at the foot of the last surviving folio page, the complete version must have run on to cover at least a portion of the recto of the first missing leaf. This would seem to be the limit of legitimate speculation about the extent of the missing text, especially since the surviving text

[7] The hand or glove with flower is one of the most common watermarks in English documents of the first half of the sixteenth century. See Edward Heawood, "Sources of Early English Paper-Supply, II: The Sixteenth Century," *The Library*, 4th Ser., X (1930), 436-438 and Fig. 137. See also Heawood's *Watermarks, Monumenta chartæ papyraceæ historiam illustrantia*, I (Hilversum, 1950), Nos. 2495, 2496, 2511, and 2534.

[8] Actually the hand in fol. 21 is upside down with thumb extended to the right, which indicates only that the scribe reversed the sheet which is now foll. 4 and 21 before writing; with the sheet in its proper position the mark would appear on fol. 4 with flower up and thumb right.

breaks off only after King John has begun his dying speech, which presumably could have brought the play to a satisfactory conclusion in relatively short order. But there are some additional clues that permit a more precise estimate. In the first place, it is certain that the original version did not end with the death of the hero. The stage direction at line A45 instructs the actor playing Cardinal Pandulphus to "go owt and dresse for Nobelyte."[9] Since Nobility does not appear in the subsequent portion of the surviving A-text, we can only conclude that he was to come onstage again after John's death, as he does in the B-text (at l. 2213). Probably he was to return to take part in a traditional conversion scene of the kind which occurs in the B-text and which is an essential feature of the English morality play. It is possible to carry speculation a step further on the strength of a contemporary description of an early version of the play. A certain Henry Totehill, who witnessed the performance of "an enterlude concernyng King John" on the evening of January 2, 1539, objected that "it was . . . nawghtely don, to put down the Pope and Saincte Thomas [à Becket]. . . ."[10] This comment hardly fits our A-text, which includes only one allusion to St. Thomas, and that one not especially conspicuous (see ll. 1283-91). It does fit the B-text, however, for Thomas is mentioned prominently three times: the dying Dissimulation exults that he dies for the Church with Thomas of Canterbury (l. 2132); Sedition, as he is led to execution, also compares himself to Thomas (ll. 2586 ff.); and Imperial Majesty criticizes Nobility and Clergy for honoring the former archbishop (ll. 2597 ff.). Since the performance referred to antedates by some years the composition of the B-text (see below, pp. 23-24), it seems likely that one or more of these passages, present only in the B-text, was included in the missing leaves of the A-text and later retained (or perhaps adapted) by Bale in preparing the B-text. We might even speculate that the missing leaves contain passages

[9] Line numbers preceded by *A* refer to the A-text lines canceled and rewritten by Bale; in the present edition these canceled lines are printed in Appendix A.

[10] Totehill's description is contained in a deposition included in a letter to Cromwell and printed in the second edition of Collier's *History of English Dramatic Poetry*, I, 124, and also in *Miscellaneous Writings and Letters of Thomas Cranmer*, ed. John Edmund Cox (Cambridge, Eng., 1846), p. 388. Pafford and Greg, p. xviii, locate the original document among the State Papers, Domestic, of Henry VIII, Vol. 142, fol. 35.

corresponding to lines 2163-92 and 2595-2649 of the B-text. These could easily have been accommodated in the two missing leaves, they provide a conclusion to John's dying speech and a significant reference to Thomas à Becket, and they include a conventional conversion scene involving Nobility. Finally, it is not unlikely that the missing leaves contained some version of the trial and sentencing of Sedition, but if so it must have been somewhat shorter than the corresponding scene in the B-text (ll. 2457-2592).

Further analysis of the A-text requires some consideration of the various inks which appear throughout the composite manuscript. Although it is possible with the proper scientific equipment to identify six different inks, only three of these occur with any regularity, and we may safely disregard the others as having no evidential value.[11] Two of the three principal inks can be associated with the scribe and the third with Bale. This is not to say that positive identification on the basis of ink alone is possible in all cases, for on occasion a word or letter unmistakably formed in Bale's characteristic manner has a shading or coloring virtually indistinguishable from those of one of the scribal inks, and in such cases it is usually safer to rely on the configuration of letters than on the texture of the ink. Nevertheless, the differences in ink are for the most part sufficiently distinctive to be of considerable value in determining more exactly the nature of the A-text.

The two scribal inks enable us to distinguish two series of alterations made by the scribe in his own work. By far the greater number of scribal alterations are in the same ink as that used in the writing of the text into which they were introduced, which suggests that the first series was made concurrently with the original writing rather than at a later date. Many of these are simply corrections of careless mistakes—e.g., *nobelyte* for *noberyte*, *clargy* for *chargy*. A few others point unmistakably to transcription from another copy (see notes at ll. 169-170, 317, 534), and none of the remaining contradicts this inference. The second series of scribal alterations—evidently completed before Bale be-

[11] See R. B. Haselden, *Scientific Aids for the Study of Manuscripts*, Supplement to the Bibliographical Society's Transactions, No. 10 ([Oxford], 1935), p. 89. Haselden was able to distinguish six inks by means of a comparison microscope and Lovibond tintometer glasses.

[7]

gan his own revision and expansion of the scribal copy (see l. 763 S.D. and note)—is much more significant. There are only twenty-six of these, of which four concern miscellaneous accidentals, eight affect dialogue, and fourteen involve stage directions. The first group consists of the addition of a carelessly omitted speech-prefix at line 1053, a bracket to join the names of three speakers supposed to speak in unison at line 526, and two symbols at line 630 to mark the point of insertion for some new material (which in fact was never added). These are hardly significant in themselves, but their location within the A-text, as we shall see, is revealing.

Except for the two spelling changes in lines 136 and 800, the scribal revisions affecting dialogue are no more than corrections of obvious errors in the original transcription—the kind of improvements one would expect from a reasonably alert proofreader. In line 316, for example, a meaningless *the* has been altered to *ther* and a macron added to *I* to produce the required *In.*[12] At the same time, a great number of such patent omissions escaped the attention of the revising scribe. The extent of his carelessness in this respect is suggested by the textual notes to lines 292, 343, 776, 868, 1478, 1581, 1770, and A36, all of which record Bale's addition of words necessary for syntactical sense. Nor does this list include any examples of syntactical nonsense resulting from errors of commission also overlooked by the scribe in his revising and eventually rectified by Bale. All of this indicates clearly enough that the scribe's revision of his finished copy was a good deal less than thorough and systematic, and an examination of his treatment of stage directions helps to explain why.

In preparing his copy the A-text scribe employed two kinds of stage directions: one, usually reserved for concise directions, appears in the right-hand margin; the other is written across the page in spaces between the lines of dialogue.[13] The space for each of these latter "centered" directions is clearly marked off by the long horizontal line which the scribe habitually drew at the end of every speech. Whenever a centered direction was called for, he simply drew his customary horizontal line terminating a speech,

---

[12] For other corrections of the same kind see notes to ll. 503 (*we*), 800 (*þe*), 1150 (*yowr*), and 1626 (third *yowr*).
[13] One unusual stage direction (at l. 1029) appears in the left-hand margin.

[8]

then left a blank (usually about the size of a single line of text), and drew another horizontal line parallel to the first. When he supplied the proper words, he generally drew two vertical bars connecting the horizontal lines, thus producing in effect a long rectangular box enclosing the stage direction. Three of these boxes were never filled (see notes to ll. 891, 1788, A33); most of the others enclose directions written in the ink of the original transcription, but a few were filled only after the scribe had changed inks and had begun to revise his work.

The centered directions at lines 763, 802, 890, and 1055 are written entirely in the ink of scribal revision, while three other centered directions are written partly in this ink, indicating the expansion of directions present in the unrevised copy. It is clear that these three expansions were not anticipated at the time of transcription, for twice (at ll. 556 and 1190) the revising scribe was forced to run outside his rectangular box and extend his horizontal lines well into the margin, and once (at l. 1120) he has interlined his addition within a box which was already filled. A similar pattern appears in the case of marginal directions: four were added complete during revision (at ll. 154, 1061, 1609, and A24) while three were expanded from their original form (see ll. 312, 626, and A79). There is no sign of provision having been made for any of these at the time of the original transcription.

If we may judge the scribe's intentions simply from the number of revisions, it is clear that he reviewed his text more with an eye for theatrical matters than anything else. But this is not the only evidence. It should also be noted that every alteration of dialogue occurs on the same page with one or more alterations in specifically theatrical features, either speech-prefixes or stage directions. Apparently the revising scribe noticed irregularities in dialogue only by chance, whenever he happened to review a page for the purpose of checking or supplementing his indications of theatrical business.

The majority of the added or expanded stage directions merely specify actions which are implied in the surrounding dialogue. A simple "Go owt" direction, for example, has been expanded by adding the names of the characters involved (l. 626 S.D.), and a specified stage clearance has been supplemented by a reference to the character whose speech begins the following scene (l. A79 S.D.). Scribal additions of the same order are found in stage directions at lines 763, 802, 890, 1055, 1120, 1190, and 1609. Five other directions supplied by the revising scribe affect doubling— i.e., the assignment of extra roles to certain actors. Two of these (at ll. 154 and 1061) simply reiterate doubling patterns which had been specified in the original copy (at ll. 1397, 1490, 1533, and A45); since both additions are complete marginal directions, the scribe probably did not foresee a need for them as he prepared his transcription. The remaining three, however, introduce patterns which contradict those of the original copy and which would have been impossible to execute in performance. These deserve special treatment.

One is contained in a marginal direction which was added entire: "Go owt Ynglond and dresse for Dyssymvlacyon" (l. A24 S.D.). Nowhere else is this distribution of roles proposed; and since England and Dissimulation must appear onstage together in a later scene (ll. A103-A129), it is clear that this direction is in error.[14] The same kind of error is contained in two notations added to stage directions already present in the unrevised copy. At line 312 the actor playing Sedition is instructed to dress for Civil Order, and at line 556 he must prepare to resume the role of Sedition. This doubling assignment, which is mentioned only in these two directions, is manifestly impossible in two fairly long scenes (ll. 1191-1275 and 2457-2592). Since two of these three directions were written in the margin and the third (that at line 556) was added to a centered direction which had been boxed in the original draft, it seems that the scribe did not anticipate the need for any of them as he transcribed the bulk of his text.

The evidence examined thus far is not conclusive, but it does suggest that the revising scribe added some stage directions on his own authority. Such a hypothesis gains some support from two

---

[14] The direction and the scene referred to are both in that part of the A-text which was later canceled and rewritten by Bale (see below, p. 13); but even in the rewritten text the doubling situation is impossible, for England and Dissimulation must be onstage together from l. 2094 to l. 2137. Pafford and Greg, p. xxxi, believe that one of these roles was split between two actors, but this seems unlikely. Tudor dramatists seldom resorted to this device. See David M. Bevington, *From "Mankind" to Marlowe: Growth of Structure in the Popular Drama of Tudor England* (Cambridge, Mass., 1962), p. 89.

unusual blunders which are not easily explained as faulty transcription. The first appears in line 556 in one of the erroneous
doubling directions mentioned above. Where he had first written
simply "Here kyng Iohn and Sivile order go owt," the scribe returning to his text felt the need to indicate a doubling situation
and added to his original direction "and Syvile order drese hym
for dyssymalacyon." Apparently he then noticed that this direction was at variance with the (erroneous) one he had added at
line 312, for he scratched out "dyssymalacyon" and wrote "Sedewsyon." In the stage direction at line 1120 he has made the same
error but failed to correct it: he has interlined in revision the
words "and dyssymvlacyon" when he obviously meant to mark
the entrance of Sedition.[15] But if the scribe did in fact add some
directions on his own initiative, it is difficult to explain why he
allowed the blanks after lines 891, 1788, and A33 to remain even
after his revision. We cannot assume that he accidentally neglected
to review those pages on which they occur, for two of the three
pages in question contain marks of his revision. Probably he was
not quite certain of the precise action expected, since the immediate context in each case reveals the dramatist's intention in
only a general way.

One further hypothesis remains to be considered. Since the
A-text scribe was so much concerned with theatrical matters, it is
just possible that his copy represents an acting version of the
play.[16] There is no compelling proof of this, although there are
two minor irregularities that may indicate cutting for performance. In a section of the A-text later canceled and rewritten by
Bale, there is a brief passage in which Cardinal Pandulphus quite
unexpectedly orders John to surrender a third of England and Ireland to Juliana, John's sister-in-law (ll. A18-A21). In the B-text
this demand originates with Sedition (alias Stephen Langton),
who explains its purpose to the Cardinal (ll. 1926-36) and thus
produces a coherence lacking in the A-text. The second irregularity, since it involves an entire role, is even more suggestive of cutting. At line A4 John condemns a certain clerk (who never speaks
and perhaps does not even appear onstage) to be hanged because

---

[15] See note to l. 1085 S.D. for the argument that this is not a scribal error.
[16] This possibility was first advanced by Pafford and Greg, pp. xxii-xxiii, on
what seem to be inadequate grounds. See below, p. 22.

[11]

"he hath falsefyed owr coyne." Nowhere in the A-text is this cryptic remark explained, and the entire matter is dismissed at line A16 when John submits to Cardinal Pandulphus and allows the clerk to be released. In the rewritten B-text this incident appears as a fully developed episode (ll. 1809-82, 1910-19) in which the clerk, called Treason, appears onstage and reveals his crimes, which include "coniurynge, calkynge, and coynynge of newe grotes, / . . . clippynge of nobles, with suche lyke pratye motes" (ll. 1859-60). Although the superior continuity of the B-text in each case might seem to indicate the existence of a fuller version of the play lying behind the A-text, it should be pointed out that since both episodes derive from identifiable sources (see below, p. 37, and Notes), it is possible to explain the differences between the A- and B-texts as no more than Bale's independent treatments of these sources on two different occasions. As will be seen in the discussion of the dating problem, this explanation involves considerably less difficulty than one which postulates a lost version earlier than that preserved in the A-text.

THE B-TEXT

The final version of *King Johan* runs to 2,691 lines of dialogue, approximately 700 lines more than the entire A-text (including the two missing leaves). As noted above, this new material was written both on the pages of the scribal manuscript and on fresh paper inserted within and added to the end of this manuscript. It is all in the highly distinctive hand of John Bale, which has been carefully described and analyzed elsewhere.[17]

Bale added relatively little to the first two thirds of the scribal manuscript, confining himself for the most part to writing his fresh material (up to twelve lines) in the margins of the folio pages. Two longer passages, however, he wrote out on separate slips of paper: the first, measuring about 6½" x 5¼" and containing twenty-one lines for insertion on page 24, is now page 23 (fol. 12); the second, measuring 6½" x 9" and containing thirty-

---

[17] See Pafford and Greg, pp. xi-xii, who note the characteristic tick over the *u*, a feature of Bale's hand which does not appear in his work before 1540. Some specimens of Bale's writing have been reproduced in facsimile by W. W. Greg in Part II of his *English Literary Autographs, 1550-1650* (Oxford, 1928), Pl. XXXI, and by Davies, after p. 244.

five lines for insertion on page 27, is now page 26 (fol. 14). As he approached the end of the scribal manuscript, Bale's revising became more extensive. He saw the need for two insertions in the A-text dialogue on page 38 and for another on the following page—page *1. These three insertions he wrote consecutively on both sides of the quarto leaf which is now paged 39 and 40. (The arrangement was rather confusing, especially after the final four leaves of the folio manuscript were detached from their proper place; but the intended sequence of lines can be determined easily enough with the help of the reference symbols which Bale has provided.) At this point Bale's method of expansion changed radically. He canceled the last seven lines on page *1, all of pages *2, *3, and *4, and no doubt the final two leaves, which are no longer extant. The canceled matter was then rewritten in greatly expanded form on the quarto leaves which are now paged from 41 to 63.

Thus the holograph section of the composite manuscript, which contains the bulk of Bale's expansion of the A-text, consists of fifteen leaves. These have been separated and mounted in the same manner as those of the folio manuscript, but the original format is much more difficult to determine. The reconstruction proposed by Pafford and Greg (p. xi), however, is probably correct and may be accepted with only slight reservations: pages 47-54 and 55-62 (foll. 27-30 and 31-34) were formerly two complete sheets with normal quarto foldings; pages 39-42 and 43-46 (foll. 23-24 and 25-26) are individual double leaves which were possibly at one time parts of the same sheet; pages 23, 26, and 63 (foll. 12, 14, and 35) are all detached leaves but of the same make of paper as that used by Bale throughout. This paper contains an unidentified watermark as well as a countermark in the form of a cross and globe over the date "1558."[18]

It is clear that when Bale undertook his extensive expansion of

[18] Apparently Pafford and Greg, who did not have access to the manuscript, derived their information from Haselden, who has included some observations on the watermarks of this paper in his *Scientific Aids*, p. 88 and Fig. VI. With ordinary magnification, it is possible to see part of the cross-and-globe countermark in foll. 25, 27, and 32, as well as an indefinite watermark in foll. 12, 14, 23, 28, and 31. The marks on foll. 26 and 30 are too indistinct to be identified as either watermark or countermark. Presumably parts of watermarks have been lost on foll. 24, 29, and 34, and part of a countermark on fol. 33.

the scribal copy he had little interest in the theatrical features of his work. No place in the holograph section of the manuscript do we find directions for doubling or disguising, and seldom do we find explicit indications of even the most necessary stage business. His indifference to theatrical matters, in fact, has produced the impossible situation in which Sedition, already onstage, is required to "cum in" in his disguise as "þe bysshop Stevyn Langton" (l. 1782 S.D.; cf. l. 1758 S.D. and note). And although two relatively long interpolations (ll. 991-1011 and 1086-1120) would have contributed incidentally to ease of production, their primary function is to reinforce the thesis of the play, either through satire or more directly through exposition and commentary.[19] Other passages added in revision reveal Bale's concern for protecting his hero and preserving his stature as the incorruptible opponent of papal domination. This is the purpose of the lengthy discussion (ll. 1666-1724) inserted just before John finally resigns the crown to Pandulphus, the pope's emissary. The effect is to postpone the actual deposition while the king first seeks the advice of Nobility, Clergy, and Civil Order (thus implicating them, to an extent, in his decision) and then explains his actions:

> I haue cast in mynde the great displeasures of warre,
> The daungers, the losses, the decayes both nere and farre,
> The burnynge of townes, the throwynge downe of buyldynges,
> Destructyon of corne and cattell, with other thynges,
> Defylynge of maydes and shedynge of Christen blood,
> With suche lyke outrages, neyther honest, true nor good.
> These thynges consydered, I am compelled thys houre
> To resigne vp here both crowne and regall poure.   (ll. 1705-12)

Both in this insert and the shorter one which follows (ll. 1773-76) the widow England is made to voice her objections to John's surrender, but in each case she eventually comes to acquiesce in his decision. Bale was evidently much concerned with extenuating and justifying his hero's actions at precisely that point where the historical evidence weighed most heavily against him.

The Interpreter's speech (ll. 1086-1120), a nondramatic summary and commentary added entire in the B-text, is a more ob-

---

[19] See also ll. 447-458, 1221-26.

vious example of Bale's polemical intent. Here John is pictured as "a faythfull Moyses," a prototype of "duke Iosue, whych was our late kynge Henrye." Henry, more successful than his predecessor, is the "stronge Dauid" who overcame "Great Golye, the pope" and thus restored true religion to England, while Pope Innocent, Cardinal Pandulphus, and the other representatives of Roman Catholicism during John's reign are identified with "proude Pharao" and the agents of "Satan the Deuyll." This is typical of the vigorous propaganda which has earned Bale the title of the "bilious bishop," but it also serves an important dramatic function by emphasizing the biblical and typological assumptions on which the theme of the play is founded (see below, pp. 59-60).

By concluding this speech with the rubric "finit actus primus," Bale has introduced a formal division not found in the A-text. In the absence of the final leaves of the scribal manuscript it is impossible to say whether or not this break represents a drastic alteration of the play's structure, but it seems likely that the two-part design is an artificial one, prompted only by the increased length of the revised and enlarged version.

In rewriting the final 140 lines of the surviving A-text (ll. A1-A140), Bale revised and expanded freely but never suppressed an entire line, with the result that each of these 140 A-text lines can be traced in the corresponding 356-line section of the B-text (ll. 1805-2161). Here, too, it is possible to see Bale's concern for securing the proper sympathy for his hero. The references to John's execution of Peter Pomfret, confined to six lines in the A-text (ll. A8-A13), extend over twenty-seven lines in the B-text (ll. 1883-1909), with the new material clearly aimed at discrediting the prophet and justifying his execution by the king. A fourteen-line addition (ll. 2144-57) to the scene dramatizing John's death serves a similar purpose by enumerating his charitable deeds and emphasizing the base motives of his enemies. Other additions in this section of the B-text seem to have been introduced for their immediate satiric value (e.g., ll. 2036-41, 2128-37) or to fatten the role of Sedition (e.g., ll. 1959-66, 1986-97). Two very brief passages (ll. 2044-45 and 2102) are of interest as supplying Dissimulation with the alias "Simon."

Presumably all this new B-text material represents fresh authorial invention and not simply the restoration of accidental scribal omissions from the A-text; at least the A-text shows no serious lack of integrity of the kind which would result from such omissions. But if the scribal copy represents a deliberately cut stage version (see above), it is conceivable that the B-text incorporates material from the antecedent, unabridged version. Although the evidence does not permit a conclusive decision on this point, it would be difficult to explain why Bale expanded the scribal manuscript as he did if a copy of the unabridged play were available to him.

Although the errors in his own writing corrected by Bale at lines 2062, 2120, 2198, and 2410 are sure signs of transcription, there is no guarantee that all of the material unique to the B-text was transcribed. It is even possible that the errors noted here resulted from Bale's careless copying from the lost leaves of the scribal manuscript and that most of the additions to the A-text were invented and written down for the first time as Bale gave the manuscript its present form. The general appearance of the holograph section of the manuscript, however, does not suggest foul papers, and on the whole it is probably safer to regard the additional text in the quarto leaves as a fair copy of new material composed some time after the completion of the A-text.

From the appearance of pages *1-*4, which contain the A-text passages canceled and rewritten by Bale, we may infer that the authorial corrections and interpolations which occur throughout the scribal manuscript were part of the same reviewing process which produced the substantial amount of new material in the quarto leaves. Although Bale did make some minor changes on these pages before canceling them, these are so few that it is obvious that he was not working according to his usual policy: he made only five substantive changes (see ll. A21, A36, A82, 2086-91, A124, and notes) and did not bother to alter the scribal punctuation, as he did with more than fair consistency throughout the rest of the scribal text. If the quarto leaves had been added some time after the review of the scribal text, presumably we would find that the canceled material had been more thoroughly worked over before being discarded and rewritten.

In reviewing the A-text, Bale made at least one verbal emendation or interpolation on every page of the scribal manuscript. His
usual practice in making verbal corrections was to delete the
A-text reading and write his replacement above the line, inserting
a caret at the point of substitution. On occasion, however, he
neglected to delete the original, with the result that both words
stand in the revised text. In line 1260, for example, *tyckle* appears
above and is obviously meant to replace *tycle*, although neither
word has been deleted. In a few instances there is genuine ambiguity, as in line 2026, where *great* has been interlined above a
scribal *foule* and neither word deleted. Although Collier believed
that in this case Bale was "apparently leaving it to the choice of
the speaker which word he would use,"[20] the syntax, at least,
would permit both words to stand. This problem and others of
the same nature are treated individually in the Notes.

PREVIOUS EDITIONS

As noted above, when Collier prepared his edition of *King
Johan* for the Camden Society, the final four leaves of the original
scribal manuscript were missing. Collier of course had no way of
knowing that all but the first of these had been completely canceled and rewritten by Bale; but since the first thirty-four lines
from the first leaf had been retained by the author as an integral
part of his revised and enlarged version, Collier was immediately
aware of the irregularity resulting from their absence, which he
attributed to "some confusion or omission . . . in the MS."[21] On
the basis of his interpretation of Bale's explicit, which refers to
the ".ij. playes of kynge Johan," he speculated further that an
authorial addition containing some device for dividing the work
into two plays had been lost.[22] It is clear, however, that there is no
formal division of the play other than the one after line 1120.

Collier understood fairly well the nature of the manuscript,
and consequently his text, although incomplete, is accurate enough

[20] Collier, p. 108; cf. Pafford and Greg, pp. 115, 123, and 127 (notes to ll. 2252,
2423, and 2486 of their text).

[21] Collier, p. 68.

[22] Ibid., p. xi. Since he was aware of the division into two acts introduced into
the B-text, Collier must have taken the explicit to indicate some further division
of the work.

with respect to its general features. He recognized the existence of authorial revision and interpolation, but unfortunately made no attempt to indicate precisely where in his text they occurred. This deficiency, together with his incomplete description of the manuscript, misled subsequent editors who had no access to the manuscript or a facsimile to "reconstruct" the order of certain passages, with the result that their texts are inferior to Collier's. In matters of detail, however, Collier's text is a good deal less than satisfactory. His modernization of i/j, u/v, and the like is not a serious defect, but the numerous errors of transcription and omission make his text unreliable for any close study of the play.

The text of *King Johan* included in Manly's *Specimens of the Pre-Shaksperean Drama* (Boston: Athenæum Press Series, 1897) and the modernized version in John S. Farmer's *Dramatic Writings of John Bale, Bishop of Ossory* (London: Early English Drama Society, 1907) are both based on Collier's Camden Society text. The two selections from the play (ll. 1277-1397 and 2086-2192) in Alfred W. Pollard's *English Miracle Plays, Moralities and Interludes*, 8th ed., rev. (Oxford, 1927), are also based on Collier. Both Manly and Farmer have attempted ingenious (though mistaken) rearrangements of some passages (see note at l. 1703), and Manly has also introduced a number of emendations and conjectural readings, some of which are attributed to Kittredge, who was one of the general editors of the Athenæum Press Series.[23] Farmer's "Note-Book and Word-List" is of value and has been consulted frequently in the preparation of the present edition.

The Malone Society's type-facsimile, the first printed version to include the complete text of *King Johan*, was prepared by Pafford and Greg from the photographic facsimile published by W. Bang (see above, n. 2). Following the policy for The Malone Society Reprints series, the editors have attempted to reproduce as closely as possible the physical dress of the manuscript, including the interpolations, successive revisions and erratic arrangement of the

---

[23] Some of these emendations would have been unnecessary had Manly used another copy of the Camden Society text, which exists in at least two states. Of the three copies I have seen, one (from the Goldwin Smith collection in the Cornell University Library) contains eight readings not found in the others. Two of the Goldwin Smith readings are obvious misprints, while six preserve genuine manuscript readings which Collier apparently emended during the press run. Manly must have used an uncorrected copy.

leaves, with the result that their text is not only extremely awkward to use but occasionally obscures the nature of the work which Bale has left us. And although their text is remarkably accurate, especially in view of the difficult original, it does suffer from its reliance on a facsimile. With a firsthand examination of the manuscript, Pafford and Greg would have improved on certain readings and eliminated any number of uncertainties, particularly from their textual apparatus.

Two anthologies containing texts of *King Johan*, both evidently intended primarily for classroom use, have appeared since the present work was submitted for publication. William A. Armstrong's *Elizabethan History Plays* (London, 1965) includes a modernized version of Pafford and Greg's text together with a very few explanatory notes. Edmund Creeth's *Tudor Plays: An Anthology of Early English Drama* (Garden City, 1966) is a much more ambitious but in some respects less satisfactory editorial undertaking. Like Pafford and Greg, Creeth has worked not from the manuscript but from Bang's photographic facsimile, with some assistance from the Malone Society's text. He has given a reasonably full but very untrustworthy collation of manuscript variants and has supplied a generous amount of annotation. It has not seemed necessary to record all of Creeth's numerous departures from the manuscript, many of which are either unacknowledged modernizations or careless misreadings of his original—misreadings which in most cases could have been corrected by checking the Malone Society's text. I have, however, revised my Notes in about a dozen places to comment on some of his deliberate emendations and explanatory notes.

DATE

ONE witness to "an enterlude concernyng King John," which was performed before Cranmer on January 2, 1539, objected that "it was petie and nawghtely don, to put down the Pope and Saincte Thomas [à Becket]"; another discovered that the villainous John depicted by the priests was in fact "as noble a prince as ever was in England . . . [and] he was the begynner of the puttyng down of the Bisshop of Rome. . . ."[1] These reactions, which fit no other known play of the period, point convincingly to the existence of some form of Bale's *King Johan* early in 1539. One further piece of documentary evidence may establish a slightly earlier date. In a letter to Cromwell dated October 9, 1538, Robert Ward reveals his distress over "the bysshopys off Rome vsurpyd power" and then complains of a particular unreformed priest at Barking who "neu*er* came yet in plac*e* but he causyd sedycyo*n* and stryfe, as m*r* bale can gyfe yow informacyo*n*."[2] If (as seems likely) the troupe of players which Cromwell is known to have patronized from about 1538 to 1540 is to be identified with the troupe which Bale was leading at the time,[3] we may well suspect that Ward is indeed alluding to John Bale the playwright, and also to Usurped Power and Sedition, two prominent characters from *King Johan*. The one piece of internal dating evidence from the A-text (see l. 1229 and note) is consistent with a 1538 date and strongly suggests that the play was written not more than four or five months before Ward's letter.

The earliest explicit reference to *King Johan* occurs in one of Bale's catalogs of British writers, the *Anglorum Heliades*, where the item "Pro Rege Ioanne, Li. ii." appears in the section devoted to the author's own comedies and tragedies written in English.[4]

[1] See the letter from Cranmer to Cromwell dated January 11, 1539, printed in Cranmer's *Miscellaneous Writings and Letters*, ed. Cox, p. 388 (cited above, p. 6 and n. 10). The interest in St. Thomas at this time is also reflected in Henry's proclamation of November 1538, by which he decreed that the archbishop's name be eliminated from the calendar of saints and his images removed from their places of veneration. See *Tudor Royal Proclamations*, ed. Paul L. Hughes and James F. Larkin, I (New Haven, 1964), No. 186.

[2] P.R.O., S.P., 1/137.

[3] See Honor McCusker, *John Bale: Dramatist and Antiquary* (Bryn Mawr, 1942), pp. 75-76, and the two items from Cromwell's account books printed by Pafford and Greg, p. xvii.

[4] Brit. Mus. MS. Harl. 3838, fol. 112ᵛ (I cite the most recent of three foliations).

Since in the dedicatory letter to Leland (fol. 4$^\text{v}$) and again in the account of his own life near the end of the work (fol. 111$^\text{v}$) Bale claims that the *Heliades* was completed in 1536, it seems that our tentative dating of *King Johan* is off by at least two years. It should be noted, however, that Bale's date cannot be accepted uncritically: in the body of the work the date 1538 occurs twice, and there is a reference to an event which took place in 1539 (foll. 43$^\text{v}$ and 110$^\text{v}$). Although these discrepancies can be explained,[5] the significant issue for the present discussion is the date of the play-list itself, which can be determined independently. The list includes Bale's *Three Laws* ("De triplici dei lege"), but not his *God's Promises, John the Baptist's Preaching,* or *Temptation of Christ*; and since each of these was printed about 1547 with a colophon stating that it had been "compyled" in 1538, it follows that the *Heliades* list (which presumably was complete when drawn up) was also made in 1538, after the *Three Laws* but before the *Promises, Preaching,* and *Temptation* were "compyled."[6] From the play-list alone it is impossible to say whether *King Johan* belongs to the same year, but at least it is not necessary to push the date of composition back to 1536.[7]

The *King Johan* entry in the *Anglorum Heliades* raises other questions related to the dating of the play. First of all, the *incipit*—"Quum domino pro suo beneplacito"—does not agree with the opening line of the A-text, which reads, "To declare the powres and the strenght [sic] to enlarge." It has been argued that it does agree with a lost prologue to the play—an explanation suggested

The manuscript is still unpublished, but there are useful excerpts in Davies, pp. 231-232, and McCusker, p. 99.

[5] Pafford and Greg, p. xx, assume that the post-1536 references are additions made by the scribe at the time of transcription and that the bulk of the manuscript, including the play-list, was composed in 1536. McCusker, p. 100, offers a convincing objection to this hypothesis and concludes that the scribe was probably copying from an original which had been updated to 1539 or 1540.

[6] "Compyled" could indicate either original invention or something closer to the modern sense of *compilation*; there is nothing to suggest that it could mean *revision, production,* or the like.

[7] Cf. Jesse W. Harris, *John Bale: A Study in the Minor Literature of the Reformation* (Urbana, 1940), pp. 67-71. Harris assumes a 1536 date for the *Heliades* play-list and on this basis tries to show that all the plays in the list, including *King Johan,* were probably composed "by about 1533-34." Even if his dating of the play-list were accepted, Harris' faulty reasoning would not support this conclusion.

by the fact that Bale's *incipits* to his other surviving plays are all taken from the prologues.[8] Pafford and Greg (pp. vii, xxi-xxiv) rejected this solution when they were able to establish through bibliographical evidence that the folio section of the composite manuscript was not defective at the beginning; and since they were committed to an early date for the *Heliades* play-list (see n. 5), they saw in the anomalous *incipit* a reference to a lost 1536 version of the play lying behind the A-text. However, it is more reasonable to assume that an original prologue became detached from the scribe's copy-text, or that a prologue written for a specific occasion was purposely omitted from the later transcription. At least the bibliographical evidence is not in itself strong enough to force an appeal to a hypothetical lost version.

The description of *King Johan* as a play in two *libri* raises a second problem. This designation obviously cannot refer to the two acts of the B-text, but neither does it fit the A-text, which has no formal divisions of any kind. Just what Bale meant by the "books" of his play, then, is uncertain, and his use of the term elsewhere in his catalogs sheds no light on the question.[9] Perhaps a "book" in this context means simply as much of a play as could be presented conveniently without a break; it is even possible that the *King Johan* entry indicates that there was once a companion piece to the existing play which constituted one unit of a King John cycle.[10] Pafford and Greg attempted a more ingenious solution by supposing that the hypothetical 1536 version was in two parts and that the surviving A-text is an abridgment of this earlier version for acting purposes.[11] Although this attractive hypothesis gains some support from internal signs of a cut A-version over-

[8] Collier, p. 105; Davies, p. 211.

[9] Each of his extant plays except *King Johan* he described as composed of a single *liber*; even *God's Promises*, printed in seven acts, and the *Three Laws*, printed in five, were invariably cataloged as of one *liber* each, while a lost play on John the Baptist was said to have been in fourteen *libri*. Bale's use of the term in describing nondramatic works is quite conventional (see, e.g., Appendix B).

[10] Pafford and Greg, p. xxii, rather hastily assume that Bale has exhausted all the suitable historical material in the play which has survived. But John's early life, his relations with Richard, his dealings with Arthur, all afford matter for dramatic treatment.

[11] Pp. xxi-xxiii. Pafford and Greg further conjectured that the explicit in Bale's hand which appears at the end of the composite manuscript was taken over from the original two-part play and that the ".ij. playes" of this explicit thus refers not to the two acts of the B-text but to the two parts of the 1536 version.

looked by Pafford and Greg (see above, pp. 11-12), it seems an unnecessarily elaborate way of explaining Bale's *libri* notation. Of
course it was proposed to resolve other difficulties as well, but, as
we have seen, these are also capable of much simpler solutions.

The composition of the A-version, then, probably belongs to
the latter part of 1538—certainly no later than the end of that
year. The evidence for dating the authorial revisions and expansions is, unfortunately, much less conclusive. It is certain that the
text in the added quarto leaves was transcribed no earlier than
1558, the date which appears in the watermark of these leaves,
and there is nothing in this section of the manuscript which suggests that the transcription was not all done at one time. Furthermore, the authorial corrections, revisions, and occasional additions which appear on the pages of the scribal manuscript were
evidently introduced at the same time as the transcription of the
added leaves.[12] But even though we may conclude that the composite manuscript attained its present state during or after 1558,
this reveals little about the date at which the fresh B-text material
was composed. The evidence bearing on this more important
question is confined to a few passages from the play itself.

The reference to "our late kynge Henrye" (l. 1112, absent from
the A-text) proves that at least some of the B-text additions were
written after Henry's death on January 28, 1547; and since this
reference is part of an early interpolation, it is probable that none
of the additions was written before this date. If the "slumbre"
from which Verity wishes to rouse John Leland (l. 2198) refers
to Leland's death in 1552, it would offer a helpful terminus; but
it could as easily refer to his insanity, which seems to have inca-
pacitated him throughout the last seven years of his life.[13]

The passage in which Imperial Majesty looks forward to the
suppression of the Anabaptists (see ll. 2626-31, 2680-81, and notes)
was evidently written before Elizabeth's proclamation of September 22, 1560, which would have been understood as the fulfill-
ment of Imperial Majesty's hopes. A subsequent reference to the
Anabaptists, however, regards the proclamation as an accomplished fact (see ll. 2680-81 and note). Since this later passage is

[12] See above, p. 16.
[13] See Pafford and Greg, pp. xv-xvi.

part of what is in effect an epilogue, it is probable that the entire epilogue (ll. 2650-91) was added after September 1560 without thought of the minor inconsistency involved. And since the earlier passage occurs within twenty lines of the epilogue, it is safe to infer that the bulk of the fresh B-text material was composed before Elizabeth's proclamation. Incidentally, the proclamation of September 1560 would also set the earlier limit for Bale's transcription of the added leaves.

From internal evidence, then, we can do no more than locate the bulk of the B-text additions between 1547 and 1560, and nothing that is known of Bale's career during the middle years of the century helps in narrowing these limits. Shortly after Henry's death he ended his eight-year exile and returned to England. He was appointed by Edward to the bishopric of Ossory but was once more forced to flee to the Continent when Mary came to the throne. In 1558 he again returned to England and spent the last five years of his life at Canterbury, still engaged in active religious controversy.[14] Nothing argues against his having composed all the fresh B-text material except the epilogue during his stay in Ireland or during his second period of exile. It is even possible that the improvement of the A-text was prompted specifically by the hope of presenting the play before Edward at his coronation, or before Elizabeth on her visit to Ipswich in 1561.[15] In any event, this new material must have been copied into the composite manuscript between September 1560 and Bale's death in the fall of 1563.

[14] A recently discovered work by Bale, a holograph manuscript entitled "A Returne of Iames Cancellers raylynge Boke vpon his owne heade," is dated from Canterbury, July 6, 1561. The manuscript is now at the Lambeth Palace Library.

[15] See below, p. 39.

BALE's view of John as a martyr-king, forced against his will to submit to papal tyranny, evidently derives from William Tyndale's *Obedience of a Christen Man*, first printed in 1528.[1] Although Tyndale's treatment of John is relatively brief, it sets forth the essential features of his character and reign as these were understood by Bale and later sixteenth-century reformers. In his denunciation of the hypocritical papists Tyndale first asserts that "All kynges are compelled to submitte them selves to them," and then urges his readers to "Reade the story of kynge Iohn / and of other kynges" to understand how "They [i.e., the papists] will have their causes avenged / though hoole Realmes shulde therfore parish."[2] The idea is dropped at this point only to be developed at greater length in a later passage:

Reade the cronycles of Englonde (out of which yet they [i.e., the papists] have put a greate parte of their wekednisse) and thou shalt fynde them all wayes both tebellious [sic] & disobediente to the kynges & also churlysh & vnthankefull / so that / when all ye realme gave the kynge some what to mayntene hym in his ryghte / they wolde not geve a myte. Considre the story of kynge Iohn / where I doute not but they have put the best and fayrest for them / selves and the worst of kinge Iohn / For I suppose they make the cronycles them selves. Compare the doinges there of holy church (as they ever call it) vnto the lernynge of Christe and of his Apostles. Did not the legate of Rome assoyle all the lordes of the realme of their due obedience which they oughte to the kynge by the ordinaunce of God? wolde he not have cursed the kynge with his solemne pompe / because he wolde have done that office which God commaundeth every kynge to do and wherfore God hath put the swerde in every kynges hande? that is to wete / because kynge Iohn wolde have punished a weked clerke that had coynned false money. The laye men that had not done halfe so greate fautes must dye / but the clerke must goo scapfre. Sent not the Pope also vnto the kynge of France remission of his synnes to goo and conquere kynge Ihons realme. So now remission of synnes cometh not by fayth in the testa-

---

[1] Bale first mentions this work in his *Summarium*, fol. 221. See also his *Catalogus*, I, 658. The principal parallels between the *Obedience* and *King Johan* were first noted by McCusker, pp. 90-94.

[2] Fol. 86.

men̄te yᵗ God hath made in Christes bloude: but by fyghtinge & murtheringe for the popes pleasure. Last of all was not kinge Iohn fayne to delyver his crowne vnto the legate & to yeld vp his realme vnto yᵉ Pope / wherfore we pay Peterpen̄ce.³

Although Simon Fish had a few years earlier presented essentially the same interpretation of John's dealings with the papacy,⁴ there are enough parallels of thought and expression between *King Johan* and the *Obedience* to indicate that Bale's direct inspiration was Tyndale. At the same time, John's trouble with the pope would naturally have had a special relevance for Englishmen living through the religious and political turmoil of the 1530's. Henry himself is reported to have made an explicit connection between his own predicament and the errors of Henry II and John which had allowed papal influence to spread so extensively throughout Europe.⁵ It is also interesting to note the case of a certain clerk who was convicted of treason and executed at Tyburn in 1535 for expressing his hope that Henry, whom he considered a tyrant comparable to King John, would soon meet the same death as his predecessor.⁶ Perhaps the interest in John's career reflected in these incidents owes something to the opening of his grave at Worcester in 1529, an event which Bale celebrated in verse.⁷ In any case, with this interest to draw on and with Tyndale's example before him, Bale was able to appreciate the dramatic and polemic value of the King John story.

King Johan itself, however, provides a strikingly different account of the historical material behind it. Near the end of the play, in a speech found only in the B-text, Verity offers what amounts to a formal documentation of Bale's portrayal of John:

³ Ibid., fol. 157ʳ⁻ᵛ.
⁴ See *A Supplication for the Beggars*, ed. Edward Arber (London, 1880), pp. 6-7. W. Maskell, in the Preface to his reprint of the *Supplication* (London, 1845), dates it 1524 or 1525. Bale cites Fish and his work in the *Catalogus*, II, 102.
⁵ *Letters and Papers*, VI (London, 1882), No. 235. Henry had read the *Obedience*, and despite his continued opposition to Tyndale, thoroughly enjoyed it: see Henry Walter, ed. *Doctrinal Treatises and Introductions to Different Portions of the Holy Scriptures, by William Tyndale* (Cambridge, Eng., 1848), p. 130.
⁶ *Letters and Papers*, VIII (1885), No. 609.
⁷ The poem is printed by Pafford and Greg, p. xxxiv. See also Bale's *Catalogus*, I, 266.

For hys valeauntnesse many excellent writers make,
As Sigebertus, Vincentius and also Nauclerus;
Giraldus and Mathu Parys with hys noble vertues take—
Yea, Paulus Phrigio, Iohan Maior and Hector Boethius.
Nothynge is allowed in his lyfe of Polydorus
Whych discommendeth hys ponnyshmentes for trayterye,
Aduauncynge very sore hygh treason in the clergye.

(ll. 2200-2206)

According to Verity, then, all of these historians, with the exception of Polydore Vergil, attest to John's noble virtues or specifically to his valor—and even Polydore's history contains ample evidence to justify John's actions against the clergy. As a diligent student of British antiquities, Bale was certainly in a position to utilize his formidable knowledge of historical writings in support of his hero, but as it turns out, this catalog of witnesses is at best highly misleading.

Of these historians, John Major, the noted Scotch theologian and author of a history of Great Britain published in 1521, comes closest to the favorable view of John which Verity advances. After narrating the circumstances of the king's poisoning, including the fact that the guilty monk had first received absolution from his superior, Major reflects on the entire affair as follows:

> Multa hic deliramenta contemplor: Regem auctoritate propria occidere huic monacho grande nefas erat. licet enim malis regibus vitam in mortem commutare reipublicae expediat, nullo tamen pacto vero auctoritate privata & signanter monacho eos occidere licet. Insuper Abbatis absolutio ante factum vulpina erat.[8]

Here Major is obviously concerned more with the abstract issue of regicide than with John's personal merits, although he does perhaps suggest that John should be counted among the wicked kings—a suggestion made more definite in another passage in which John is called "vir inconstans & imperii avidus," as evidenced particularly by his taxation of the clergy.[9]

The inclusion of Giraldus Cambrensis in Verity's list is equally

---

[8] *Historia Maioris Britanniae, tam Anglię quam Scotię* ([Paris], 1521), foll. 56ᵛ-57.
[9] Ibid., fol. 55ᵛ.

inappropriate. While it is true that Gerald on at least one occasion expended his impressive rhetoric in extolling the promise of the young Count John, then Lord of Ireland,[10] on another occasion he felt the need to criticize him—apparently in person as well as in writing—for returning to England in violation of his oath and for his reluctance to invade Ireland.[11] And what seems to be his most fully considered opinion, set down only after the king's death, resolves any possible ambiguity about his attitude. John, he says, unable to equal his brothers and parents in good qualities, strove to outdo them in depravity, and so applied himself that his tyranny surpassed that of all other tyrants, past and present.[12] The account continues in much the same vein with an anecdote about a certain Maurice of Glamorgan, who was said to have experienced a vision in which a dead knight delivered a cryptic verse about the destruction of the kingdom by a double misfortune ("duplice plaga"). Gerald expounds this vision by applying it to King John, who is held personally responsible for the troubles that befell England during his reign. It is curious to discover that Bale has included this story (but without Gerald's interpretation) in *King Johan*. Although there is no guarantee that Gerald was Bale's direct source (for the story had been repeated by at least two later historians who chose to omit the application to King John), it is almost certain that Bale was acquainted with the earlier version and that he was therefore aware of the violent attack on John with which it is associated.[13] That he should suppress Gerald's application is understandable; that he should cite

[10] *Topographia Hibernica*, ed. James F. Dimock, in *Opera*, Rolls Series 21, V (London, 1867), 199-201 (*Dist.* III, *cap.* lii). Giraldus praises John in a stylized comparison with his brother Geoffrey, although he introduces some qualifications of his praise in the latter part of this chapter. The entire chapter is repeated in Giraldus' *De principis instructione liber*, ed. George F. Warner, in *Opera*, VIII (London, 1891), 177.

[11] *De rebus a se gestis*, ed. J. S. Brewer, in *Opera*, I (London, 1861), 86.

[12] *De principis instructione liber*, in *Opera*, VIII, 310: "Dictus etenim Johannes . . . , quoniam fratres egregios atque parentes in bonis æquiparare non potuit, puta, sicut annis inferior, sic animis amaris et actibus pravis longe deterior existens, non solum ipsos in malis, verum etiam in vitiis enormibus vitiosos vincere cunctos et maxime tyrannos omnes, quos vel præsens ætas vel longævæ memoriæ recolere potuit antiquitas, detestandis pravæ tyrannidis actibus totis transcendere nisibus elaboravit." In the epilogue to this work Gerald apparently attacks John again, although his allusions are not perfectly clear (see pp. lii-liii and 328).

[13] See ll. 1899-1906 and note.

Gerald as one who attests to John's virtues, however, is certainly misleading, although not out of keeping with his treatment of other historical authorities.

Both Matthew Paris and Hector Boece give rather full coverage to John's reign, and neither is especially sympathetic to the king.[14] Phrigio, Nauclerus, and Sigebertus (i.e., a continuator of the *Chronographia* of Sigebert of Gemblours), whose histories are much broader in scope, contain only brief, factual notices of King John and are completely noncommittal about his virtues or lack of them.[15] The *Speculum Historiale* of Vincent of Beauvais is more concerned with the French king Philip and his son Louis than with King John, but its incidental references to English affairs are revealing. Philip's invasion of England, for example, is defended in part as a justifiable punishment of John for his many wrongdoings, including the murder of his nephew Arthur:

> ... & vt regem ipsum iohannem qui nepotem suum arcturum occiderat: qui & plurimos paruulos obsides suspenderat & innumera flagicia perpetrauerat: vel pene condigne subiceret: vel a regno prorsus expellens *secundu*m interpretationem agnominis sui sine terra efficeret.[16]

Similarly, in a chapter entitled "De malicia regis Ioannis Anglie ..." Vincent recounts John's alleged refusal to ransom his own son when he had been captured in battle.[17] Other comments on John are more factual and less uncomplimentary, but none of them supports Verity's assertion.

Polydore Vergil also presents a decidedly unflattering picture of King John, but it is John's failure to act, his torpor which occasionally borders on cowardice, that is given particular emphasis. According to Polydore, this weakness is seen even in John's early dealings with the French:

Ioannes uero ut semper imparatus, dum hostis domesticis calamita-

---

[14] On Matthew Paris, see Appendix B. Boece treats John in *Lib.* XIII of his *Scotorum historiae a prima gentis origine* ([Paris, 1527]), foll. 288ᵛ-291. This work comprises the three historical works attributed to Boece in Bale's *Summarium,* fol. 222ᵛ, and *Catalogus,* II, 220-221. Boece insists on the reasonableness of Innocent's actions against John; he also makes a point of John's avarice.

[15] See note to ll. 2201-04.

[16] Venice, 1494, fol. 381ᵛ (*Lib.* XXX, *cap.* v). See also note to ll. 2201-04.

[17] Ibid., fol. 407ᵛ (*Lib.* XXX, *cap.* lxiii).

tibus turbabatur, sponte quieuit, quia homo laboris fugiens, minime*que* audax, omnia mallebat, quam dimicare armis.[18]

And he finally concludes that John's virtues were so meager that it is impossible to say anything about them.[19] Verity's comments on Polydore's hostility to John, then, are just, but at the same time they could have been applied with equal justice to most of the other historians in Verity's list. The Italian's treatment of John is, in fact, very much in the tradition of the English chroniclers on whom he relied, and it is apparent that Bale was serving his own polemical ends in attempting to saddle him with the full blame for the traditional antipathy toward King John.

There is little point in searching for corroboration of Verity's claim in the numerous other histories known to Bale.[20] Medieval chroniclers, almost exclusively ecclesiastics, naturally sided with the pope in his long and bitter struggle with the recalcitrant English king and were therefore inclined to see and emphasize the worst in John's behavior. In some cases their censure is severe and overt, in others it is only implicit; there is even a kind of disinterested neutrality in those chroniclers who refrain from commenting on the events they record, but there seems to be no example of a medieval historian who actually championed John's cause or defended his character.[21] Since later historians were to a great extent dependent on their ecclesiastical predecessors, it is not

[18] *Anglicae historiae libri XXVI* (Basle, 1534), p. 260. For similar comments see pp. 264, 277, etc.

[19] Ibid., p. 284.

[20] Many of the historical works cited in Bale's bibliographical lists have been lost or else cannot be identified from his descriptions. A few of these seem to have dealt specifically with John's life or reign. See, e.g., his *Catalogus*, I, 258 and 265, for references to a life of John by John Ford or Fordham; the work in question is unknown today, but see John of Ford's observations on King John's reign in his commentary on the Song of Songs, ed. J. C. Holdsworth, *EHR*, LXXVIII (1963), 708-714. The life of John attributed to Walter Hunt (or Venantius) in the *Catalogus*, I, 265 and 616, has not been traced beyond Tanner's reference in 1784. The life mentioned in the *Catalogus*, I, 265 and 266, as the work of Ralph Niger is apparently the same one cited by Bale in his *Index*, p. 486, as Roger of Hoveden's; it is probably the history found in CCCC MS. 264 with the inscription "Radulphus Niger" in Bale's hand (see Montague Rhodes James, *A Descriptive Catalogue of the Manuscripts in the Library of Corpus Christi College Cambridge* [Cambridge, 1912], II, 13). It is simply an extract from Roger of Wendover; Ralph Niger's chronicle stops short of John's reign.

[21] See Ruth Wallerstein, *King John in Fact and Fiction* ([Philadelphia, 1917]), pp. 1-20, and Herbert Barke, *Bales "Kynge Johan" und sein Verhältnis zur zeitgenössischen Geschichtsschreibung* (Würzburg, 1937), pp. 46-66.

surprising that they came to the same conclusions about John's reign, and particularly about John himself. The image of the king perpetuated in this way was perhaps, as Bale insisted, a distorted one, and it is even possible that modern historians are still affected by the bias of monastic chroniclers.[22] In any case, it was the thoroughgoing change in religious sentiment brought about by the Reformation which first made this image suspect and eventually altered it beyond recognition. This last development was largely due to the labor of the English Protestant historians and apologists who wrote after Bale's time, or at least after the first version of his *King Johan*; but, as we have seen, the seeds of the new interpretation had at least been planted by Fish and Tyndale in the 1520's.

Although Tyndale supplied the essential inspiration for *King Johan*, Bale evidently turned to more traditional sources for most of his historical material. This material was so widespread that it is seldom possible to determine which accounts Bale has used; on occasion, however, his reliance on one authority has forced him into disagreement with others, and in such cases we have a reliable guide to sources.

His version of King John's death by poisoning is the most significant instance. John is poisoned by Dissimulation, who has adopted the disguise of a Cistercian monk, Simon of Swynsett (ll. 2044, 2102). Simon extracts the poison from a toad which he found in the garden (ll. 2009-10). Before administering the poison, he takes care to confess and be absolved (ll. 2017-49), excusing his act by claiming that the king would have raised the price of a penny loaf of bread to a shilling (l. 2023). As he approaches the king, he sings a wassailing song (ll. 2086-91), and to persuade the king to drink from the poisoned cup he praises the extraordinary virtues of his "pocyon" (ll. 2107-10, 2113-15). The king, however, insists that Simon drink first (ll. 2111, 2116). Simon drinks and is taken to the infirmary ("the farmerye"), where presumably he dies (ll. 2121-37); but he has been assured that five monks of

---

[22] Some recent historians, however, have insisted on the importance of public records for correcting and supplementing the chroniclers. See, e.g., C. R. Cheney, "King John and the Papal Interdict," *Bulletin of the John Rylands Library*, XXXI (1948), 307, and Wilfred Lewis Warren, *King John* (New York, 1961), pp. 3-16 and passim.

Swynsett Abbey will pray for his soul daily until Judgment Day
(ll. 2042, 2125). John has also drunk of the poisoned cup, and
when he begins to feel the effects of the poison and calls for
Simon, he is told of the monk's deception (ll. 2138-44). Then
after a brief farewell he dies (l. 2185).

The earliest accounts of John's death, which probably come
closest to the truth of the matter, say nothing about poisoning.
They speak of an attack of dysentery (sometimes attributed to
the king's accustomed gluttony) aggravated by excessive grief
over his military losses; the illness, and sometimes death itself, is
said to have occurred at Swineshead Abbey, a Cistercian monastery in Lincolnshire.[23] Numerous later accounts introduce the
idea of poisoning as an alternative version of what actually happened; these are generally offered as unsubstantiated ("ut dicitur," "fama refert," etc.) and relate none of the circumstantial
details of the affair beyond its Swineshead locale and the use of
some treated fruit, usually plums or peaches.[24] It was a much
more fully developed and even formalized legend, but one which
still retained some obvious connections with these rather meager

[23] See, e.g., Roger of Wendover, II, 196; Matthew Paris, *Chronica*, II, 667-668;
Paris, *Historia*, II, 190-192; Ralph of Coggeshall, p. 183.

[24] See *Annales . . . Thomae Wykes*, Ann. mon., IV, 59; Bermondsey annals, in
Ann. mon., III, 453 (poison administered by a black monk of Worcester); "A
Short English Chronicle, from Lambeth MS. 306," in *Three Fifteenth-Century
Chronicles*, ed. James Gairdner (London, 1880), p. 19; *The Chronicle of Ihon
Hardyng*, ed. Richard Grafton (London, 1543, i.e., 1544), fol. 150ᵛ; Fabyan, p.
322; Hector Boece, *Scotorum historiae*, fol. 291; Polydore Vergil, *Historia*, p. 283.
Thomas Duffus Hardy, *Descriptive Catalogue of Materials Relating to the History
of Great Britain and Ireland, to the End of the Reign of Henry VII*, Rolls
Series 26, III (London, 1871), 273, says that an illumination in Trin. Coll. Cambr.,
MS. R. 17.7 (an Abingdon chronicle from the early fourteenth century) shows John
being poisoned at Swineshead; cf. Montague Rhodes James, *The Western Manuscripts in the Library of Trinity College, Cambridge: A Descriptive Catalogue*
(Cambridge, Eng., 1901), II, 414-415, who notes only one picture of John in this
manuscript (No. 993): the king "crowned and throned, with foliated sceptre."
An illumination like the one Hardy describes, with the king taking poison from
a cup rather than from a piece of fruit, is to be found in Brit. Mus., MS. Cotton
Vit. A. xiii.

A peculiar variation on this legend which does not seem to have circulated very
widely is found in the fourteenth-century *Chronicle* of Walter of Guisborough
(formerly attributed to Walter of Hemingford or Hemingburgh), ed. Harry
Rothwell (London, 1957), pp. 155-156: the Swineshead poisoner is driven to his
deed partly to protect the abbot's sister, the prioress of a neighboring convent,
from the king's lust; he manages to escape death by selecting the unpoisoned
fruit from a dish of fresh pears when the king commands him to act as taster.

and qualified poisoning narratives, that Bale chose for inclusion in *King Johan*.

The legend seems to be French in origin. Its earliest appearance is in a mid-fourteenth-century revision of the Brut chronicle in French prose; the unrevised French Brut, composed shortly after 1332, does not include the story.[25] Despite its French origin, the legend gained its widest circulation as part of the English prose Brut, translated sometime before 1400 and printed for the first time by Caxton in 1480.[26] It was reprinted many times thereafter and soon came to be known as Caxton's Chronicle. For the reign of King John, at least, it is substantially identical with the work printed by Wynken de Worde in 1497, 1502, and later as the St. Albans Chronicle, or the Fruit of Times, and it is under this last title that later writers, including Bale, frequently refer to it.[27] There is no evidence that Bale was acquainted with the legend in the original French, but he certainly knew at least two Latin versions in addition to the English. One was the late fourteenth-century *Eulogium*, the other John Major's translation from Caxton.[28] But it is obviously the English version, quoted here from the edition of Friedrich Brie, that Bale has used:

And so it bifel, þat he [i.e., the king] wold haue gon to Nichole; and as he went þiderward, he come by þe Abbay of Swyneshede, and þere he abode ij dayes. & as he satte at þe mete, he axede a monk of þe hous, 'how miche a lofe was worþ, þat was sette bifore him oppon þe table.' & þe monk saide þat 'þe lof was worþ but an halpeny.' "O," quod he, "þo here is grete chepe of brede. Now," quod þe Kyng, "and y may leue, soche a lof shal bene worþ xx s., or halfe

[25] See Frederic Madden, "Prose Chronicles of England Called the Brute," *N&Q*, 2nd Ser., I (1856), 2; William Hardy, ed. *Recueil des Croniques et Anchiennes Istories de la Grant Bretaigne . . . par Jehan de Waurin*, Rolls Series 39, I (London, 1864), lxii, n. 2, and lxxxviii; Friedrich W. D. Brie, *Geschichte und Quellen der mittelenglischen Prosachronik, The Brute of England; oder, The Chronicles of England* (Marburg, 1905), p. 27.

[26] See Friedrich W. D. Brie, ed. *The Brut, or the Chronicles of England*, I, EETS, OS 131 (London, 1906), x. Brie describes Bodl., MS. Rawl. B. 171, written about 1400, as the earliest known copy of the English translation. For a list (incomplete) of other manuscript copies, see Brie, *Geschichte und Quellen*, pp. 1-5.

[27] *Summarium*, fol. 208ᵛ; *Catalogus*, I, 618.

[28] Bale mentions the *Eulogium* in his *Catalogus*, I, 163; in the *Catalogus*, II, 219, he paraphrases a section of Major's description of John's poisoning. Major's statement in the *Historia*, fol. 56ᵛ, that he has translated *ad literam* from Caxton applies only to his account of John's death.

ȝere be gone." and when he hade saide þis word, michel he þouȝt, and ofte-tyme sichede, and toke & ete of þe brede, & saide: "by God, þe worde þat y haue saide, hit shal ben soth." þe monk þat stode bifore þe Kyng, for þis word was ful sory in hert, and þouȝ[t], raþer he wolde him-self soffre pitouse deþ, & þouȝt to ordeyn þerfor somme maner remedy. And anone þe monk went to his Abbot, and was shryuen of him, and tolde þe Abbot al þat þe Kyng saide, and praiede his Abbot forto assoile him, for he wolde ȝeue þe Kyng soche a wassaile þat al Engeland shal be þerof glade and ioyful. Tho went þe monk into a gardeyn, & founde a grete tode þerin, & tok her vp, & put here in a coppe, & prickede þe tode þrouȝ wiþ a broche meny tymes, til þat þe venyme come out on eueryche side into þe coppe. and þo tok he þe coppe, and fellede hit wiþ god ale, & brouȝ[t] hit bifore þe Kyng, & knelyng saide: "Sir," quod he, "Wassaile! for neuer, dayes of ȝour lyue, dranke ȝe of soche a coppe." "Bygynne, monk," quod þe Kyng, and þe monk dranke a grete drauȝt, and toke þe Kyng þe coppe; & þe Kyng drank also a grete drauȝte, and sette doune þe coppe. þe monk anone right went into þe fermory, & þere deide anon, on whos soule God haue mercy, Amen! & v monkes singeþ for his soule, & shal whiles þat Abbay stant. The Kyng aros vp anone ful euel at ese, & commanded anon to remeve þe table, & axede after þe monk; and men tolde him þat he was dede, for his wombe was broken in sondre. When þe Kyng herde þis tidynges, he comandede forto trusse; but al it was for nouȝt, for his bely biganne to swelle, for þe drynk þat he drank, þat he deide wiþin ij daies, þe morwe after Seynt Lukes day.[29]

John Major's translation of this passage is generally close and accurate, but it is abridged just enough to make it clear that Bale was not relying on it: the toad, the "wassail" (found in all other versions), and the infirmary are omitted, and in general the dramatic features are much less prominent.[30] The *Eulogium*, although somewhat closer to Bale, mentions only three monks (rather than five) as praying for the soul of the guilty monk, gives slightly different figures for John's inflationary design, and omits the monk's praise of the poisoned drink.[31] The account in

[29] I, 169-170. Brie's text, based on three manuscripts, agrees substantially with the editions of 1482 (Caxton), 1502 (de Worde), 1504 (Julian Notary), and 1510 (Pynson). Bale's use of this popular work was first noted by Barke, *Bales "Kynge Johan,"* pp. 118 ff.
[30] *Historia*, fol. 56ᵛ.
[31] III, 109-111.

Higden's *Polychronicon* has some of the details peculiar to the versions derived from the Brut, but it is virtually innocent of the dramatic characteristics of the *Eulogium* and the English versions, nor can it account for several particulars in *King Johan* which are also in the Brut.[32]

Only in his use of the name "Simon" does Bale depart from his source; in the Brut and all other early versions connected with it the poisoner is nameless, being identified only as a certain monk of Swineshead Abbey. The name does occur in the later retellings of the legend by Foxe and Grafton, however, and although they could have borrowed it from Bale, this is unlikely since neither gives any indication of having known *King Johan*: Grafton cites only a version of Caxton's Chronicles and the *Polychronicon* as his authorities (although in fact he probably copied from Foxe), and Foxe, who supplies one of the fullest bibliographies on record for the poisoning of King John, does not include Bale's name in his list.[33] This suggests a source common to Bale and Foxe and possibly Grafton rather than a chain of borrowings. The existence of such a source is also suggested by the appearance of "Dan Symon" as the poisoner of John in three manuscripts of an anonymous chronicle in English verse. Although the manuscripts are of different dates, they all preserve a King John legend composed not later than about 1307.[34] Parts of this chronicle have a close connection with the prose Brut, but all the significant John material is independent.[35] In all three manuscripts the narrative of the poisoning differs markedly from Bale's version, however, and there is no reason to think that Bale was acquainted with it.

Two striking historical errors in *King Johan* confirm Bale's use of the English prose Brut. The first involves the four English

[32] Higden (VIII, 196) omits all the dialogue between John and the monk, does not specify the kind of poison used, and says nothing of the prayers to be offered for the soul of the poisoner. The account in the Meaux Abbey chronicle (I, 397) is obviously derived from Higden.

[33] See Foxe (1576), I, 260 (the edition of 1563, fol. 69^{r-v}, gives a somewhat briefer account), and especially I, 760, where Foxe cites a host of Latin, French, and English authorities. This latter passage seems to be absent from the 1563 edition. See also Grafton, II, 115-116. Grafton's earlier histories (1543-44, 1563, 1565), which treat John's death much more summarily, do not mention Simon.

[34] See Ewald Zettl, ed. *An Anonymous Short English Metrical Chronicle*, EETS, OS 96 (London, 1935), pp. xi, xvi, xviii-xx, xcvii-xcviii, and for "Dan Symon," pp. 42-43.

[35] Ibid., p. xcviii.

bishops—William of London, Eustace of Ely, Walter of Winchester, and Giles of Hereford—whom Bale represents as publishing the sentence of excommunication against King John (ll. 931-934). The official sources as well as the majority of medieval chroniclers make it clear that John's excommunication in 1209 was published by three bishops, the same three instructed by Innocent to execute and enforce the interdict the year before. These were William of London, Eustace of Ely, and Mauger of Worcester.[36] This error, which also appears in Foxe and Grafton, has been discovered in only three pre-Bale accounts of the interdict—the English prose Brut, the Meaux Abbey chronicle, and Fabyan.[37] Since only the first of these includes both the poisoning episode and the second historical inaccuracy (to be discussed below) as they appear in *King Johan*, it is the most probable source. The fact that Foxe and Grafton agree with Bale against historical fact need indicate nothing more than their reliance on one of the many manuscript or printed versions of the Brut.[38]

The second factual error appears in Bale's dramatization of John's capitulation to Pandulph, the pope's legate. Sedition proposes as a condition to the relaxation of the interdict that John be forced to grant the "dowrye and the pencyon" to "Iulyane," the wife of Richard Coeur de Lion (ll. 1927-28). The payment amounts to the "thirde part of Englande and of Irelande" (l.

[36] The pertinent documents for both the excommunication and the interdict are printed in *Selected Letters of Pope Innocent III concerning England (1198-1216)*, ed. C. R. Cheney and W. H. Semple (London, 1953), Nos. 30, 31, 34, 37 (all unmistakably addressed to London, Ely, and Worcester), and 41. See also Roger of Wendover, II, 45-46, 52; Paris, *Historia*, II, 114-115; Waverley annals, in *Ann. mon.*, II, 260; Winchester annals, in *Ann. mon.*, II, 80; *The Historical Works of Gervase of Canterbury*, ed. William Stubbs, Rolls Series 73, II (London, 1880), 107, and (from the "Canterbury Chronicle") lxiv, lxxvii, lxxxvii, xc-xcix; Walter of Guisborough, p. 146; Nicholas Trivet, *Annales*, ed. Thomas Hog (London, 1845), p. 180; etc.
Here and elsewhere Bale has not carefully distinguished between the excommunication and the interdict. See notes at ll. 1034 and 1357.

[37] Brie, I, 155; Meaux Abbey chronicle, I, 342; Fabyan, p. 315. The *Eulogium*, III, 94, also lists four bishops, but they are not the four in the Brut or in Bale. As noted above, John Major translated from Caxton only the account of John's death; he says nothing about the manner in which the interdict was executed.

[38] See Grafton, II, 103. The unorthodox list of four bishops is not included in any of Grafton's earlier works. The error is silently corrected in the fourth modern edition of Foxe's *Acts and Monuments*, ed. George Townsend (London, 1843), II, 864, although the more authentic reading from the 1563 edition (p. 62) is preserved in an appendix.

1944). But before John is compelled to submit to this agreement, England announces that Juliana has died (l. 1953), and John is thus released from his obligation.

The episode does have a historical basis, for John was involved in dispute over a payment to Richard's widow, first during the early years of his reign and again in connection with the settlement with the pope in 1213. But the terms were not quite so harsh as Bale would have them, and in fact they were not agreed upon until 1215, a year after the interdict had been withdrawn.[39] Over and above these inaccuracies, which might indeed be explained as purposeful departures from historical truth for the sake of emphasizing the pope's unreasonable demands, is the fact that Richard's wife was not "Iulyane" or Juliana, but Berengaria of Navarre, who outlived John by some fifteen years.[40] The source of Bale's peculiar mixture of half-truth and historical error is clearly the English prose Brut, which presents almost the same episode in precisely the same context:

> When Kyng Iohn hade done his homage to þe legat þat shewede him þe Popes lettre, þat he shulde paye to Iulyan and ȝelde aȝeyn, þat was Kyng Richardes wif, þe þridde part of þe londe of Engeland & of Irland þat he hade wiþholde siþ þat Kyng deide,—when Kyng Iohn herde þis, he was wonder wroþ, for vtterliche þe enterdityng might nouȝt bene vndone til þat he hade made gree & restitucion to þe forsaide Iulian of þat she axed. The legate went þo aȝeyn to þe Pope after Cristesmasse, and þe Kyng sent þo messagers ouere see to Iulian, þat was Kyng Richardes wif, forto haue a relesse of þat she axede. And so hit bifelle þat Iulian deide anone after Ester, and insomiche þe Kyng was quyt of þat she axede. . . .[41]

Bale has compressed the sequence of events by eliminating the legate's return to Rome and the dispatch of messengers to Richard's widow; he has also changed Juliana's role from an active to

[39] See Innocent's letters to John in *Patrologia Latina*, Vol. CCVI, cols. 1218-19, and in Thomas Rymer, comp. *Foedera* (London, 1816), I, i, 102. See also Roger of Hoveden, *Chronica*, ed. William Stubbs, Rolls Series 51, IV (London, 1871), 164, 172-173; Waverley annals, in *Ann. mon.*, II, 278.
[40] See *DNB*, "Berengaria."
[41] Brie, I, 166. Except for *King Johan*, only the Meaux Abbey chronicle (relying on the Brut) contains a comparable episode: John was ordered to pay to Berengaria (not "Juliana") one third of the English lands held by Richard at his death, but Berengaria died before the payment was made (I, 393-394).

a passive one by having the demands originate with Sedition rather than with Juliana herself. But in all other respects he has followed his source with fidelity.

Most of the additional historical material in *King Johan* can be found in both the Brut and in the more orthodox medieval chronicles. It seems likely that this material was also drawn from the Brut. But there are numerous details of European history exclusive of England, as well as the episode of Peter of Pomfret, which Bale could not have found in this source. It is possible to document most of these details by reference to authorities known to Bale, but the evidence does not permit the kind of certainty which prevails in regard to his use of the Brut. These doubtful cases are treated individually in the Notes.

THE description of the interlude presented before Cranmer early in 1539 (see above, p. 20) is the only record of performance of *King Johan* which has survived. Certain entries in the Revels' accounts have been taken to indicate that the play was presented at Edward's coronation, but the evidence is far from compelling.[1] It has also been suggested that the play was performed at Ipswich when Elizabeth visited that city in August 1561.[2] This proposal, though not unreasonable, rests solely on the fact that the manuscript was discovered among some papers probably belonging to the Corporation of Ipswich. But despite the lack of documentary evidence regarding performance, it is obvious that the play was meant to be acted, and it is even possible to derive from the text itself some idea of the kind of production intended by the author.

The playing area—the "place" (l. A129 S.D.) or *locus* (l. 1377 S.D.)—must have been relatively large, judging from the action beginning at line 761. A stage direction at line 763 instructs Usurped Power and Private Wealth to "cum in"; it is clear from what follows, however, that at this point they merely speak from offstage or perhaps from a corner of the stage, for Dissimulation must "go and bryng them" at line 768. Dissimulation returns with Private Wealth nine lines later, and shortly thereafter both characters, together with Sedition, leave the stage (or the center of the stage) to return momentarily, with Sedition now being carried by Private Wealth, Usurped Power, and Dissimulation (l. 802 S.D.). All this action, of course, exists principally for its allegorical meaning, but it also suggests a playing area of some size, and one which would permit rapid and easy exits and entrances. Whether it was actually a raised platform stage or simply a cleared space it is impossible to say. It may be that the play was specifically designed to be adaptable to the different acting conditions that a traveling troupe (such as Bale himself seems to have supervised)

---

[1] See Pafford and Greg, pp. xviii-xix. Evidently Bale did not return from exile until at least a year after the coronation. Of course it is possible that the play was produced by someone else (see J. H. Walter, *MLR*, XXVIII [1933], 508), but there is nothing in the Revels' accounts of the coronation festivities that points convincingly to a performance of *King Johan*.

[2] See J. Payne Collier, *History of English Dramatic Poetry*, new ed. (London, 1879), II, 163; cf. Pafford and Greg, pp. xix, xxiii.

would be likely to encounter.³ Certainly there is nothing in the other theatrical features of the play to contradict such an idea.

The text gives no indication of scenery, and no doubt the play could have been performed satisfactorily on a bare stage. Most of the action is set in England during the reign of King John, although there is one scene laid in Rome (see note at l. 627), and in the concluding scene the action is shifted suddenly to sixteenth-century England (see ll. 2193 ff.). These settings, however, can only be inferred from casual references in the dialogue, and the general impression is that geographical locale is of no real consequence. Nor does the text give any evidence of the use of permanent *sedes* or stations ("houses," "mansions," or the like) such as might serve to localize the action theatrically.

The props required for production would have been neither numerous nor elaborate. The king's crown and scepter, referred to explicitly when John is forced to submit to the pope's representative (l. 1729), may also have been part of Imperial Majesty's equipment. John's book, which Nobility, Clergy, and Civil Order are required to kiss as a sign of their fidelity to the king (l. 521), was no doubt meant to represent the Bible, a conventional symbol of virtue in sixteenth-century Protestant drama.⁴ The same prop could have served Cardinal Pandulphus (l. 1971), although in this case the "boke" is probably not to be taken as a Bible. A piece of writing, apparently some kind of scroll, is called for on three other occasions: Dissimulation must "deleuer þe wrytynges [i.e., some letters] to Vsurpyd Powr" (l. 890 S.D.); Sedition, when he first appears as Stephen Langton, flourishes what he calls "þe bull of myn avctoryte" (l. 1211 and cf. l. 1181); and John must hand over to Pandulphus an "oblygacyon" (l. 1778 S.D.)—a document binding the king and his heirs as vassals of the pope. The same prop could have been used in all three situations. John must also transfer some money to Cardinal Pandulphus (l. 1780), and Dissimulation carries a cup for the poisoned drink to which both he and John succumb (ll. 2104 ff.). In a passage found only in the B-text, Treason is said to be in chains (l. 1917), and perhaps some kind of prop was required for that scene of low comic satire in which Sedition as Stephen Langton displays his relics (ll. 1215-

³ See Craik, p. 9.   ⁴ Craik, p. 64.

[40]

30); at least the opening formula, "Here ys fyrst a bone," suggests a prop, although the catalog becomes so ridiculous that it is impossible to imagine a representational display of these objects.

More interesting are the props associated with Roman Catholic religious ritual, specifically the cross, bell, book, and candle, called for explicitly in one stage direction (at l. 983) and obviously required for John's formal excommunication (ll. 1034-51). They may appear again when Cardinal Pandulphus curses John in person (ll. 1357-58). In actual performance there may have been other props of a similar nature, but only these few used for the rite of excommunication are indicated explicitly. Their function is obviously satiric: they become in effect emblems of the elaborate religious ceremony and ritual to which Bale's Protestantism objected so strenuously, and as such they are closely related to Bale's use of costume.

The evidence for costuming derives principally from the directions for disguising and doubling which appear frequently throughout the play. From an actor's point of view these two practices, each involving a costume change, are indistinguishable. In a disguise situation, however, the dramatist uses costume change as a meaningful thematic device, while doubling is simply a theatrical expedient for enabling a small acting company to stretch its resources by having some actors assume two or more roles. The importance of costume under such conditions is obvious: an audience must be able to realize that a given character has adopted an assumed personality (and that the assumed personality is only a masquerade), and it must also be able to distinguish one character from another played by the same actor.

Although we must, therefore, assume a certain amount of distinctive costuming in a performance of *King Johan*, it is not always possible to determine the precise details of dress that Bale had in mind. In fact, such evidence as we find is restricted to indications of certain kinds of clerical attire. The character called Treason, for example, is immediately recognizable as a priest:

Come hyther, fellawe. What? Me thynke thu art a pryste.

(l. 1809)

The three major representatives of evil also adopt distinctive clerical disguises. When Sedition, disguised as Stephen Langton,[5] first appears to Nobility, he is immediately identified as a religious:

> Yowr habyte showyth ye to be a man of relygeon.
>
> (l. 1135)

Clergy is even able to identify him as the Archbishop of Canterbury, presumably because of his dress (l. 1191). In his role as Stephen Langton, Sedition is equipped with a stole, which on at least one occasion he puts on before hearing confession (l. 1148). Private Wealth disguises himself as a cardinal, and Bale's direction, which reads simply "Privat Welth cum in lyke a cardynall" (l. 1303 S.D.), seems to assume that this label is a self-explanatory description of costume. Usurped Power, who disguises himself as the pope, probably wears some distinctive mark of his office, perhaps the triple crown, keys, and cope mentioned in line 838. Dissimulation at his first appearance seems to be dressed as a monk (see l. 665); he later describes his robe as parti-colored, symbolic of the numerous orders of religious (ll. 724-733).

It is no accident that clerical garb is mentioned or implied so frequently. One of Bale's principal concerns in *King Johan* is to disparage the Roman clergy, and the association of evil figures with religious habits provides a suitable kind of continuous visual satire. The costume of some of the morally good or neutral figures must have been distinctive; but since it is not meant to carry the thematic burden imposed on the clerical dress, there is almost no reference to it in either dialogue or stage direction. The roles of Clergy, Civil Order, and Nobility, for example, are all involved in doubling, and consequently each of these characters must have been distinguishable by his dress. But although Nobility is immediately identified by Sedition (ll. 1138-39), there is no clue to his appearance. For King John himself we may safely assume some kind of distinctive regal attire, but aside from the occasional references to his crown and scepter, there is no indication of his physical appearance. England, the only female character and a widow (see ll. 22, 106 ff.), looks "wan and pale" (l. 57) and is poorly dressed (see l. 59), but otherwise there are no suggestions

---

[5] For purposes of convenience, I assume here and below that a character's first appearance represents his undisguised condition. But see note to l. 983 S.D.

as to her appearance. For the remaining characters there are no suggestions whatever.

In *King Johan* costume does not serve the symbolic function that it does in other Tudor moral plays. Typically in these plays a change in costume represents a change in the moral condition of a character, usually the principal character.[6] In *Everyman*, for example, the protagonist receives a "garmente of sorowe" to signify his new state of moral regeneration. Variations on this device are found in plays like John Skelton's *Magnificence*, where the hero has his clothes spoiled by Adversity in token of his loss of material prosperity, and in John Redford's *Wyt and Science*, where Idleness exchanges the garments of Ignorance and Wyt. In *King Johan*, however, costume is used more to conceal than reveal moral or intellectual states. Thus Dissimulation assumes his religious habit in order to conceal his true nature and thus make possible the poisoning of the king (see ll. 2102-03). Similarly Sedition realizes that he will be able to succeed only by hiding his real nature beneath a clerical exterior (see ll. 296-299). Within the satiric context of the play, of course, the clerical dress does finally serve to reveal the moral condition of the evil characters, at least to the audience; but this is still different from the usual practice in which costume symbolizes the shifting allegiances of a neutral (and hence morally changeable) character. In *King Johan*, where symbolic costuming involves only those characters representative of abstract and unchanging evil, costume can function as disguise and as emblem simultaneously.

The most remarkable and at the same time the most complicated theatrical feature of *King Johan* is revealed in the directions for doubling. As noted earlier, these are found only in the scribal portion of the manuscript, although all but a few seem to represent the author's own plan. They deserve close attention, especially for the light they shed on the kind of troupe for which Bale has designed his play.

The final (B-text) version of the play includes fourteen speaking parts, only eight of which are explicitly marked for doubling.[7]

[6] See Craik, pp. 78-87.
[7] These figures purposely leave out of account the aliases adopted by several characters. Cf. William J. Lawrence, *Pre-Restoration Stage Studies* (Cambridge, Mass., 1927), p. 52, who calculates nineteen roles to be played by twelve actors.

The arrangement specified in the directions scattered throughout the text is set forth in the following table:

Actor A: Nobility
     Private Wealth (alias Cardinal Pandulphus)
Actor B: England
     Clergy
     Dissimulation (alias Simon of Swynsett)
Actor C: Sedition (alias Stephen Langton)
     Civil Order
     Commonalty

We have already seen (p. 10) that this particular distribution of roles involves each of two actors (B and C) in the impossible situation of impersonating two characters simultaneously, and that the inconsistencies probably arose from the A-text scribe's supplying some doubling instructions on his own authority. If these suspect instructions—three of the five added by the scribe in revision—are disregarded, we are left with the following explicit distribution of roles:

Actor A: Nobility
     Private Wealth (alias Cardinal Pandulphus)
Actor B: England
     Clergy
Actor C: Sedition (alias Stephen Langton)
Actor D: Civil Order
     Commonalty

The reduction of Actor C's load appears to be an unnecessary loss of economy, but it could be argued that the actor filling the role of Sedition, the chief Vice of the play, would not have been expected to carry the burden of additional roles.[8] More important, it is the arrangement set forth in the scribe's initial draft and, presumably, in his original. It is also perfectly consistent and practicable, as the other arrangement was not.

Lawrence's first figure is understandable though illogical, for he apparently counts each disguise and proposed alias as a separate role; but there seems no way to account for his tabulation of the number of actors.

[8] Lawrence, p. 54, and Craik, p. 39, agree that it is unusual to find the actor assigned the role of the Vice playing a second part.

It seems likely that the remaining seven roles were also meant to be doubled in actual performance, although the manuscript offers no evidence of this. Four of these roles appear only in passages added by Bale in the course of his extensive revision and expansion of the scribal copy, and these passages contain very few stage directions of any kind. But the fact that entrances and exits have been so arranged that even in the greatly enlarged version there are never more than five characters onstage at one time suggests that Bale was still conscious of the demands of doubling. The distribution of roles proposed below, although entirely speculative, does at least agree with the dramatist's evident interest in economy and practicality.

Actor E: King John
           Imperial Majesty
Actor F: Usurped Power (alias Pope Innocent III)[9]
           Treason
           Verity

The feasibility of this arrangement may be demonstrated briefly.

Imperial Majesty appears only in the long final scene (ll. 2193-2691) following the death of King John: an actor playing both roles would have 126 lines to make the one necessary costume change. Treason, a decidedly minor character who in the A-text does not speak and perhaps does not even appear, is involved in only one brief episode in the B-text (ll. 1809-1919), more than 700 lines after Usurped Power's final exit. Obviously the doubling of these roles would present no problem, and it could be that the same actor played the part of Verity, another minor character whose one appearance onstage (ll. 2193-2363) does not coincide with either Usurped Power's or Treason's. Only Dissimulation and the Interpreter are presently unaccounted for in this hypothetical reconstruction. The former could have been played easily by Actor D, while the latter's only function is to deliver a non-dramatic speech from an empty stage (ll. 1086-1120), the kind of task which Bale may well have reserved for himself.[10] The

---

[9] See ll. 831-838 and note.
[10] Craik, p. 32, assigns this role to the actor playing England and Clergy.

character known as Baleus Prolocutor fills such a part in all of Bale's other plays which have survived.

With the fourteen speaking parts thus distributed among six regular actors and the author, we would have an acting company much closer in size to the typical early Tudor troupe than at first appears.[11] The versatility of this group which Bale expected to perform his play can be illustrated from the activities of Actor A, whose assignment also reveals something of the care with which the dramatist, anticipating the need for doubling roles, must manage the comings and goings of his dramatis personae.

Early in the play Actor A appears onstage for about 300 lines in the role of Nobility (ll. 314-626). When he makes his first exit he must prepare for the role of Private Wealth, who appears onstage some 140 lines later (l. 763). Another costume change is required shortly after Actor A's second appearance, for Private Wealth is directed to assume the disguise of a cardinal at line 983. No more than 49 lines are allowed for this change.[12] Private Wealth disguised as a cardinal is then instructed to "go owt and dresse for Nobylyte" (l. 1061 S.D.); 60 lines later Nobility makes his entrance and remains onstage for less than 100 lines (ll. 1121-89) before Actor A again prepares to assume the role of Private Wealth (alias Cardinal Pandulphus). The Cardinal's presence is not required for more than 100 lines, but when he does appear his stay is a brief one (ll. 1304-97), and the actor must soon dress again for Nobility. He has at the most 49 lines for this change and remains onstage as Nobility for only a short time (ll. 1446-1533) before he must leave and prepare to return 65 lines later as the Cardinal. Actor A now remains onstage for more than 400 lines (ll. 1598-2005) before he is required to change for Nobility; for this final change he has more than 200 lines (ll. 2005-2214).

All told, the actor doubling in the roles of Nobility and Private Wealth (alias Cardinal Pandulphus) must make seven costume changes during the course of the play. One of these is a disguising

---

[11] Until the 1560's and 1570's the ordinary professional troupe seems to have operated with four to six players. See Lawrence, pp. 43-52; Craik, p. 28; David M. Bevington, *From "Mankind" to Marlowe: Growth of Structure in the Popular Drama of Tudor England* (Cambridge, Mass., 1962), p. 71.

[12] The Cardinal's entrance is not noted in the manuscript, but it cannot be later than l. 1033, which is marked with the rubric "say þis all thre."

rather than a doubling change, but the other six are all dictated by the need for economy in presentation. Although the necessary costume change is not always noted explicitly at the appropriate place in the manuscript, there are no inconsistencies in Actor A's assignment, and there are reasonable allowances for changes whenever they are required. The average time for these changes is 89 lines, the minimum 49 lines.[13] Even this minimum is seen as a generous one when we realize that Tudor performers were frequently allowed less than 30 lines for their changes, even when the number of changes during a single performance was comparable to that of Bale's Actor A.[14]

[13] In the A-text Actor A has less time for some of his changes, but the difference is not significant.
[14] See Bevington, pp. 91-92.

VERSE

ALTHOUGH the verse of *King Johan* has attracted a fair amount of attention, there remains substantial disagreement about some of its most basic features. For example, where Schipper saw the "four-beat long line" as the underlying metrical unit, Saintsbury proposed to scan the lines as Alexandrines, and Bernard has described them as "tumid pentameters."[1] No doubt this fundamental disagreement is explained to some extent by Bale's own metrical ineptitude. When he turned to dramatic composition he unfortunately abandoned that vigorous and generally effective prose which characterizes his controversial religious tracts. The plays—written almost entirely in rhymed couplets interspersed with rhyme-royal stanzas—reveal his difficulty in controlling rhyme and rhythm simultaneously, and it is usually the rhythm which suffers. Nevertheless, once its principles are understood, the verse of *King Johan* is seen to be not altogether artless.

The meter of the play is decidedly accentual rather than syllabic or accentual-syllabic.[2] There is no discoverable system either in the number of syllables or in the distribution of stressed and unstressed syllables in each line; in fact, the only consistent feature of this verse is the caesura, which is used very mechanically, often distorting the normal syntactical and rhetorical sense of particular lines. One example is the following, reproduced here with the medial punctuation of the B-text (see below, p. 66):

> For I am his gostly, father and techear amonge.
>
> (l. 277)

Here the caesura, marked by a comma, separates an adjective from its noun in such a way as to produce a highly unnatural syntactical grouping and an awkward line of verse. Lines like this, partly because of their awkwardness, prove to be very useful in the analysis of verse: when considered in conjunction with certain

---

[1] Jacob Schipper, *A History of English Versification* (Oxford, 1910), p. 110; George Saintsbury, *A History of English Prosody from the Twelfth Century to the Present Day* (London, 1906), I, 336-337; Jules Eugène Bernard, Jr., *The Prosody of the Tudor Interlude* (New Haven, 1939), p. 90.

[2] Bernard, p. 3, finds this to be true of the Tudor interlude generally, although he seems to consider the meter of *King Johan* exceptional in this respect: "It is a matter more of dodecasyllabics than of five or six stresses" (p. 90).

corrections and improvements introduced by the author in the course of his revising the scribal text, they make it possible to demonstrate that the metrical scheme which Bale had in mind was basically a five-stress line divided in two by a break after the second stress.

In at least nine instances Bale has carefully altered an A-text line from four to five stresses. These lines are reproduced below as they stand in both the A- and B-texts; the punctuation is that of the manuscript, a raised point in the A-text and a comma in the B-text.

1. She shall ráther kýsse · where yt dó not ýtche (A-text)
   She shall ráther kýsse, whereás it dóth not ýtche (B-text)
   (l. 96)

2. Whan we sýng full lówde · owr hártes be aslépe (A-text)
   Whan we sýng full lówde, owr hártes be fást aslépe (B-text)
   (l. 731)

3. Than mýst I haue hélpe · by swéte Benettes cúppe (A-text)
   Than mýst I haue hélpe, by swéte saynt Bénettes cúppe (B-text)
   (l. 738)

4. I máke ther cómmons · agénst them to bé (A-text)
   I máke ther cómmons, agénst them fór to bé (B-text)
   (l. 753)

5. And shów owt of Énglond · þe caússe of þi pássage (A-text)
   And shów owt of Énglond, þe caússe of þi fárre pássage (B-text)
   (l. 874)

6. Yèa kýnges wyll be glád · to géve hym alégyance (A-text)
   Yèa kýnges wyll be glád, to géve hym théir alégyance (B-text)
   (l. 987)

7. I wóld owt of hánd · resáyue this remýssyon (A-text)
   I wóld owt of hánd, resáyue this cleáne remýssyon (B-text)
   (l. 1146)

8. I hére by his wórdes · he wyll nót obéye yt (A-text)
   I hére by his wórdes, that hé wyll nót obéye yt (B-text)
   (l. 1449)

9. To þe chýrch besýdes · for the scáthe ye haue dóne (A-text)
   To þe chýrch besýdes, for the gréat scáthe ye haue dóne (B-text)
   (l. 1743)

[49]

Conceivably some of these lines as they stand in the A-text could be made to yield three stresses after the caesura: the third and fourth, for example, could be read "swéte Bénettes cúppe" and "agénst thém to bé." But by inserting the extra syllable in the second half line, Bale has resolved any possible doubt about his intention; in their revised form both lines conform much less ambiguously to the five-stress pattern.

The deletion of a nonessential word before the caesura, as in the following examples, also helps to enforce this pattern:

10. A kýng tó [i.e., also] my bróther · lýke as to hým ded fáll (A-text)
    A kýng my bróther, . . .   (B-text)
                                                                 (l. 12)

11. Defénde the póre wýdowe · whan shé is ín dystrésse (A-text)
    Defénde the wýdowe, . . .   (B-text)
                                                                  (l. 134)

12. Why mérvell yów at mé? Téll me yowr véry ményng (A-text)
    Why mérvell at mé? . . .   (B-text)
                                                                  (l. 320)

Only the second of these three deletions can be attributed with certainty to Bale, but all reveal clearly his preference for the five-stress line.

The pattern of Bale's verse becomes even clearer in two additional cases in which an original six-stress line has been altered to five stresses. The first of these reads in the A-text (l. A109)

    I ám as iéntell a wórme · as éuer yów dyd sé.

In the B-text (l. 2100) this becomes

    I ám as géntle, a wórme as éuer ye sée.

Here an almost perfect Alexandrine has been altered in rewriting to produce the customary five-stress line. The change involves no textual clarification or improvement of any kind; in fact the shifting of the caesura results in an awkward separation of noun and adjective which does violence to a natural reading of the line.[3] Similarly, where the A-text reads

[3] The change does reduce a thirteen-syllable line to twelve syllables, but this is apparently accidental. Note that in examples 5, 10, and 11 above Bale has revised a twelve-syllable line to produce thirteen syllables, and in examples 1 to 4 he has added a syllable to a ten-syllable line.

By the mésse and þát is nót · wórth a rótyn wárdon,

Bale has moved the caesura forward (and made one insignificant spelling change) to produce the following:

By the mésse and þát, is not wórth a róttyn wárdon.

(l. 971)

Again the alteration imposes a metrical pattern at odds with the normal flow of speech, and in this case the rhythm is affected as well. In the original version the line is essentially a hexameter, with the rising rhythm of the first half line reversed at the caesura, while in the revised version Bale seems to be striving to suggest a rising rhythm—"iambic" or "anapestic"—throughout.

In *King Johan*, as in Bale's other plays, the rhymed couplet predominates. It is varied by occasional rhyme-royal stanzas, especially (but not exclusively) in set speeches intended to expound the doctrine of the play, and less frequently by the addition of an extra or redundant rhyme line. In a few cases (e.g., ll. 60, 67, 74) the redundant rhyme seems to mark an aside, but more often it has no special significance. Bale sometimes runs a single rhyme through four, six, or eight lines, and twice he rhymes ten consecutive lines (ll. 44-53, 1544-53). Aside from some passages in Latin and a single line of song (l. 2457), there are only two unrhymed lines (ll. 1242 and 2552). These are perhaps the result of faulty transcription, although in neither situation is there any more definite sign of textual irregularity.

Rhymes in *King Johan* are for the most part "true" rather than "eye" or "slant" rhymes, although phonological developments since Bale's time sometimes obscure this fact. The following survey is restricted to certain types of apparent (and some real) irregularities; a few individual peculiarities are treated in the Notes.

1. *haue* frequently rhymes with *knaue* and also with *depraue* and *saue*. These may be eye rhymes, but more likely they reflect an alternative pronunciation developed from the accented form of *have*.[4]

---

[4] See Henry Cecil Wyld, *Studies in English Rhymes from Surrey to Pope* (London, 1923), p. 106; Eric John Dobson, *English Pronunciation, 1500-1700* (Oxford, 1957), II, 453-454.

2. *masse* rhymes with *asse* and *passe*, but the same word in the alternate spelling *messe* rhymes with *hedlesse*.[5] In unrhymed positions *masse* and *messe* seem to be used indiscriminately, although the spelling in *e* is usually preferred in exclamatory phrases like *by the messe*. The rhyme *messys : assys* (ll. 423-424) shows an indifference to spelling.

3. Presumably the *ī* in *mynde* and its rhyme words *kynde, behynde, bynde,* and *blynde* had become diphthongized by the time Bale was writing; consequently it is difficult to account for the two instances of *mynd(e) : fynd(e)* 'fiend' and the six instances of *mynd(es) : frynd(es)* 'friends.' Both *fynd* and *frynd* developed from OE *eo* forms, but neither underwent diphthongization: *feond* seems not to have developed *ī* until after *mynd, kynd,* etc., had been diphthongized, and the vowel of *freond* was shortened early in the ME period.[6]

The single instance of the rhyme *geve* 'give' : *greve* 'grieve' is unusual, but perhaps represents a rhyme on [i:].[7]

4. Polysyllabic words ending in unaccented *ĭ* produce peculiar rhymes only when rhymed with monosyllables. Thus *iniurye* rhymes with *dewtye, mercy, grevosly, truly,* and *resonably,* but also (in the plural) with *spyes.* Similarly, *ceremony* rhymes with *hartely,* but also (in the plural) with *lyes* and *pyes.* We also find (*by and*) *bye : heresye : verelye : remedye,* as well as *lye : godlye : clergye,* and *I : dewtye : resonably : cytie.* Probably some of the monosyllabic words in question (like *bye* and *I*) had alternative pronunciations capable of producing true rhymes with polysyllabic *-ĭ* words, but some seem to be eye rhymes only.

A related phenomenon occurs in the rhyming of *iustyce* with *vyce, intyce* and *sacrifyce.* These last two, although not monosyllabic, carry a stress (either primary or secondary) on their final syllable.

5. The rhyming of *done* with *alone* (twice) and *grone* shows the existence of an unshortened ME *ǭ* in the first word, which is also attested by mid- and late-sixteenth-century orthoëpists.[8] Ap-

---

[5] Cf. *Three Laws,* ll. 741-742, for the rhyme *gesse : Messe.*

[6] Wyld, p. 102, lists a few rhymes of the type *fiend : friend,* but his examples are neither numerous nor conclusive.

[7] See Dobson, II, 477, and cf. Bale's *God's Promises,* ed. Emrys E. Jones (Erlangen, 1909), ll. 888-889, for the rhyme *beleue : geue.*

[8] Dobson, II, 505.

parently the verbs 'to loose' and 'to lose' (both spelled *lose*) also retained ME $\bar{\varrho}$; they are not rhymed with each other, but the first is rhymed with *depose* and the second with *hose*.

6. The rhyming of *amonge* with such words as *longe* (three times), *wronge* (three times), and *songe* reflects a recognized sixteenth-century pronunciation.[9]

7. Rhyming words in *ow* seem to fall into two distinct groups. The pronoun *yow* is consistently rhymed with *now* and *inow / ynough*, and once each with *alowe* 'allow' and *avowe*, while the verb *trowe* rhymes only with *crowe* (sb.), *growe*, *knowe*, and *blowe*. Bale's apparent consistency in keeping these classes distinct may be illusory; sixteenth-century poets generally felt free to mix the two.[10]

8. Certain rhyming words in *ur* plus consonant present an unusual problem. The five examples of *Turke(s)* : *wur(c)ke(s)* are obviously true rhymes; but the second of these words, in the spelling *worch(e)* or *wurche*, also rhymes with *church(e)* in three instances.[11] We also find *churche* rhyming with the verb *lurche* (l. 1897) meaning 'to cheat,' while the related verb *lurke* (l. 1770) meaning 'to hide' rhymes with *Turke*. Perhaps Bale was drawing on an alternate pronunciation in [k] for some of these words, but it is also possible that some of the rhymes are only eye rhymes.

One of the most conspicuous features of Bale's rhyming practice is the use of feminine or double rhymes. By far the greater percentage of these are perfectly regular, whether of the type *order* : *bordere, straunger* : *daunger, prayers* : *players*, or of the type *abusyd* : *refusyd, knoweth* : *groweth*, where the final syllable is an inflectional ending. There are a few examples of the equally regular feminine rhyme made up of two words, as in *turne them* : *burne them, lecherovs man* : *relygyovs man, forsake hym* : *shake hym*. But there is in addition a substantial number of irregular rhymes in which the similarity of sound is restricted to a final unaccented syllable. For example, *troubled* : *maynteyned, rebelled* : *accursed, declared* : *appoynted, appoynted* : *prophecyed* were all apparently felt by Bale as true rhymes,

[9] Ibid., 584.
[10] See the rhymes cited by Dobson, II, 694-695.
[11] The *churche* : *wurche* rhyme also occurs in *Three Laws*, ll. 1381-82.

although we would expect the identity of sound to be extended to the syllable preceding the unaccented -*ed*.[12] Of a similar type are the many faulty rhymes in -*y(e)* or -*ly(e)* : *myrye* : *purgatorye, many* : *mony* 'money,' *shortly* : *surely, bytterlye* : *purgatorye, Norwayes* : *nowayes*, etc. This practice of rhyming unaccented final syllables is a common feature of Bale's other plays as well.[13]

[12] See also *thred* : *graunted* (ll. 1070-71) and *thred* : *dyrectyd* (ll. 1306-07), where the principles of masculine and feminine rhyming have been mixed.
[13] See Moser, pp. 7-10.

KING JOHAN
AND SIXTEENTH-CENTURY DRAMA

MOST students of the Elizabethan drama agree that *King Johan* exerted no direct influence on either the *Troublesome Raigne* or Shakespeare's *King John*. W. W. Greg's opinion that all three plays "follow in common a Protestant tradition" in their treatment of King John has not won universal acceptance, but it has at least discouraged attempts to link Bale's play very closely with the later King John plays.[1] Certainly it seems unlikely on the face of it that a playwright from the 1580's or 1590's would be familiar with a manuscript play written at least fifty years earlier and which has left no record of performance later than 1539. Only through very compelling internal evidence could a direct relationship be established, and such evidence has not been found.

The only noteworthy attempt to overturn the prevailing consensus is far from successful. John Elson, who comes just short of proposing *King Johan* as an immediate source of the *Troublesome Raigne*, claims to have discovered "more than a hundred parallel passages and instances of similarity."[2] Although Elson believes that "some forty" of these "carry appreciable weight," he cites only six, the most interesting of which involve the following two passages from Bale's play, the first spoken by the Interpreter and the other by John. Both rest on an analogy between John and the biblical David.

> As a stronge Dauid at the voyce of verytie,
> Great Golye, the pope, he strake downe with hys slynge,
> Restorynge agayne to a Christen lybertie
> Hys lande and people. . . .   (ll. 1114-17)

> Most mercyfull God, as my trust is in the,
> So comforte me now in this extremyte;
> As thow holpyst Dauid in his most hevynes,
> So helpe me this hour of thy grace, mercye and goodnes.
>   (ll. 1650-53)

---

[1] See "Bale's *Kynge Johan*," *MLN*, XXXVI (1921), 505. Greg's judgment, at least as it applies to Bale's relationship with the *Troublesome Raigne*, is accepted by John Dover Wilson as a general assumption (New Cambridge *King John* [Cambridge, Eng., 1954], p. xix).

[2] "Studies in the King John Plays," in *Joseph Quincy Adams Memorial Studies*, ed. James G. McManaway et al. (Washington, D.C., 1948), pp. 191-192.

[55]

The John-David analogy also appears in the *Troublesome Raigne*,
but with an obviously different application:

> But in the spirit I cry vnto my God,
> As did the Kingly Prophet *Dauid* cry,
> (Whose hands, as mine, with murder were attaint)
> I am not he shall buyld the Lord a house,
> Or roote these Locusts from the face of earth:
> But if my dying heart deceaue me not,
> From out these loynes shall spring a Kingly braunch
> Whose armes shall reach vnto the gates of *Rome*,
> And with his feete treads downe the Strumpetes pride,
> That sits vpon the chaire of *Babylon*.   (II.viii.98-107)[3]

Although all three passages are flattering to King John, they illustrate more the richness of the biblical figure than any meaningful
connection between the two plays. And if, as Elson suggests, Bale
was influenced by a passage in Matthew Paris in which the same
analogy is drawn to emphasize John's claim to the throne by
election rather than by strict descent, we have still another example
of how the same figure could be variously interpreted.[4]

It is equally unlikely that *King Johan* played a significant part
in disseminating the "Protestant tradition" of King John as the
determined opponent of papal domination.[5] Writers of the last
three or four decades of the century could have found a fully developed Protestant interpretation of John and his reign in Foxe
and Grafton, not to mention Tyndale's *Obedience*. These works,
with perhaps Holinshed's somewhat less doctrinaire treatment of
the subject, would seem to represent the main channels by which
the tradition reached both dramatic and nondramatic writers of

[3] *Tr. Reign.* The reference is to part, scene, and line.

[4] See Elson, pp. 192-193. The original is to be found in Paris' *Chronica*, II, 454-455, and also (with variations) in his *Historia*, II, 80. In both works the passage is part of a sermon supposedly delivered by Archbishop Hubert at John's coronation.

[5] The existence of such a "tradition" is undeniable: see the references to William Allen, Thomas Smith, William Lambarde, and others in the New Arden edition of Shakespeare's *King John*, ed. E. A. J. Honigmann (London, 1959), p. xxvi. But see also Lily B. Campbell, *Shakespeare's "Histories": Mirrors of Elizabethan Policy* (San Marino, 1947), Ch. xii. Miss Campbell's sources indicate that the later Elizabethans could derive more than one lesson from John's career. Henry Chettle and Anthony Munday's *Robert, Earl of Huntington* plays also attest the existence of a quite different King John tradition.

the later sixteenth century. It is just possible, however, that Bale personally contributed something to Foxe's story of John as it appears in the first and later English editions of the *Actes and Monuments*. The two lived and worked together at different times after 1548, and there is reason to believe that Foxe formed some of his ideas, particularly his attitude toward English history, under the informal tutelage of his older contemporary.[6] But beyond this it is difficult to go.

Attempts to determine Bale's indebtedness to particular plays or individual dramatists have been only moderately successful. C. H. Herford's suggestion that Bale drew some details from Sir David Lindsay's *Satyre of the Thrie Estaitis* is now quite properly discounted: the similarities between the two plays are not close, Bale gives no indication in his catalogs of having known Lindsay's play, and the A-version of *King Johan* almost certainly antedates the *Satyre*.[7] Herford is also responsible for the theory that *King Johan*, particularly in its construction, is modeled on Thomas Kirchmeyer's famous neo-Latin Antichrist play, the *Pammachius*, first printed at Wittenberg on May 13, 1538—less than eight months before the earlier version of *King Johan* was presented before Cranmer.[8] The chronology here does not of course rule out the possibility that Bale knew the *Pammachius* even before he composed the A-version of *King Johan*, although it does at least suggest that any influence of Kirchmeyer's play would be confined to the B-text. And in fact the few places in which Bale's play does closely resemble specific passages in the *Pammachius* are B-text additions or interpolations (see especially notes at ll. 991 and 2193). There are other less tangible similarities (discussed below) which may also indicate that Bale had read the *Pammachius* in the interval between the composition of the A- and B-texts and as a result deliberately heightened certain effects in

[6] See William Haller, *The Elect Nation: The Meaning and Relevance of Foxe's "Book of Martyrs"* (New York, 1964), pp. 67, 70, 72, 162.

[7] Charles H. Herford, *Studies in the Literary Relations of England and Germany in the Sixteenth Century* (Cambridge, Eng., 1886), p. 135. Cf. Douglas Hamer, ed. *The Works of Sir David Lindsay of the Mount* (Edinburgh, 1936), IV, xxvi, 138, and especially 160.

[8] Pages 136-138. Herford seems to have assumed a relatively late date for *King Johan*, even though he was aware of the 1539 performance before Cranmer. Bale first mentions his translation of the *Pammachius* in his *Summarium* (1549).

revision. But in any case it is sufficiently obvious that Bale's most important dramatic models are to be found not in the Continental drama of contemporary reformers but in the tradition of the native morality play.

Bale's debt to this tradition is usually said to consist in his use of "allegorical" personae, by which is meant personified abstractions like Sedition and Usurped Power and more or less generalized types like Nobility, Clergy, and Civil Order. It is also generally held that his distinctive advance over the morality genre lies in his combining in one way or another these kinds of characters with literal, historical individuals. Sedition, for example, not only exists throughout much of the play as the historical Stephen Langton, he also operates, even in his nonliteral mode of existence, in the same world with King John, who is consistently presented as a particular historical person. This conventional view of Bale's achievement in *King Johan*, although fundamentally sound, is seriously limited by its tendency to view the play almost exclusively in terms of its characters. The allegorical personae provide an obvious clue to Bale's dramatic antecedents, but once we are led to the morality play, it is not enough simply to point to these personae and note how Bale's characters differ from them. It is at least equally important for a proper historical and critical understanding of the play to attend to Bale's use and adaptation of the means by which the morality dramatist put his figures in action and developed this action according to a predetermined homiletic purpose. This necessarily involves a consideration of allegory, structure, and theme, as well as character.

The distinguishing trait of the English morality play is that it makes significant use of one or more traditional allegories or extended metaphors which exist independently of the play itself. The allegory may be exploited fully, as it is in *The Castle of Perseverance* where both the spiritual war (or, more specifically, the siege) and the debate of the Four Daughters of God are simply translated from narrative into dramatic form. On the other hand, it may be treated only allusively as a kind of objective reference point which reinforces the dramatic action. In *Everyman*, for example, one of the underlying allegories is that of the spiritual journey, according to which death and judgment are viewed as inevitable stages in a progress through time. Yet even though Everyman explicitly undertakes a journey, the basic metaphor is never thoroughly developed. It does nonetheless exert a significant measure of control over the play's plot and thematic development, and in this respect it is essentially no different from the traditional allegories which govern *The Castle of Perseverance*.

Obviously there is no such traditional allegory lying behind *King Johan*. Its place is taken partly by more or less authoritative historical narrative, which determines to an extent the plot development of the play, but more basically by a schematic view of history which for Bale gave the historical data their special interest and relevance. According to this view—one espoused by a number of sixteenth-century Protestant thinkers—the key to the understanding of history is to be found in the perennial opposition between the forces of Christ and Antichrist as expounded mystically in the Apocalypse. Except for the thousand-year period from the Nativity to Pope Sylvester II, during which time Satan remained bound and sealed in the bottomless pit (Apoc. xx.1-3), the faithful few in each age have been persecuted by the various manifestations of the general Antichrist—particularly the papacy. This state of affairs is to continue until the glorious Second Coming and the descent of the New Jerusalem, understood in a spiritual sense as a return to the uncorrupted doctrine and practice of the primitive Church.[9]

Bale does not attempt to prove or even explain any of this in *King Johan*; instead, he assumes it as an independent structure with an established and generally accepted validity, much as the morality dramatist assumed the validity of his received allegory. Nevertheless this apocalyptical theory of history does have its effect on the play. It accounts for the frequent reference to Antichrist and related eschatological matters (see, for example, ll. 677, 1091, 2081, 2190, 2645, 2679—many of these in B-text additions), but more important it underlies and reinforces the analogy between John and Henry VIII which is implicit through much of

---

[9] See Bale's lengthy commentary on the Apocalypse, *The Image of Both Churches*, particularly the third part (1548?, reprinted in *Select Works of John Bale*, ed. Henry Christmas [Cambridge, Eng., 1849]). See also Haller, pp. 64-70, and Ernest Lee Tuveson, *Millennium and Utopia: A Study in the Background of the Idea of Progress* (Berkeley and Los Angeles, 1949), Ch. ii.

the play and spelled out fully in the Interpreter's speech (ll. 1086-1120). Since John was one of those called upon to champion the true faith at a time when Satan was at large and held sway (ll. 1091-92), his defeat was virtually inevitable. But given the apocalyptical orientation of Bale's theory of history, this defeat could only be a prelude to the ultimate victory of the Church, which Bale, conscious of living in the "latter time" of spiritual regeneration prophesied by St. John, was prepared to see in Henry's successful defiance of Rome. John is thus in a very real sense a type of Henry, and Bale has obviously selected and arranged the historical data to emphasize this fact. He has also contrived to bring Henry (in the guise of Imperial Majesty) onstage in the last scene of the play. This is perhaps a somewhat unsubtle device, but it cannot be dismissed as simply a clumsy anachronism. It represents a consistent working out of the structural plan which governs the entire play, and as such it forms an integral part of Bale's dramatic design.

Kirchmeyer's *Pammachius*, which is much more heavily and explicitly eschatological, presents Julian, the last Roman emperor, in what amounts to a very similar historical framework. In accordance with popular eschatological thinking, his submission to Pope Pammachius, the Antichrist, signals the approach of the last days. The parousia of course is not represented; as explained in the epilogue, it is to be the subject of a fifth act, which Kirchmeyer has purposely left unwritten. But it is clearly foreshadowed by the advent of "Theophilus" (Luther), whose doctrine is expounded throughout much of Act IV. Julian, then, is not strictly a type of Luther as John is of Henry, nor is he in most other respects comparable to Bale's hero. But like John he does have a recognizable place in the apocalyptical view of history which saw the Reformation as a glorious victory over the forces of Antichrist comparable to—if not precisely identical with—the ultimate victory foretold by St. John. In terms of dramatic structure, with the Reformation standing as an essentially comic resolution to an otherwise tragic story, the two plays are thus closely parallel, and it may be that this resolution in *King Johan*—absent from the surviving A-text— was added by Bale in revision under the influence of Kirchmeyer's play. It is more likely, however, that the eschatological concept and the resulting structural design were implicit in Bale's plan from the beginning and that Kirchmeyer's work simply encouraged him to give these elements a greater prominence.

The dualistic scheme derived from the Apocalypse and applied to the history of the Church has a counterpart in the traditional view of the opposition between Virtue and Vice in the spiritual life of the individual Christian. As modified and formalized in the most popular type of English morality play, this conflict presented a neutral protagonist poised between the representatives of moral good and evil and aligning himself with each in turn.[10] The plot of these plays is thus defined by a series of reversals, each representing a moral choice by which the protagonist commits himself to Virtue or Vice. The number of reversals might vary from one to four, but theological considerations required that the protagonist's final movement be toward the forces of good.[11] Nor was this pattern confined to the earlier moralities, operating within the realm of specifically Christian ethics. Humanistic and secularized "moralities" like John Rastell's *Four Elements* exhibit the same form even though the protagonist's choices are no longer strictly moral.

Bale must have seen in this dramatic formula a microcosmic reflection of that larger conflict which governed the movement of history. He has accordingly used the formula extensively, at the same time adjusting it freely to accommodate it more effectively to his apocalyptical view of English history. While King John is obviously the central figure of the play, he does not stand in the position of a neutral protagonist like Mankind or Magnificence. The fundamental difference is that his will is unchanging. At his first appearance he reveals himself as a noble ruler concerned above all for the welfare of his subjects:

> I haue worne the crown and wrowght vyctoryouslye,
> And now do purpose by practyse and by stodye
> To reforme the lawes and sett men in good order,
> That trew iustyce may be had in euery bordere.
>
> (ll. 18-21)

---

[10] See Robert Lee Ramsay, ed. *Magnyfycence: A Moral Play by John Skelton*, EETS, ES 98 (London, 1908), pp. cxlvii-cl.

[11] See Spivack, pp. 244-245, who observes that the traditional morality, because of its application to humanity in general, could not end tragically without implying a kind of blanket damnation contrary to Christian thought; tragedy in a Christian morality play could become possible only when the central character had lost his universal signification.

His dying speech is a reiteration of these sentiments seasoned with a Christian resignation born of experience:

> I haue sore hungred and thirsted ryghteousnesse
> For the offyce sake that God hath me appoynted;
> But now I perceyue that synne and wyckednesse
> In thys wretched worlde, lyke as Christe prophecyed,
> Haue the ouerhande; in me is it verefyed.
> Praye for me, good people, I besych yow hartely,
> That the lorde aboue on my poore sowle haue mercy.
>
> (ll. 2167-73)

At no point does he embrace evil. His one questionable act—the resignation of the crown to Cardinal Pandulphus—has been carefully extenuated by Bale in passages bearing the marks of careful and thorough revision, with the result that the capitulation is a sign not of the king's frailty but of his compassion. This attitude is made explicit in John's appeal to the widow England:

> O Englande, Englande, shewe now thyselfe a mother;
> Thy people wyll els be slayne here without nomber.
> As God shall iudge me, I do not thys of cowardnesse
> But of compassyon, in thys extreme heauynesse.
>
> (ll. 1717-20)

Bale's hero, in short, is unsuited for the role of neutral protagonist precisely because his will is unalterably committed to good. The forces of evil which oppose and eventually subdue him create crises and reversals in the action, but these are no longer illustrative of moral choice on the part of the principal character.

Bale has assigned the essential characteristics of the neutral protagonist to Nobility, Clergy, and Civil Order, and it is these characters who engage in the familiar movement between good and evil formerly reserved for the central figure. Clergy first appears as one already corrupted by the forces of evil: his entrance is marked by an argument with John, which he concludes with a disrespectful "Yowr grace ys fare gonne; God send yow a better mynd" (l. 372). The fact that he is capable of conversion, however, is proof that he is not inherently evil.[12] Nobility and Civil

[12] See the discussion of *New Custom* in William Roy Mackenzie, *The English Moralities from the Point of View of Allegory* (Boston, 1914), p. 50 and n. 1.

Order are also presented as characters essentially innocent although inclined toward wickedness. In their initial encounter with John, they at first give evidence of a rebellious spirit; but soon, together with Clergy, they request and willingly accept instruction from the king (ll. 526 ff.). At this point the forces of good have reached a temporary ascendancy by winning the allegiance of the tripartite protagonist. In Act II Bale makes use of the temptation motif employed extensively in the moralities to motivate the series of moral choices which defined the plot, and, significantly, it is not John but Nobility, Clergy, and Civil Order who are tempted. Sedition approaches each in turn and gains his support against the king. While Nobility at first offers resistance (ll. 1176-79), his eventual fall is swift and decisive: "Than I submyt me to the chyrches reformacyon" (l. 1183). Clergy and Civil Order submit even more readily to Sedition's proposals (ll. 1207-12). Then, as the play draws to a close, all three undergo a sudden conversion in the manner of the neutral protagonist of the morality plays:

> *Nob.* For Gods loue, nomore! Alas, ye haue sayde ynough.
> *Cler.* All the worlde doth knowe that we haue done sore amys.
> *C. Ord.* Forgyue it vs, so that we neuer heare more of thys.
>
> (ll. 2306-08)

In these successive reversals we have the conventional plot of the conflict morality, preserved in a strikingly different context through a redistribution of the functions assigned the various characters.

The purpose of these modifications is clear. The neutral figure of a morality must, of course, suffer a fall from virtue, and such a fall would obviously be unsuitable to Bale's martyr-king. Furthermore, by making Nobility, Clergy, and Civil Order collectively the morally neutral protagonist, Bale has been able to reserve for John the position normally occupied by the chief representative of virtue, the character pitted against the vice-tempters in the struggle for domination over the neutral hero. At the same time, insofar as John is also mortal and not precisely a personified abstraction, his encounter with the forces of Antichrist leads to his death, with the result that he becomes, as Samuel Frederick John-

[63]

son has pointed out, the earliest example in English drama of the isolated hero whose essential virtue and nobility in a world of evil bring about his tragic downfall.[13] Bale, however, was not writing tragedy, and the tragic implications of his hero's death are purposely thwarted by the comic resolution inherent in the play's eschatological framework. Although John is human and consequently susceptible to tragedy, he is at the same time a prototype of Henry VIII and an embodiment of "imperial majesty" as Bale conceived it. These latter considerations more than John's predicament as a particular individual have dictated the play's structure and made it a comedy.

Although the structure of *King Johan* owes much to a theory of history which is fundamentally religious, Bale's ultimate concern is not so much religious as political. Both plot and theme center on Pope Innocent's appointment of Stephen Langton as Archbishop of Canterbury in opposition to John's wishes. It is the power of the king to assert his sovereignty in his own realm that is at stake, and Bale's purpose of course is to defend the royal authority as supreme in matters spiritual as well as temporal. The issue touches religion as well as politics, and this fact, together with Bale's violently polemical disposition, accounts for the vicious satire of Roman Catholic religious practices and institutions which fills the play and obscures some of its artistic qualities. To call *King Johan* a theological play, however, is clearly a mistake.[14] Although the standard topics of sectarian dispute—the papacy, indulgences and pardons, "voluntarye workes," the mass, the Scriptures in English, etc.—are mentioned frequently enough, these are never considered theologically but only as they impinge on problems of social harmony. Auricular confession, together with the whole Catholic penitential system, is thoroughly satirized, travestied, and otherwise denounced,[15] not on the basis of doctrinal dispute over the sacrament of penance but because private confession supposedly offered a threat to political stability. Nor is the play a "moral" play in the strictest sense. In place of the essen-

[13] "The Tragic Hero in Early Elizabethan Drama," in *Studies in the English Renaissance Drama*, ed. Josephine W. Bennett et al. (New York, 1959), p. 170.
[14] Cf. Elbert N. S. Thompson, "The English Moral Plays," *Transactions of the Connecticut Academy of Arts and Sciences*, XIV (New Haven, 1910), 363. Thompson refers to *King Johan* as an "exponent of Puritan dogma."
[15] See Miller, pp. 802-822.

tially unchanging and universal questions of salvation which occupied earlier homiletic dramatists, we find secular topics of particular concern to thirteenth- and sixteenth-century Englishmen presented in a deliberately modified version of the literary formula popularized by the morality playwrights. And it is this calculated use of a traditional artistic form that makes *King Johan* more than a curious survival of sectarian propaganda.

Bale, to be sure, was not the only early Tudor dramatist to adapt the methods and conventions of the morality genre to nonmoral purposes. As William O. Harris has demonstrated, Skelton had earlier set himself a similar task, and, by modifying the traditional English morality in the light of the Stoic-Christian tradition of fortitude, had given effective dramatic presentation to his ideas on the nature of kingship and the royal virtues.[16] Other plays of the period, like the so-called youth and educational plays, while retaining the formal characteristics of the traditional morality are similarly limited in scope even though not specifically political in intent. In the earlier *Hickscorner,* and even in the traditional *Wisdom,* there is precedent for Bale's practice of substituting a multiple for a single protagonist. *Hickscorner* also illustrates the tendency—somewhat less clearly observable in *The Interlude of Youth*—to obscure the moral neutrality of the central figure in the traditional conflict plot. Nevertheless *King Johan* stands out as one of the most ambitious and thoroughgoing attempts by an early Tudor playwright to exploit the resources of the native English religious drama. It also reveals the extent to which this drama, unaffected by classical precepts or models, could be made to retain its appeal and relevance in an age uncongenial to its most fundamental presuppositions.

[16] *Skelton's "Magnyfycence" and the Cardinal Virtue Tradition* (Chapel Hill, 1965), pp. 145 ff.

NOTE ON THE TEXT

THE present text is based on the B-text, which clearly represents the author's final intentions so far as these can be determined.

The spelling of the manuscript has been retained with the following exceptions: (*a*) ȝ and *z*, frequently indistinguishable in both the scribe's and Bale's hand, have been differentiated; (*b*) Bale's *y* has been printed as *þ* whenever appropriate (see below); (*c*) the different forms of *r* and *s* have not been distinguished; (*d*) speech-prefixes have been abbreviated arbitrarily and consistently throughout.

I have freely altered the erratic and idiosyncratic capitalization of the scribal writing to make it conform more closely with Bale's own practice, which agrees for the most part with modern standards. The capitalization in passages written by Bale himself, even when it is at variance with his usual practice, has been followed except in those few instances in which a line of verse or a stage direction begins with a minuscule.

The pointing of the original, in both the scribal and authorial sections of the manuscript, follows no discernible logical, syntactical, rhetorical, or dramatic principle. The first end-stop mark of punctuation, for example, does not occur until line 30, even though this opening passage is divided between two speakers. Almost every line of the play, however, is broken into two metrical units—in the scribal text by a raised point (usually altered by Bale to a comma), in Bale's own writing by a comma. Under these circumstances it seems necessary to impose a more meaningful system of punctuation on the original, and consequently the pointing of the present text is entirely editorial. Where another editor has introduced a significantly different punctuation, this fact is recorded in the Notes.

The spacing of words in the scribal text is frequently doubtful or careless and has not always been adhered to. For example, *beleve* (l. 50) and *inow* (l. 327), each clearly written as two words, have been silently corrected; conversely, *thynke yt* (l. 8) has been printed as two words, although it is written as one in the manuscript. In cases where a peculiar spacing might conceivably represent an accepted spelling alternate, however, the original has been allowed to stand. As a result, certain forms (e.g., *because, besides, without*) are printed sometimes as two words, sometimes as one, according to the scribe's apparent intention in each instance.[1]

Contractions, suspensions, and abbreviations in the manuscript have been silently expanded.[2] Wherever there is doubt about the intended form, the aim has been to expand in accordance with the usual unabbreviated spelling of the writer involved. Thus in Bale's hand the superior *r*, which appears only in *yor*, is taken to indicate the omission of *u* since Bale's more common spelling is *your*. Other superior letters in Bale's hand all occur in conjunction with *y* when this character represents *þ*; consequently even though *y* and *þ* are indistinguishable in Bale's hand, there is no chance of confusing *ye* (= *ye*) with *y^e* (= *þe*), or *yt* (= *yt*) with *y^t* (= *þat*).[3] In the scribal text the pronoun *þ^u* has been rendered as *þou* by analogy with the scribe's alternate spelling *thow*. (Bale's *thu* is evidently not a contraction.) Apparently the superior *r* in the scribal hand does not always have a special significance: see, for example, *cu^r sse* (l. 661), *cu^r ssys* (l. 1386), *e^r lles* (l. 1371). It appears often in *yow^r* (sometimes *yor*), *ow^r*, *pow^r* (once *pow^r r*), (*h*)*ow^r* 'hour' (once *how^r rs*), *sow^r* 'sour,' *he^r* 'here,' and *the^r*. A comparison with other spellings in the scribal text fails to reveal any consistent treatment of these words; for example, we find *pow(e)res* (ll. 1, 7, 1506) and *powrs* (ll. 1019, 1408) as well as *powers* (l. 1417), *howre* (l. 239) as well as *hower* (l. A81). The superior letter in the scribal text has therefore been rendered as an ordinary letter.

I have italicized foreign words and phrases and set off rhyme-royal stanzas with spaces. In the manuscript these stanzas are usually marked with a paragraph symbol, which I have omitted.

Stage directions have been printed, in italics, either across the page or in the margin, according to their position in the manu-

---

[1] The Malone Society's text is unreliable in matters of spacing.

[2] There are a number of peculiar marks in the scribal text which have been judged mere flourishes and therefore ignored. The most common of these are the short horizontal bar through the ascender of *h* and the curl used to join a final double *l*. Most of these meaningless symbols are reproduced in the Malone Society's text.

[3] The scribe's *y* and *þ* bear a superficial resemblance to each other, but the two are distinctive enough to prevent ambiguity. But see textual notes at ll. 110 and 270 for exceptional cases in which the scribe has himself confused the two, obviously through carelessness.

script (see above, pp. 8-9). I have occasionally noted in square brackets an entrance or exit not marked in the manuscript.

Speech-prefixes in the original are frequently misleading where a disguising situation occurs. When Sedition becomes Stephen Langton, for example, his speeches as they appear in the scribal text are generally labeled with the latter name, although in the parallel sections of the rewritten text the former name is used under the same circumstances. In the present edition clarity and consistency have been achieved by using the name of the assumed personality whenever extended disguising takes place.

The purpose of the textual apparatus is to note instances in which the present text departs from the B-text and to point out the more significant details of Bale's treatment of the A-text. I have not recorded those corrections introduced by the scribe into his own work since few of these, as we have seen, are more than mechanical; those of consequence are recorded in the Notes. Variations between the A- and B-texts are noted only when they are substantive in nature; but since this standard is frequently difficult to apply, I have tended to be rather inclusive than otherwise. Bale's corrections of his own writing, whether substantive or not, have also been recorded. Readings from the printed editions, which have no independent authority, are generally excluded from the apparatus; those of special interest are discussed in the Notes.

The usual practice in recording emendations and other variations from the B-text has been to repeat the reading of the present edition for reference, except where this reading represents a silent editorial regularizing of the B-text capitalization or punctuation (as described above), in which case the manuscript reading is reproduced exactly, with contracted and suspended elements printed in italics. When this first element is derived from the B-text, no siglum is supplied; otherwise the lemma is identified as *A* (A-text), *ed.* (the present editor), or as the reading of one of the printed editions. In noting Bale's corrections of his own writing, the symbol *b* has been used to identify the uncorrected reading. An asterisk indicates that further information on textual matters is to be found in the Notes.

It has been necessary to adopt a different system of recording variants in lines 1804-2161, the passage which constitutes Bale's expansion and revision on fresh paper of 140 canceled A-text lines from the last two surviving leaves of the scribal manuscript. The final version is printed in its logical place and the corresponding section of the A-text in Appendix A. Textual notes in both places indicate the correspondences in detail.

KING JOHAN

[DRAMATIS PERSONAE

King John
England, a widow
Nobility
Clergy
Civil Order
Commonalty
Sedition (alias Stephen Langton)
Dissimulation (alias Simon of Swynsett)
Usurped Power (alias Pope Innocent III)
Private Wealth (alias Cardinal Pandulphus)
Treason, a priest
Verity
Imperial Majesty
The Interpreter]

[ACT I]

[Enter King John and England.]

K. *John.* To declare the powres and their force to   (p. 1, fol. 1)
    enlarge
The scriptur of God doth flow in most abowndaunce;
And of sophysteres the cauteles to dyscharge
Bothe Peter and Pawle makyth plenteosse vtterauns;
5   How that all pepell shuld shew there trew alegyauns
To ther lawfull kyng Christ Iesu dothe consent,
Whych to þe hygh powres was evere obedyent.

To shew what I am I thynke yt convenyent.
Iohn kyng of Ynglond þe cronyclys doth me call.
10   My granfather was an emperowre excelent,
My fathere a kyng by successyon lyneall.
A kyng my brother lyke as to hym ded fall;

1 their force] the strenght *A.*   7 was] were *A.**
2 doth] to *A.*   12 kyng my] kyng to my *A.**
3 cauteles] fantesyes *A.*

[70]

Rychard Curdelyon they callyd hym in Fraunce,
Whych had ouer enymyes most fortynable chaunce.

15   By the wyll of God and his hygh ordynaunce
In Yerlond and Walys, in Angoye and Normandye,
In Ynglond also, I haue had the governaunce.
I haue worne the crown and wrowght vyctoryouslye,
And now do purpose by practyse and by stodye
20   To reforme the lawes and sett men in good order,
That trew iustyce may be had in euery bordere.

Eng. Than I trust yowr grace wyll waye a poore wedowes cause,
Vngodly vsyd, as ye shall know in short clavse.
K. John. Yea, that I wyll swer, yf yt be trew and iust.
25 *Eng.* Lyke as yt beryth trewth, so lett yt be dyscust.
K. John. Than gentyll wydowe, tell me what þe mater ys.
Eng. Alas, yowr clargy hath done very sore amys
In mysvsyng me, ageynst all ryght and iustyce;
And for my more greffe, therto they other intyce.
30 *K. John.* Whom do they intyce for to do the inivrye?
Eng. Soch as hath enterd by false hypocrysye,
Moch worse frutes havyng than hathe þe thornes vnplesaunt.
For they are the trees that God dyd never plant,
And as Christ dothe saye, blynd leaders of the blynd.
35 *K. John.* Tell me whom thow menyst, to satysfy my mynd.
Eng. Suche lubbers as hath dysgysed heades in þer hoodes,
Whych in ydelnes do lyve by other menns goodes:
Monkes, chanons and nones, in dyvers coloure and shappe,
Bothe whyght, blacke and pyed. God send ther increase yll happe!
40 *K. John.* Lete me know thy name or I go ferther with the.
Eng. Ynglond, syr, Ynglond my name is, ye may trust me.
K. John. I mervell ryght sore how thow commyst chaungyd thus.
[Enter Sedition.]
Sed. What, yow ij alone? I wyll tell tales, by Iesus,
And saye that I s[e y]ow fall here to bycherye.
45 *K. John.* Avoyd, lewde person, for thy wordes are   (p. 2, fol. 1ᵛ)
    vngodlye.
Sed. I crye yow mercy, sur. I pray yow be not angrye.
    Be my fayth and trowth, I cam hyther to be merye.

14 ouer] of *A.*   23 vsyd, as] vsyd ᐧ as *A.**
20 lawes] lawe *A.*

K. John. Thow canst with thy myrth in no wysse dyscontent me,
    So that thow powder yt with wysdom and honeste.
50 *Sed.* I am no spycer, by þe messe, ye may beleve me!
K. John. I speke of no spyce, but of cyvyle honeste.
Sed. Ye spake of powder, by the holy trynyte!
K. John. Not as thow takyst yt, of a grosse capasyte,
    But as saynt Pawle meanyth vnto the Collessyans playne:
55   So seasyne yowr speche þat yt be withowt dysdayne.
    Now, Ynglond, to the: go thow forth with thy tale
    And showe þe cawse why thow lokyst so wan and pale.
Eng. I told yow before, the faulte was in þe clergye
    That I, a wedow, apere to yow so barelye.
60 *Sed.* Ye are a wylly wat and wander here ful warelye.
K. John. Why in þe clargye, do me to vnderstande.
Eng. For they take from me my cattell, howse and land,
    My wodes and pasturs, with other commodyteys.
    Lyke as Christ ded saye to þe wyckyd pharyseys,
65   Pore wydowys howsys ye grosse vp by long prayers,
    In syde cotys wandryng lyke most dysgysed players.
Sed. They are well at ese þat hath soch soth sayers.
K. John. They are thy chylderne; þou owghtest to say them good.
Eng. Nay, bastardes they are, vnnatvrall, by þe rood!
70   Sens ther begynnyng they ware neuer good to me.
    The wyld bore of Rome—God let hym neuer to thee—
    Lyke pyggys they folow, in fantysyes, dreames and lyes,
    And euer are fed with his vyle cerymonyes.
Sed. Nay, sumtyme they eate bothe flawnes and pygyn pyes.
75 *K. John.* By the bore of Rome I trow thow menyst þe pope.
Eng. I mene non other but hym. God geve hym a rope!
K. John. And why dost thow thus compare hym to a swyne?
Eng. For that he and his to such bestlynes inclyne.
    They forsake Godes word, whych is most puer and cleane,
80   And vnto the lawys of synfull men they leane.
    Lyke as the vyle swyne þe most vyle metes dessyer
    And hath gret plesure to walowe them seluys in myre,
    So hath this wyld bore, with his church vnyversall—
    His sowe with hyr pygys and monstres bestyall—
85   Dylyght in mennys draffe and covytus lucre all.
    Yea, *aper de sylua* the prophet dyd hym call.

68 them] *Collier*; then *B.*   84 monstres] *Manly*: monstros *B.*

Sed. Hold yowr peace, ye whore, or ellys by masse   (p. 3, fol. 2)
    I trowe
  I shall cawse the pope to curse the as blacke as a crowe!
K. John. What arte thow, felow, þat seme so braggyng bolde?
90 *Sed.* I am Sedycyon, that with þe pope wyll hold
  So long as I haue a hole within my breche.
Eng. Commaund this felow to avoyd, I yow beseche,
  For dowȝtles he hath don me great inivry.
K. John. Avoyd, lewd felow, or thow shalt rewe yt truly.
95 *Sed.* I wyll not awaye for that same wedred wytche;
  She shall rather kysse whereas it doth not ytche.
  Quodcumque ligaueris I trow wyll playe soch a parte
  That I shall abyde in Englond, magry yowr harte.
  Tushe, the pope ableth me to subdewe bothe kyng and keyser.
100 *K. John.* Off that thow and I wyll common more at leyser.
Eng. Trwly of the devyll they are þat do onythyng
  To the subdewyng of any Christen kyng,
  For be he good or bade, he is of Godes apoyntyng:
  The good for the good, þe badde ys for yll doyng.
105 *K. John.* Of þat we shall talke here after. Say forth thy mynd now
  And show me how þou art thus becum a wedowe.
Eng. Thes vyle popych swyne hath clene exyled my hosband.
K. John. Who ys thy husband, telme good gentyll Yngland.
Eng. For soth, God hym selfe, the spowse of euery sort
110 Þat seke hym in fayth to þer sowlys helth and comfort.
Sed. He ys scant honest that so many wyfes wyll haue.
K. John. I saye hold yowr peace and stand asyde lyke a knave.
  Ys God exylyd owt of this regyon? Tell me.
Eng. Yea, that he is, ser, yt is the much more pete.
115 *K. John.* How commyth yt to passe þat he is thus abusyd?
Eng. Ye know he abydyth not where his word ys refusyd,
  For God is his word, lyke as seynt Iohn dothe tell
  In the begynnyng of his moste blyssyd gospell.
  The popys pyggys may not abyd this word to be hard
120 Nor knowyn of pepyll or had in anye regard.
  Ther eyes are so sore they maye not abyd þe lyght,
  And þat bred so hard ther gald gummes may yt not byght.
  I, knowyng yowr grace to haue here the governance

89 braggyng] braggyn *A.*   110 þer] *ed.;* yer *B;* the *Collier,*
96 whereas it doth] where yt do   *Manly, Farmer, Creeth.*
    A.

By the gyft of God, do knowlege my allegeance,
125 Desyeryng yowr grace to waye suche iniuryes
As I daylye suffer by thes same subtyll spyes.
And lett me haue ryght as ye are a ryghtfull kyng,
Apoyntyd of God to haue such mater in doyng;
For God wyllyth yow to helpe þe pore wydowes cause,
130 As he by Esaye protesteth in this same clause: (p. 4, fol. 2ᵛ)
Querite ivdicium, subuenite oppresso,
Ivdicate pupillo, defendite vidvam.
Seke ryght to poore, to the weake and faterlesse,
Defende the wydowe whan she is in dystresse.
135 *Sed.* I tell ye, the woman ys in great hevynes.
K. John. I may not in no wyse leve þi ryght vndyscuste,
For God hath sett me by his apoyntment ivst
To further thy cavse and to mayntayne þi ryght,
And therfor I wyll supporte þe daye and nyght.
140 So long as my symple lyffe shall here indewer,
I wyll se þe haue no wrong, be fast and swer.
I wyll fyrst of all call my nobylyte,
Dwkis, erlyes and lordes, yche on in ther degre.
Next them þe clargy, or fathers spirituall,
145 Archebysshopes, bysshoppes, abbottes and pryers all.
Than þe great ivges and lawers everychon,
So opynyng to them þi cause and petyfull mone,
By þe meanys wherof I shall þer myndes vnderstande.
Yf they helpe þe not, my selfe wyll take yt in hande
150 And sett such a waye as shall be to þi comforte.
Eng. Than for an answere I wyll shortly ageyne resort.
K. John. Do, Ynglond, hardly, and thow shalt haue remedy.
Eng. God reward yowr grace, I beseche hym hartely,
And send yow longe dayes to governe this realme in peace.
Go owt Ynglond and drese for Clargy.
155 *K. John.* Gramercy, Yngland, and send the plentyvs increse.
Sed. Of bablyng matters, I trow, yt is tyme to cease.
K. John. Why dost thow call them bablyng maters? Tell me.
Sed. For they are not worth þe shakyng of a pertre
Whan the peres are gon; they are but dyble dable.

---

130 protesteth] protest *A.*   137 apoyntment] *ed.*; apoyntmemt
134 the wydowe] the pore wydowe   *B.*
    A.   147 opynyng] *Manly*; opynnyg *B.*

160   I marvell ye can abyd suche byble bable.
      K.John. Thow semyst to be a man of symple dyscrescyon.
      Sed. Alas, þat ye are not a pryst to here confessyon.
      K.John. Why for confessyon? Lett me know þi fantasye.
      Sed. Becawse þat ye are a man so full of mercye,
165   Namely to women þat wepe with a hevy harte
      Whan they in þe churche hath lett but a lytyll farte.
      K.John. I perseyve well now thow speakyst all this in   (p. 5, fol. 3)
          mockage
      Becawse I take parte with Englandes ryghtfull herytage.
      Say thu what thow wylt, her mater shall not peryshe.
170 *Sed.* Yt is ioye of hym that women so can cheryshe.
      K.John. God hathe me ordeynned in this same princely estate
      For þat I shuld helpe such as be desolate.
      Sed. Yt is as great pyte to se a woman wepe
      As yt is to se a sely dodman crepe;
175   Or as ye wold say, a sely goose go barefote.
      K.John. Thow semyste by thy wordes to haue no more wytt
          than a coote.
      I mervell thow arte to Englond so vnnaturall:
      Beyng her owne chyld, þou art worse than a best brutall.
      Sed. I am not her chyld! I defye hyr, by þe messe!
180   I her sonne, quoth he? I had rather she were hedlesse.
      Thowgh I sumtyme be in Englond for my pastaunce,
      Yet was I neyther borne here, in Spayne nor in Fraunce,
      But vnder the pope in the holy cyte of Rome,
      And there wyll I dwell vn to the daye of dome.
185 *K.John.* But what is thy name? Tell me yett onys agayne.
      Sed. As I sayd afore, I am Sedycyon playne.
      In euery relygyon and mvnkysh secte I rayne,
      Havyng yow prynces in scorne, hate and dysdayne.
      K.John. I pray þe, good frynd, tell me what ys thy facyon.
190 *Sed.* Serche and ye shall fynd in euery congregacyon
      That long to the pope, for they are to me full swer,
      And wyll be so long as they last and endwer.
      K.John. Yff thow be a cloysterer, tell of what order thow art.
      Sed. In euery estate of þe clargye I playe a part:
195   Sumtyme I can be a monke in a long syd cowle,

160 byble] beble *A*.	178 than a best] than best *A*.
166 lytyll] *A*; lysyl *B*.*	182 neyther] nowther *A*.
169 Say thu what] Say what *A*.	193 of] me *A*.

Sumtyme I can be a none and loke lyke an owle,
Sumtyme a channon in a syrples fayer and whyght,
A chapterhowse monke sumtym I apere in syght,
I am ower syre Iohn sumtyme, with a new shauen crowne,
200 Sumtym þe person and swepe þe stretes with a syd gowne,
Sumtyme þe bysshoppe with a myter and a cope,
A graye fryer sumtyme, with cutt shoes and a rope;
Sumtyme I can playe þe whyght monke, sumtyme þe fryer,
The purgatory prist and euery mans wyffe desyer.
205 This cumpany hath provyded for me morttmayne,
For þat I myght euer among ther sort remayne.
Yea, to go farder, sumtyme I am a cardynall;
Yea, sumtyme a pope, and than am I lord ouer all,
Bothe in hevyn and erthe and also in purgatory,
210 And do weare iij crownes whan I am in my glorye.
K. John. But what doeste thow here in England? Tell me shortlye.
Sed. I hold vpp þe pope, as in other places many,   (p. 6, fol. 3ᵛ)
For his ambassador I am contynwally,
In Sycell, in Naples, in Venys and Ytalye,
215 In Pole, Sprvse and Beine, in Denmarke and Lumbardye,
In Aragon, in Spayne, in Fraunce and in Germanye,
In Ynglond, in Scotlond, and in other regyons elles.
For his holy cawse I mayntayne traytors and rebelles,
That no prince can haue his peples obedyence,
220 Except yt doth stand with the popes prehemynence.
K. John. Gett the hence, thow knaue and moste presumptuows wreche,
Or as I am trew kyng, thow shalt an halter streche!
We wyll thow know yt, owr powr ys of God,
And therfor we wyll so execute the rod
225 Þat no lewde pryst shall be able to mayneteyne the.
I se now they be at to mych lyberte.
We wyll short ther hornys, yf God send tyme and space.
Sed. Than I in Englond am lyke to haue no place?
K. John. No, þat thow arte not, and therfor avoyd apace.
230 *Sed.* By the holy masse, I mvst lawgh to here yowr grace!
Ye suppose and thynke þat ye cowd me subdewe.
Ye shall neuer fynd yowr supposycyon trewe,
Thowgh ye wer as strong as Hector and Diomedes,
Or as valyant as euer was Achylles.

208 ouer] of *A*.   228 Englond] *Collier*; Englong *B*;
                                                         ynglong *A*.

235 Ye are well content that bysshoppes contynew styll?
  K. John. We are so in dede, yf they ther dewte fullfyll.
  Sed. Nay, than, good inowgh. Yowr awtoryte and powrr
   Shall passe as they wyll; they haue sawce bothe swet and sowr.
  K. John. What mennyst thow by þat? Shew me þi intente this howre.
240 *Sed.* They are Godes vycars, they can both saue and lose.
  K. John. Ah, thy meenyng ys that they maye a prynce depose.
  Sed. By þe rood they may, and þat wyll appere by yow.
  K. John. Be þe helpe of God, we shall se to þat well inow.
  Sed. Nay, þat ye can not, thowgh ye had Argus eyes,
245 In abbeyes they haue so meny suttyll spyes.
   For ones in the yere they haue secret vysytacyons,
   And yf ony prynce reforme ther vngodly facyons,
   Than ij of the monkes mvst forthe to Rome by and by
   With secrett letters to avenge ther inivry.
250 For a thowsand pownd they shrynke not in soch matter,
   And yet for the tyme the prynce to his face they flater.
   I am euer more ther gyde and þer advocate.
  K. John. Than with þe bysshoppes and monkes þou art checke mate?
  Sed. I dwell among them and am one of ther sorte.
255 *K. John.* For thy sake they shall of me haue but small comforte;
   Loke, wher I fynd the, þat place wyll I put downe.
  Sed. What yf ye do chance to fynd me in euery towne (p. 7, fol. 4)
   Where as is fownded any sect monastycall?
  K. John. I pray God I synke yf I dystroye them not all!
260 *Sed.* Well, yf ye so do, yett know I where to dwell.
  K. John. Thow art not skoymose thy fantasy for to tell.
  Sed. Gesse. At a venture ye may chance þe marke to hytt.
  K. John. Thy falssed to shew, no man than thy selfe more fytt.
  Sed. Mary, in confessyon, vndernethe *Benedicite.*
265 *K. John.* Nay, tell yt ageyne that I may vnderstond þe.
  Sed. I saye I can dwell whan all other placys fayle me
   In ere confessyon, vndernethe *Benedicite,*
   And whan I am ther þe pryst may not bewray me.
  K. John. Why, wyll ere confesshon soch a secret traytor be?
270 *Sed.* Whan all oþer fayle, he is so swre as stele.
   Offend holy churche and I warant ye shall yt fele,
   For by confessyon the holy father knoweth
   Throw owt all Christendom what to his holynes growyth.

244 eyes] eyer *A.*   252 eu*er* more ther] eu*er* ther *A.**
245 spyes] spyer *A.*   270 oþer] *ed.*; oyer *B.*

K. John. Oh, where ys Nobylyte, þat he myght knowe thys falshed!
275 *Sed.* Nay, he is becum a meyntener of owr godhed.
    I know þat he wyll do holy chyrche no wronge,
    For I am his gostly father and techear amonge.
    He belevyth nothyng but as holy chyrch doth tell.
K. John. Why, geueth he no credence to Cristes holy Gospell?
280 *Sed.* No, ser, by the messe, but he callyth them herytyckes
    Þat preche þe Gospell, and sedycyows scysmatyckes.
    He tache them, vex them, from preson to preson he turne them,
    He indygth them, ivge them, and in conclusyon he burne them.
K. John. We rewe to here this of owr nobylyte;
285   But in this behalfe, what seyst of the spretuallte?
Sed. Of this I am swer: to them to be no stranger,
    And spesyally whan ther honor ys in dawnger.
K. John. We trust owr lawers haue no such wyckyd myndes.
Sed. Yes, they many tymys are my most secrett fryndes.
290   With faythfull precheres they can play leger demayne,
    And with falce colores procure them to be slayne.
K. John. I perseyve this worlde is full of iniquite.
    As God wold haue yt, here cummyth Nobylyte.
Sed. Doth he so in dede? By owr lord, than wyll I hence!
295 *K. John.* Thow saydest þou woldyst dwell where he kepyth resydence.
Sed. Yea, but fyrst of all I mvst chaunge myn apparell
    Vnto a bysshoppe, to maynetayene with my quarell,
    To a monke or pryst or to sum holy fryer.
    I shuld neuer elles accomplych my dysyre.
300 *K. John.* Why, art thow goyng? Naye, brother, thow   (p. 8, fol. 4ᵛ)
    shalte not hence.
Sed. I wold not be sene as I am for fortye pence.
    Whan I am relygyovse I wyll returne agayne.
K. John. Thow shalt tary here, or I mvst put the to payne.
Sed. I haue a great mynd to be a lecherovs man—
305   A wengonce take yt! I wold saye, a relygyovs man.
    I wyll go and cum so fast as euyre I can.
K. John. Tush, dally not with me. I saye þou shalt abyde.
Sed. Wene yow to hold me þat I shall not slyppe asyde?
K. John. Make no more prattyng, for I saye þou shalt abyde.
310 *Sed.* Stoppe not my passage; I mvst over see at þe next tyde.
K. John. I wyll ordeyne so, I trowe, þou shalt not ouer.

274 myght knowe thys] myght   290 they can play] they play *A.*
    thys *A.*   292 this worlde is,] this is ˙ *A.*

Sed. Tush, tush, I am sewer of redy passage at Douer.

Her go owt Sedwsion
and drese for Syvyll ordere.

K. John. The devyll go with hym! Þe vnthryftye knaue is gon.

[*Enter Nobility.*]

Nob. Troble not yowr sylfe with no soch dyssolute persone,

315   For ye knowe full well, very lyttell honeste
    Ys gote at ther handes in every commynnalte.

K. John. This is but dallyaunce; ye do not speke as ye thynke.

Nob. By my trowthe I do, or elles I wold I shuld synke!

K. John. Than mvst I marvell at yow of all men lyvynge.

320 *Nob.* Why mervell at me? Tell me yowr very menyng.

K. John. For no man levyng is in more famylyerite
    With that wycked wrech, yf it be trew þat he told me.

Nob. What wrech speke ye of, for Iesus love intymate.

K. John. Of þat presumtous wrech þat was with me here of late,

325   Whom yow wyllyd not to vexe my selfe withall.

Nob. I know hym? Not I, by þe waye þat my sowll to shall!

K. John. Make yt not so strange, for ye know hym wyll inow.

Nob. Beleve me yff ye wyll, I know hym not, I assuer yow.

K. John. Ware ye neuer yett aquantyd with Sedissyon?

330 *Nob.* Syns I was a chyld, both hym and his condycyon
    I euer hated for his iniquite.

[*Enter Clergy.*]

K. John. A clere tokyn þat is of trew nobelyte;
    But I pray to God we fynde yt not other wyse.
    Yt was neuer well syns þe clargy wrowȝt by practyse

335   And left þe scriptur for menns ymagynacyons,
    Dyvydyng them selvys in so many congrygacyons
    Of monkes, chanons and fryers, of dyvers colors and facyons.

Cler. I do trust yowr grace wyll be as lovyng now
    As yowr predysessours haue bene to vs before yow.

340 *K. John.* I wyll suer wey my love with yowr behavers: (p. 9, fol. 5)
    Lyke as ye deserve, so wyll I bere yow fauers.
    Clargy, marke yt well; I haue more to yow to say
    Than, as þe sayeng is, þe prist dyd speke a Sonday.

Cler. Ye wyll do vs no wrong, I hope, nor inivrye.

345 *K. John.* No, I wyll do yow ryght in seyng yow do yowr dewtye.

---

314 dyssolute] dysolate *A.**   330 both] I hath *A.**
320 mervell at] mervell yow at *A.**   339 haue] hathe *A.*
324 me here of] me of *A.*   343 sayeng is, þe] sayeng þe *A.*

We know þe cawtelles of yowr sotyll companye.
Cler. Yf ye do vs wrong we shall seke remedy.
K.John. Yea, that is the cast of all yowr company.
Whan kynges correcte yow for yowr actes most vngodly,
350   To þe pope, syttyng in the chayer of pestelens,
Ye ronne, to remayne in yowr concupysens.
Thus sett ye at nowght all princely prehemynens,
Subdewyng þe ordere of dew obedyens.
But with in a whyle I shall 'so abate yowr pryde
355   That to yowr popet ye shall noyther runne nor ryde;
But ye shall be glad to seke to me, yowr prynce,
For all such maters as shall be with in this provynce,
Lyke as God wyllyth yow by his scripture evydente.
Nob. To the church I trust ye wyll be obedyent.
360   *K.John.* No mater to yow whether I be so or no.
Nob. Yes, mary, is yt, for I am sworne thervnto:
I toke a great othe whan I was dubbyd a knyght
Euer to defend the holy churches ryght.
Cler. Yea, and in her quarell ye owght onto deth to fyght.
365   *K.John.* Lyke backes, in þe darke ye alweys take yowr flyght,
Flytteryng in fanseys, and euer abhorre the lyght.
I rew yt in hart that yow, Nobelyte,
Shuld thus bynd yowr selfe to þe grett captyvyte
Of blody Babulon, þe grownd and mother of whordom—
370   þe Romych churche I meane, more vyle than euer was Sodom,
And to say the trewth, a mete spowse for the fynd.
                    [*Enter Civil Order.*]
Cler. Yowr grace ys fare gonne; God send yow a better mynd.
K.John. Hold yowr peace, I say; ye are a lytyll to fatte.
In a whyle, I hope, ye shall be lener sumwhatte.
375   We shall loke to yow, and to Cyuyle order also.
Ye walke not so secrett but we know wher abowght ye goo.
C.Ord. Why, yowr grace hath no cawse with me to be dysplesyd.
K.John. All thynges consyderyd, we haue small cause to be plesyd.
C.Ord. I besech yowr grace to graunt me a word or too.
380   *K.John.* Speke on yowr pleasur and yowr hole mynd also.

C.Ord. Ye know very well to set all thynges in order

355 noyther] nowther *A.*	365 ye] *Collier*; y *B.*
361 yes] ys *A.**	370 vyle] vyler *A.**
361 thervnto] therto *A.*	371 mete] met *A.*

I haue moche ado, and many thynges passe fro me
For yowr common welth—and þat in euery border—
For offyces, for londes, for lawe and for lyberte.
385 And for traungressors I appoynt the penalte,
That cytes and townes maye stand in quiotose peace, (p. 10, fol. 5ᵛ)
That all theft and mvrder, with other vyce, maye seace.

Yff I haue chaunsed for want of cyrcumspeccyon
To passe þe lymytes of ryght and equite,
390 I submyte my selfe vnto yowr graces correccyon,
Desyryng pardon of yowr benyngnyte.
I wot I maye fall throwgh my fragylyte;
Therfor, I praye yow, tell me what þe mater ys,
And amendes shall be where as I haue done amyse.

395 *K. John.* Aganste amendement no resounable man can be.
Nob. That sentence rysyth owt of an hygh charyte.
K. John. Now that ye are her assembled all together,
Amongeste other thynges ye shall fyrst of all consyder
Þat my dysplesure rebounyth on to yow all.
400 *Cler.* To yow non of vs ys preiudycyall.
K. John. I shall proue yt. Yes, how haue ye vsyd England?
Nob. But as yt becommyth vs, so fare as I vnderstand.
K. John. Yes, þe pore woman complayneth her grevosly,
And not withowt a cawse, for she hath great iniurye.
405 I mvst se to yt, ther ys no remedy,
For it ys a charge gevyn me from God allmyghtye.
How saye ye? Clargye, apperyth it not so to yow?
Cler. Yf it lykyth yowr grace, all we knowe þat well ynow.
K. John. Than yow, Nobelyte, wyll affyrme yt, I am suer.
410 *Nob.* Ye, that I wyll, sur, so long as my lyfe indure.
K. John. And yow, Cyvyll order, I thynke wyll graunte þe same?
C. Ord. Ondowȝted, ser; ȝea, elles ware yt to me gret shame.
K. John. Than for Englandes cavse I wyll be sumewhat playne:
Yt is yow, Clargy, that hathe her in dysdayne
415 With yowr Latyne howrrs, serymonyes and popetly playes.
In her more and more Godes holy worde decayes,

383 common welth] *common*   409 affyrme] affyrnee *A.**
    welth*es A.*   412 elles] ell *A.*
407 apperyth it not] apperyth not   416 her more and more *godes*]
    A.   here more *godes A.*
408 knowe] knoweth *A.**

And them to maynteyn vnresonable ys þe spoyle
Of her londes, her goodes, and of her pore chylderes toyle.
Rekyn fyrst yowr tythis, yowr devocyons and yowr offrynges,
420   Mortuaryes, pardons, bequestes and other thynges,
Besydes that ye cache for halowed belles and purgatorye,
For iwelles, for relyckes, confessyon and cowrtes of bavdrye,
For legacyes, trentalles, with scalacely messys,
Wherby ye haue made þe people very assys;
425   And over all this ye haue browght in a rabyll
Of Latyne mvmmers and sectes desseyvabyll,
Evyn to dewore her and eat her vpp attonnys.
Cler. Yow wold haue no churche, I wene, by thes sacred bones.
K. John. Yes, I wold haue a churche, not of dysgysyd shavelynges,
430   But of faythfull hartes and charytable doynges,
For whan Christes chyrch was in her hyeste glory,   (p. 11, fol. 6)
She knew neyther thes sectes nor ther ipocrysy.
Cler. Yes! I wyll prove yt by Dauid substancyally:
Astitit regina a dextris tuis
435   *In vestitu deaurato, circumdata varietate.*
A quene, sayth Davyd, on thy ryght hond, lord, I se,
Apparrellyd with golde and compassyd with dyversyte.
K. John. What ys yowr meanyng by that same scriptur? Tell me.
Cler. This quene ys þe chyrch, which thorow all Cristen regions
440   Ys beawtyfull, deckyd with many holy relygyons—
Mvnkes, chanons and fryeres, most excellent dyvynis,
As Grandy Montensers and other Benedictyns,
Premonstratensers, Bernardes and Gylbertynys,
Iacobytes, Mynors, Whyght Carmes and Augustynis,
445   Sanbonites, Cluniackes, with holy Carthusyans,
Heremytes and auncors, with most myghty Rodyans,
Crucifers, Lucifers, Brigettes, Ambrosyanes,
Stellifers, Ensifers, with purgatoryanes,
Sophyanes, Indianes and Camaldulensers,
450   Iesuytes, Ioannytes, with Clarimontensers,
Clarynes and Columbynes, Templers, newe Niniuytes,
Rufyanes, Tercyanes, Lorytes and Lazarytes,
Hungaryes, Teutonyckes, Hospitelers, Honofrynes,

424 made] mad *A.*
427 attonnys] *Collier*; attonyns *B.*
439 thorow all] thorow owt all *A.**
440 deckyd] *Collier*; dectyd *B.**

447-458 *Added in B.*
450 *Omitted in Collier, Manly, Farmer.*

Basyles and Bonhams, Solauons and Celestynes,
455 Paulynes, Hieronymytes and monkes of Iosaphathes valleye,
Fulygynes, flamynes, with bretherne of the black alleye,
Donates and Dimysynes, with Canons of S. Mark,
Vestals and Monyals—a worlde to heare them barke!—
Abbottes and doctors, with bysshoppes and cardynales,
460 Archedecons and pristes, as to ther fortune falles.
 C. Ord. Me thynkyth yowr fyrst text stondeth nothyng with yor reson,
For in Davydes tyme wer no such sectes of relygyon.
 K. John. Davyd meanyth vertuys by þe same diversyte,
As in the sayd psalme yt is evydent to se,
465 And not mvnkysh sectes; but yt is euer yowr cast
For yowr advauncement þe scripturs for to wrast.
 Cler. Of owr holy father in this I take my grownd,
Which hathe awtoryte þe scripturs to expownd.
 K. John. Naye, he presumyth þe scripturs to confownd.
470 Nowther thow nor the pope shall do pore Englond wronge,
I beyng governor and kyng her peple amonge.
Whyle yow for lucre sett forth yowr popysh lawys
Yowr selvys to advaunce, ye wold make vs pycke strawes.
Nay, ipocrytes, nay. We wyll not be scornyd soo
475 Of a sort of knavys. We shall loke yow otherwyse too.
 Nob. Sur, yowr sprytes are movyd, I persayve by yowr langage.
 K. John. I wonder þat yow for such veyne popych baggage
Can suffyre Englond to be impoveryshyd
And mad a begger; ye are very yll advysyd.
480 *Nob.* I marvell grettly that ye saye thus to me.
 K. John. For dowghtles ye do not as becummyth nobelyte;
Ye spare novther landes nor goodes, but all ye geve
To thes cormerantes. Yt wold any good man greve
To se yowr madnes, as I wold God shuld saue me.
485 *Nob.* Sur, I suppose yt good to bylde a perpetuite
For me and my frendes, to be prayed for evermore.
 K. John. Tush, yt is madnes all to dyspayre in God (p. 12, fol. 6ᵛ)
    so sore
And to thynke Christes deth to be vnsvfficient.
 Nob. Sur, that I haue don was of a good intent.
490 *K. John.* The intente ys nowght which hath no sewer grovnde.

466 scripturs] scriptur *A.*
468 expownd] *ed.*; expond *B.**

488 thynke christes deth to be]
 thynke that christes deth ys
  A.

Cler. Yff yow continue, ye wyll holy chyrch confunde.
K. John. Nay, no holy chyrch nor feythfull congregacyon,
  But an hepe of adders of Antecristes generacyon.
C. Ord. Yt pyttyth me moche that ye are to them so harde.
495 *K. John.* Yt petyeth me more þat ye them so mych regarde.
  They dystroye mennys sowllys with damnable supersticyon,
  And decaye all realmys by meyntenaunce of sedycyon.
  Ye wold wonder to know what profe I haue of this.
Nob. Well, amenment shalbe wher any thyng is amysse,
500   For vndowtted, God doth open soche thynges to prynces
  As to none other men in the Cristyen provynces;
  And therfor we wyll not in this with yowr grace contend.
C. Ord. No, but with Godes grace we shall owr mysededes amend.
Cler. For all such forfetes as yowr pryncely mageste
505   For yowr owne person or realme can prove by me,
  I submytte my selfe to yow bothe body and goodes.   *Knele.*
K. John. We pety yow now, consyderyng yowr repentante modes,
  And owr gracyovs pardone we grante yow vpon amendment.
Cler. God preserve yowr grace and mageste excelent.
510 *K. John.* Aryse, Clargy, aryse, and ever be obedyent,
  And as God commandeth yow, take vs for yowr governere.
Cler. By þe grace of God, þe pope shall be my rulare.
K. John. What saye ye, Clargy? Who ys yowr governer?
Cler. Ha! Ded I stomble? I sayd, my prynce ys my ruler.
515 *K. John.* I pray to owr lord this obedyence maye indewre.
Cler. I wyll not breke yt, ye may be fast and suer.
K. John. Than cum hether all thre; ye shall know more of my mynde.
Cler. Owr kyng to obeye the scriptur doth vs bynde.
K. John. Ye shall fyrst be sworne to God and to þe crowne
520   To be trew and iuste in every cetye and towne,
  And this to performe set hand and kysse the bocke.
C. Ord. With the wyffe of Loth we wyll not backeward locke
  Nor turne from owr oth, but euer obeye yowr grace.
K. John. Than wyll I gyue yow yowr chargys her in place
525   And accepte yow all to be of owr hyghe councell.
Cler.   ⎫
Nob.   ⎬ To be faythfull, than, ye vs more streytly compell.
C. Ord. ⎭
K. John. For the love of God, loke to the state of Englond!
  Leate non enemy holde her in myserable bond.
  Se yow defend her as yt becummyth nobilite,

[84]

530 Se yow instructe her acordyng to yowr degre,
Fovrnysh her yow with a cyvyle honeste. (p. 13, fol. 7)
Thus shall she florysh in honor and grett plente.
With godly wysdom yowr maters so conveye
That the commynnalte the powers maye obeye,
535 And ever beware of that false thefe Sedycyon,
Whych poysennyth all realmes and bryng them to perdycyon.
Nob. Sur, for soche wrecches we wyll be so circumspectte
That neyther ther falsed nor gylle shall vs infecte.
Cler. I warrant yow, sur, no, and that shall well apere.
540 *C. Ord.* We wyll so provyde yff anye of them cum here
To dysturbe the realme, they shall be full glad to fle.
K. John. Well, yowr promyse includeth no small dyffyculte.
But I put the case that this false thefe Sedycyon
Shuld cum to yow thre and call hym selfe Relygyon.
545 Myght he not vnder the pretence of holynes
Cawse yow to consent to myche vngodlynes?
Nob. He shall never be able to do yt, veryly.
K. John. God graunt ye be not deceyvyd by hypocresye.
I say no more, I. In shepes aparell sum walke
550 And seme relygeyose þat deceyvably can calke;
Beware of soche hipocrites as þe kyngdom of hevyn from man
Do hyde for awantage, for they deceyve now and than.
Well, I leve yow here; yche man consyder his dewtye.
Nob. With Godes leve, no favte shall be in this companye.
555 *K. John.* Cum, Cyvyle order, ye shall go hence with me.
C. Ord. At yowr commandmente I wyll gladlye wayte vpon ye.
Here kyng Iohn and Sivile order go owt,
and Syvile order drese hym for Sedewsyon.
Nob. Me thynke the kyng is a man of a wonderfull wytt.
Cler. Naye, saye þat he ys of a vengeable craftye wytt;
Than shall ye be sure the trewth of the thyng to hytt.
560 Hard ye not how he of the holy church dyd rayle?
His extreme thretynynges shall lytyll hym avayle;
I wyll worke soch wayes þat he shall of his purpose fayle.
Nob. Yt is meet a prince to saye sumwhat for his plesure.
Cler. Yea, but yt is to moch to rayle so withowt mesure.
565 *Nob.* Well, lett every man speke lyke as he hathe a cawse.

530 instructe] *Manly*; Instrutte *B.*   551 man] men *A.*
538 neyther] nowther *A.**   559 than] & than *A.*
543 the] a *A.*

[85]

Cler. Why, do ye say so? Yt is tyme for me than to pawse.

Nob. This wyll I saye, sur, that he ys so noble a prince

    As this day raygneth in ony Cristyen provynce.

Cler. Mary, yt apereth well by that he wonne in Fraunce!

570 *Nob.* Well, he lost not ther so moche by marcyall chaunce

    But he gate moche more in Scotland, Ireland and Wales.

Cler. Yea, God sped vs well, Crystmes songes are mery tales!

Nob. Ye dysdayne soche mater as ye know full evydent.

    Are not bothe Ireland and Wales to hym obedyent?

575   Yes, he holdyth them bothe in pessable possessyon.   (p. 14, fol. 7ᵛ)

    And—by cause I wyll not from yowr tall make degressyon—

    For his lond in Fraunce he gyueth but lytell forsse,

    Havyng to Englond all his love and remorse;

    And Angoye he gaue to Artur his nevy in chaunge.

580 *Cler.* Owr changes are soch that an abbeye turneth to a graunge.

    We are so handled we haue scarce eyther horse or male.

Nob. He that dothe hate me þe worse wyll tell my tale.

    Yt is yowr fassyon soche kynges to dyscommend

    As yowr abuses reforme or reprehend.

585   Yow pristes are þe cawse þat Chronycles doth defame

    So many prynces and men of notable name,

    For yow take vpon yow to wryght them euermore;

    And therfor kyng Iohn ys lyke to rewe yt sore

    Whan ye wryte his tyme, for vexcyng of þe clargy.

590 *Cler.* I mervell ye take his parte so ernestlye.

Nob. Yt becommyth Nobelyte his prynces fame to preserue.

Cler. Yf he contynew, we are lyke in a whyle to starve:

    He demaundeth of vs the tenth parte of owr lyvyng.

Nob. I thynke yt is, then, for sum nessessary thyng.

595 *Cler.* Mary, to recover that he hath lost in Fraunce,

    As Normandy dewkedom and his land beyond Orleaunce.

Nob. And thynke ye not that a mater nessesary?

Cler. No, sur, by my trowth, he takyng yt of þe clergy.

Nob. Ye cowde be content that he shuld take yt of vs?

600 *Cler.* Yea, so þat he wold spare the clargy, by swet Iesus!

    This takyng of vs myght sone growe to a custom,

    And than holy churche myght so be browght to thraldom,

    Whych hath ben euer from temporall prynces free

574 Are] ys *A*.   582 tale] talle *A*.

577 gyueth] geve *A*.   583 fassyon] *Collier*; sassyon *B*.

581 eyther] owther *A*.   596 and] as *A*.

As towchyng trybute or other captyvyte.

605 *Nob.* He that defendeth yow owght to haue parte of yowr goodes.
Cler. He hath the prayers of all them þat hathe hoodes.
Nob. Why, ys that inowgh to helpe hym in his warre?
Cler. The churche he may not of lyberte debarre.
Nob. Ded not Crist hym selfe paye trybytt vnto Cesere?

610 Yf he payd trybute, so owght his holy vycar.
Cler. To here ye reson so ondyscretlye I wonder!
Ye mvst consyder that Cryst þat tyme was vnder,
But his vycar now ys aboue þe prynces all.
Therfor beware ye do not to herysy fall.

615 Ye owght to beleve as holy churche doth teche yow,
And not to reason in soche hygh materes now.
Nob. I am vnlernyd, my wyttes are sone confowndyd.   (p. 15, fol. 8)
Cler. Than leue soch materes to men more depely growndyd.
Nob. But how wyll ye do for the othe þat ye haue take?

620 *Cler.* The keyes of þe church can all soche materes of shake.
Nob. What call ye those kyes? I pray yow hartly, tell me.
Cler. Owr holy fathers powr and his hygh avtoryte.
Nob. Well, I can no more say; ye are to well lernyd for me.
My bysynes ys soche that here now I mvst leve ye.

625 *Cler.* I mvst hence also so fast as euer maye be,
To sewe vnto Rome for the churches lyberte.

> *Go owt Nobylyte and Clar[gy].*
>
> *Here Sedycyon cummyth in.*

Sed. Haue in onys ageyne, in spyght of all myn enymyes,
For they can not dryve me from all mennys companyes.
And thowgh yt wer so þat all men wold forsake me,

630 Yet dowght I yt not but sume good women wold take me.
I loke for felowys þat here shuld make sum sporte.
I mervell yt is so longe ere they resorte.
By þe messe! I wene þe knaves are in þe bryers,
Or elles they are fallen in to sum order of fryers.

635 Naye, shall I gesse ryght? They are gon into the stwes.
I holde ye my necke, anon we shall here newes.

> *[He hears someone] seyng þe leteny.*

609 ded] sayd *A.*
621 those] thes *A.*
626 vnto] onto *A.*
627 haue in onys ageyne] haue
    onys In ageyne *A.*

630 dowght I yt] dowght yt *A.*
630 women] worme *A.**
632 ere they resorte] or they
    hether resorte *A.**
634 are fallen] fall *A.*

Lyst, for Godes passyon! I trow her cummeth sum hoggherd
Callyng for his pyggys! Such a noyse I neuer herd.
Here cum Dyssymvlacyon syngyng of the letany.
Diss. (*syng*) *Sancte Dominice, ora pro nobis.*
640 *Sed.* (*syng*) *Sancte* pyld *monache*, I beshrow *vobis.*
Diss. (*syng*) *Sancte Francisse, ora pro nobis.*
Sed. Here ye not? Cockes sowle, what meaneth þis ypocryte knaue?
Diss. Pater noster, I pray God bryng hym sone to his grave;
Qui es in celis, with an vengeable *sanctificetur,*
645 Or elles holy chyrche shall neuer thryve, by saynt Petvr.
Sed. Tell me, good felowe, makyste þou this prayer for me?
Diss. Ye are as ferce as thowgh ye had broke yowr nose at þe buttre.
I medyll not with the, but here to good sayntes I praye,
Agenst soch enmyes as wyll holy chyrche decaye.
Here syng this:
650 *A Iohanne Rege iniquo, libera nos, domine.*
Sed. Leue, I saye, or by þe messe I wyll make yow grone.
Diss. Yff thow be ientyll, I pray þe leate me alone,
For with in a whyle my devocyon wyll be gone.
Sed. And wherfor dost thow praye here so bytterly,
655 Momblyng thy Pater noster and chauntyng þe letany?
Diss. For þat holy chyrch myght saue hyr patrymonye,
And to haue of kyng Iohn a tryumphant vyctorye.
Sed. And why of kyng Iohn? Doth he vexe yow so sore?
Diss. Bothe chyrchys and abbeys he oppressyth more   (p. 16, fol. 8ᵛ)
and more,
660 And take of the clergye—yt is onresonable to tell.
Sed. Owte with the popys bulles, than, and cursse hym downe to hell.
Diss. Tushe, man, we haue done so, but all þat wyll not helpe.
He regardyth no more þe pope than he dothe a whelpe.
Sed. Well, lett hym alone; for that wyll I geve hym a scelpe.
665 But what arte þou callyd of thyn owne munkych nacyon?
Diss. Kepe yt in covnsell: dane Davy Dyssymulacyon.
Sed. What, Dyssymulacyon? Cokes sowle, myn old aquentaunce!
Par me faye, mon amye, ie tote ad voutre plesaunce.

638 S.D. dyssymvlacyon] *Collier*;   654 wherfor] why *A.*
    dyssymvlacys *B.**   657 and to] to *A.*
638 S.D. letany] *Collier*; leany *B.*   657 tryumphant] *Collier*; tryum-
641 sancte] *Collier*; sacte *B.*   phnt *B.**
644 vengeable] horeble *A.**   665 thyn] thy *A.*
647 nose] fas *A.**

Diss. Gramercyes, good frend, with all my very hert.

670   I trust we shall talke more frely or we deperte.

Sed. Why, vylayn horson! Knowyst not þi cosyn Sedycyon?

Diss. I haue euer loved both the and thy condycyon.

Sed. Thow mvst nedes, I trowe, for we cum of ij bretherne:

    Yf þou remember, owr fatheres were on manns chylderne.

675   Thow commyst of falsed, and I of prevy treason.

Diss. Than infydelyte owr granfather ys by reason.

Sed. Mary, that ys trewe, and his begynner Antycrist,

    The great pope of Rome or fyrst veyne popysh prist.

Diss. Now welcum, cosyn, by þe waye þat my sowle shall to!

680 *Sed.* Gramercy, cosyn, by þe holy bysshope Benno.

    Thow kepyst þi old wont; thow art styll an abbe mann.

Diss. To hold all thynges vp I play my part now and than.

Sed. Why, what manere of offyce hast þou within the abbey?

Diss. Of all relygyons I kepe þe chyrch dore keye.

685 *Sed.* Than of a lykelyhod thow art ther generall porter.

Diss. Nay, of mvnkes and chanons I am þe suttyll sorter.

    Whyle sum talke with Besse the resydewe kepe sylence.

    Thowgh we playe þe knavys, we must shew a good pretence.

    Where so euer sum eate, a serten kepe þe froyter;

690   Where so euer sum slepe, sum must nedes kepe þe dorter.

    Dedyst þou neuer know þe maner of owr senyes?

Sed. I was neuer with them aquentyd, by seynt Denyes.

Diss. Than neuer knewyst þou the knauery of owr menyes.

    Yf I shuld tell all, I cowd saye more than that.

695 *Sed.* Now, of good felowshyppe, I beseche þe show me what.

Diss. The profytable lucre cummyth euer in by me.

Sed. But by what meane? Tell me, I hartely pray the.

Diss. To wynne þe peple I appoynt yche man his place:

    Sum to syng Latyn and sum to ducke at grace,

700   Sum to go mvmmyng and sum to beare þe crosse,   (p. 17, fol. 9)

    Sum to stowpe downeward as þer heades ware stopt with mosse;

    Sum rede þe epystle and gospell at hygh masse,

    Sum syng at þe lectorne, with long eares lyke an asse.

    The pawment of the chyrche þe aunchent faders tredes,

705   Sumtyme with a portas, sumtyme with a payre of bedes;

---

684 Relygyons] Relygyovs *A.* *　　　701 heade*s*] head *A.* *

692 aquentyd] *Collier*; aque*n*yn-　　　705 portas, su*m*tyme] portos ˙ &

    tyd *B.*　　　　　　　　　　　　su*m*tyme *A.*

700 beare] bare *A.*

And this exedyngly drawth peple to devoycyone,
Specyally whan they do se so good relygeon.
Than haue we imagys of seynt Spryte and seynt Savyer.
Moche is the sekynge of them to gett ther faver;
710   Yong whomen berfote, and olde men seke them brecheles.
The myracles wrowght ther I can in no wyse expresse.
We lacke neyther golde nor sylwer, gyrdles nor rynges,
Candelles nor tapperes, nor other customyd offerynges.
Thowgh I seme a shepe, I can play the suttle foxe:
715   I can make Latten to bryng this gere to þe boxe.
Tushe, Latten ys alone to bryng soche mater to passe;
Ther ys no Englyche þat can soche profyghtes compasse.
And therfor we wyll no servyce to be songe,
Gospell nor pystell, but all in Latten tonge.
720   Of owr suttell dryftes many more poyntes are behynde;
Yf I tolde yow all, we shuld neuer haue an ende.
    Sed. In nomine patris! Of all þat euer I hard,
Thow art alone yet of soche a dremyng bussard!
    Diss. Nay, dowst þou not se how I in my colours iette?
725   To blynd þe peple I haue yet a farther fette.
This is for Bernard and this is for Benet,
This is for Gylbard and this is for Ihenet;
For Frauncys this is, and this is for Domynyke,
For Awsten and Elen, and this is for seynt Partryk.
730   We haue many rewlles, but neuer one we kepe;
Whan we syng full lowde owr hartes be fast aslepe.
We resemble sayntes in gray, whyte, blacke and blewe,
Yet vnto prynces not one of owr nomber trewe.
And that shall kyng Iohn prove shortly, by þe rode.
735   *Sed.* But in þe meane tyme yowr selues gett lytyll good.
Yowr abbeys go downe, I here saye, every where.
    Diss. Yea, frynd Sedysyon, but thow mvst se to þat gere.
    Sed. Than mvst I haue helpe, by swete saynt Benettes cuppe.
    Diss. Thow shalt haue a chyld of myn owne bryngyng vppe.
740   *Sed.* Of thy bryngyng vppe! Cokes sowle, what knaue is that?

712 we] whe *A.*
712 neyther] nether *A.**
717 profyght*es*] prophet*es A.*
723 alone] above *A.**
724 colours] collers *A.*
725 haue yet a farther] haue a

ferder *A.*
729 for Awsten,] this is for awsten
A.
731 be fast aslepe] be aslepe *A.*
738 swete say*nt* benett*es*] swete
benett*es A.*

Diss. Mary, Pryvat Welth; now hayve I tolde þe what.
    I made hym a monke and a perfytt cloysterere,
    And in þe abbeye he becam fyrst celerer,
    Than pryor, than abbote, of a thowsand pownd land, no wors.
745   Now he is a bysshoppe and rydeth with an hondryd hors,
    And as I here say, he is lyke to be a cardynall.   (p. 18, fol. 9ᵛ)
Sed. Ys he so in dede? By the masse, than haue att all!
Diss. Nay. Fyrst Pryvat Welth shall bryng in Vsurpyd Powr
    With his avtoryte, and than the gam ys ower.
750 *Sed.* Tush, Vsurpyd Powr dothe fauer me of all men,
    For in his trobles I ease his hart now and then.
    Whan prynces rebell agenste hys autoryte,
    I make ther commons agenst them for to be.
    Twenty Mᵈ men are but a mornyng breckefast
755   To be slayne for hym, he takyng his repast.
Diss. Thow hast, I persayve, a very suttyll cast.
Sed. I am for þe pope as for þe shyppe þe mast.
Diss. Than helpe, Sedycyon, I may styll in Englond be;
    Kyng Iohn hath thretned þat I shall ouer see.
760 *Sed.* Well, yf thow wylte of me haue remedy this owr,
    Go feche Pryvat Welth and also Vsurpyd Powr.
Diss. I can bryng but one, be Mary, Iesus mother.
Sed. Bryng thow in þe one and let hym bryng in þe other.
    Here cum in Vsurpyd Powr and Private Welth,
        syngyng on after another.
Us.P. (syng this) Super flumina Babilonis suspendimus organa nostra.
765 *Pr.W. (syng this) Quomodo cantabimus canticum bonum in terra*
    aliena?
Sed. By the mas, me thynke they are syngyng of *placebo.*
Diss. Peace, for with my spectakles *vadam et videbo.*
    Cokes sowll, yt is they; at þe last I haue smellyd them owt.
        Her go and bryng them.
Sed. Thow mayst be a sowe yf thow hast so good a snowt.

770   Sures, marke well this gere, for now yt begynnyth to worke:
    False Dyssymulacyon doth bryng in Privat Welth,

741 what] all *A.*	764 flumina] *Collier*; flunina *B.*
745 Rydeth] Ryde *A.*	766 me] my *A.*
750 vsurpyd] *ed.*; vusurpyd *B.**	767 vadam] sadam *A.*
753 them for to] them to *A.*	768 them] þᵐ *A.*
759 thretned] *Collier*; threned *B.*	

And Vsurpyd Powr, which is more ferce than a Turcke,
Cummeth in by hym to decayve all spyrytuall helth;
Than I by them bothe, as clere experyence telth.
775 We iiij by owr craftes kyng Iohn wyll so subdwe
That for iij .C. yers all Englond shall yt rewe.

Diss. Of the clergy, fryndes, report lyke as ye se,
That ther Privat Welth cummyth euer in by me.
Sed. But by whom commyst þou? By þe messe, euyn by þe devyll,
780 For þe grownd þou arte of þe Cristen peplys evyll.
Diss. And what are yow, ser? I praye yow say good be me.
Sed. By my trowth, I cum by the and thy affynyte.
Diss. Feche thow in thy felow so fast as euer thow can.
Pr. W. I trow thow shalt se me now playe þe praty man.
785 Of me, Privat Welth, cam fyrst Vsurpyd Powr;
Ye may perseyve yt in pagent here this howr.
Sed. Now welcum, felowys, by all thes bonys and   (p. 19, fol. 10)
   naylys!
Us. P. Among companyons good felyshyp neuer faylys.
Sed. Nay, Vsurpid Powr, þou must go backe ageyne,
790 For I must also put þe to a lytyll payne.
Us. P. Why, fellaue Sedycyon, what wylt þou haue me do?
Sed. To bare me on þi backe and bryng me in also,
That yt maye be sayde þat fyrst Dyssymulacyon
Browght in Privat Welth to every Cristen nacyon,
795 And that Privat Welth browght in Vsurpid Powr,
And he Sedycyon, in cytye, towne and tower,
Þat sum man may know þe feche of all owr sorte.
Us. P. Cum on thy wayes, than, þat thow mayst mak þe fort.
Diss. Nay, Vsurped Powr, we shall bare hym all thre—
800 Thy selfe, he and I—yf ye wyll be rewlyd by me,
For ther is non of vs but in hym hath a stroke.
Pr. W. The horson knaue wayeth and yt were a Croked oke!
         Here they shall bare hym in,
            and Sedycyon saythe:
Sed. Yea, thus it shuld be. Mary, now I am alofte
I wyll beshyte yow all yf ye sett me not downe softe.

775 so] sone *A.*
776 that for iij] that iij *A.*
778 cummyth] *ed.*; cunnyth *B.*
786 howr] owr *A.**

802 Croked] myghty *A.*
803 I am alofte] *Collier conj.*; thu
   art alofte *B.*; alofte *A.*

[92]

805 In my opynyon, by swete saynt Antony,
      Here is now gatheryd a full honest company.
      Here is nowther Awsten, Ambrose, Hierom nor Gregory,
      But here is a sorte of companyons moch more mery.
      They of þe chirch than wer fower holy doctors,
810 We of þe chirch now are þe .iiij. generall proctors.
      Here ys fyrst of all good father Dyssymulacyon,
      Þe fyrst begynner of this same congregacyon;
      Here is Privat Welthe, which hath þe chyrch infecte
      With all abusyons and brovght yt to a synfull secte;
815 Here ys Vsurpid Powr, þat all kynges doth subdwe,
      With such avtoryte as is neyther good ner trewe;
      And I last of all am evyn sance pere Sedycyon.
Us. P. Vnder heuyn ys not a mor knaue in condycyon:
      Wher as þou dost cum, þat commonwelth can not thryve.
820 By owr lord, I marvell þat thow art yet alyve!
Pr. W. Wher herbes are pluckte vpp þe wedes many tymys remayne.
Diss. No man can vtter an evydence more playn.
Sed. Yea, ye thynke so, yow? Now Godes blyssyng breke yowr heade!
      I can do but lawgh to her yow, by this breade!
825 I am so mery þat we are mett, by saynt Iohn,
      I fele not þe grovnd þat I do go vppon.
      For þe love of God, lett vs haue sum mery songe.
Us. P. Begyne thy self, than, and we shall lepe in amonge.
                              Here syng.

Sed. I wold euer dwell here to haue such mery sporte.
830 *Pr. W.* Thow mayst haue yt, man, yf thow wylt hether resorte,
      For the holy father ys as good a felowe as we.
Diss. The holy father! Why, I pray the, whych is he?   (p. 20, fol. 10ᵛ)
Pr. W. Vsurpid Powr here, which, thowgh he apparaunt be
      In this apparell, yet hathe he avtoryte
835 Bothe in hevyn and erth, in purgatory and in hell.
Us. P. Marke well his saynges, for a trew tale he doth tell.
Sed. What, Vsurpid Powr? Cockes sowle, ye are owr pope?
      Where is yowr thre crovnys, yowr crosse keys and yowr cope?
      What meanyth this mater? Me thynke ye walke astraye.
840 *Us. P.* Thow knowest I must haue sum dalyaunce and playe,
      For I am a man lyke as an other ys.
      Sumtyme I must hunt, sumtyme I mvst Alysen kys.

807 nor] ner *A.**   838 crovnys] *ed.*; crovnyns *B.*
816 neyther] nowther *A.*

[93]

I am bold of yow, I take ye for no straungers.
We are as spirituall: I dowȝt in yow no daungers.

845 *Diss.* I owght to conseder yowr holy father hode,
From my fyrst infancy ye haue ben to me so good.
For Godes sake, wytsave to geve me yowr blyssyng here,

Knele.

A pena et culpa þat I may stand this day clere.
Sed. From makyng cuckoldes? Mary, þat wer no mery chere.

850 *Diss. A pena et culpa*; I trow thow canst not here.
Sed. Yea, with a cuckoldes wyff ye haue dronke dobyll bere.
Diss. I pray the, Sedycyon, my pacyens no more stere;
A pena et culpa I desyre to be clere,
And than all the devylles of hell I wold not fere.

855 *Us.P.* But tell me one thyng: dost þou not preche þe Gospell?
Diss. No, I promyse yow; I defye yt to þe devyll of hell!
Us.P. Yf I knewe thow dedyst, þou shuldest haue non absolucyon.
Diss. Yf I do, abiure me or put me to execucyon.
Pr.W. I dare say he brekyth no popyshe constytucyon.

860 *Us.P.* Soche men are worthy to haue owr contrybucyon:
I assoyle the here, behynde and also beforne.
Now art þou as clere as þat daye thow wert borne.
Ryse, Dyssymulacyon, and stond vppe lyke a bold knyght;
Dowȝt not of my powr thowgh my aparell be lyght.

865 *Sed.* A man, be þe messe, can not know yow from a knave;
Ye loke so lyke hym as I wold God shuld me save.
Pr.W. Thow arte very lewde owr father so to depraue.
Thowgh he for his plesure soche lyght apparell haue,
Yt is now sommer and the heate ys withowt mesure,

870 And among vs he may go lyght at his owne plesure.
Felow Sedycyon, thowgh þou dost mocke and scoffe,
We haue other materes than this to be commyned of.
Frynd Dyssymulacyon, why dost þou not thy massage
And show owt of Englond þe causse of þi farre passage?

875 Tush, blemysh not, whoreson, for I shall ever assyst þe.
Sed. The knave ys whyght leueryd, by the holy   (p. 21, fol. 11)
trynyte!
Us.P. Why so, Privat Welth? What ys þe mater? Tell me.

847 here] her *A.*
849 chere] cher *A.*
864 not of my] not my *A.*
865 messe, can] messe · I can *A.*

866 so] as *A.*
868 apparell haue] apparell *A.*
874 þi farre passage] þi passage *A.*

Pr. W. Dyssymulacyon ys a massanger for þe clergy;
 I must speke for hym, ther ys no remedy.

880 The clargy of Ynglond, which ys yowr specyall frynde
 And of a long tyme hath borne yow very good mynde,
 Fyllyng yowr coffars with many a thowsande pownde,
 Yf ye sett not to hand, he ys lyke to fall to þe grownde.
 I do promysse yow truly, his harte ys in his hose;

885 Kyng Iohn so vsyth hym þat he reconnyth all to lose.
Us. P. Tell, Dyssymulacyon, why art thow so asshamed
 To shewe thy massage? Thow art moch to be blamed.
 Late me se those wrytynges. Tush, man, I pray þe cum nere.
Diss. Yowr horryble holynes puteth me in wonderfull fere.

890 *Us. P.* Tush, lett me se them, I pray the hartely!
  Here Dissimvlacyon shall deleuer þe wrytynges
   to Vsurpyd Powr.
 I perseyve yt well, thow wylt lose no ceremony.
Sed. Yet is he no lesse than a false knave, veryly.
 I wold thow haddyst kyst his ars, for þat is holy.
Pr. W. How dost thow proue me þat his arse ys holy, now?

895 *Sed.* For yt hath an hole, evyn fytt for þe nose of yow.
Pr. W. Yowr parte ys not elles but for to playe þe knave,
 And so ye mvst styll contynew to yowr grave.
Us. P. I saye, leue yowr gawdes and attend to me this howre.
 The bysshoppes writeth here to me, Vsurped Powr,

900 Desyryng assystence of myne avctoryte
 To saue and support the chyrches lyberte.
 They report kyng Iohn to them to be very harde
 And to haue þe church in no pryce nor regarde.
 In his parlament he demaundeth of þe clargy

905 For his warres þe tent of þe chyrches patrymony.
Pr. W. Ye wyll not consent to that, I trow, by saynt Mary!
Sed. No, drawe to yow styll, but lett none from yow cary.
Us. P. Ye know yt is cleane agenst owr holy decrees
 That princes shuld thus contempne owr lybertees.

910 He taketh vppon hym to reforme þe tythes and offrynges
 And intermedleth with other spyrytuall thynges.

878 dyssymulacyon] *ed.*; dyssymu- 885 lose] losse *A.*
  lacon *B.*   889 horryble] orebyll *A.**
882 pownde] *Collier*; pwnde *B.* 889 puteth] *ed.*; putth *B.*
884 yow truly, his] yow his *A.* 891 ceremony] cerymony *A.*
884 hose] hosse *A.*   896 knave] *Collier*; knove *B.*

Pr. W. Ye mvst sequester hym, or elles that wyll mare all.
Us. P. Naye, besydes all this, before iuges temporall
He conventeth clarkes of cawses crymynall.
915 *Pr. W.* Yf ye se not to that the churche wyll haue a fall.
Sed. By the masse, than pristes are lyke to haue a   (p. 22, fol. 11ᵛ)
    pange;
For treson, mvrder and thefte they are lyke to hange.
By cockes sowle, than I am lyke to walke for treason
Yf I be taken. Loke to yt therfor in seasone.
920 *Pr. W.* Mary, God forbyd that euer yowr holy anoynted
For tresone or thefte shuld be hanged, racked or ioynted
Lyke the rascall sorte of the prophane layete.
Us. P. Naye, I shall otherwyse loke to yt, ye may trust me.
Before hymselfe also þe bysshoppes he doth convent,
925 To þe derogacyon of ther dygnyte excelent,
And wyll suffer non to þe covrt of Rome to appele.
Diss. No, he contemnnyth yowre avtoryte and seale
And sayth in his lond he wyll be lord and kyng,
No prist so hardy to enterpryse any thyng.
930 For þe whych of late with hym ware at veryaunce
Fower of his bysshoppes, and in maner at defyaunce:
Wyllyum of London and Evstace bysshope of Hely,
Water of Wynchester and Gylys of Hartford, trewly.
Be yowr avtoryte they haue hym excominycate.
935 *Us. P.* Than haue they done well, for he is a reprobate.
To þat I admytt he ys alwayes contrary.
I made this fellow here þe archebysshope of Canterbery,
And he wyll agree therto in no condycyon.
Pr. W. Than hathe he knowlege þat his name ys Sedycyon?
940 *Diss.* Dowtles he hath so, and that drownnyth his opynyon.
Us. P. Why do ye not saye his name ys Stevyn Langton?
Diss. Tush, we haue done so, but þat helpyth not þe mater;
The bysshope of Norwych for þat cawse doth hym flater.
Us. P. Styke thow to yt fast we haue onys admytted the.
945 *Sed.* I wyll not one iote from my admyssyon fle;
The best of them all shall know þat I am he.
Naye, in suche maters lett men be ware of me.

Us. P. The monkes of Caunterbery ded more at my request

932 wyllum] wyllem *A.*   948 Caunterbery] *ed.;* caunterbey
936 alwayes] euer *A.*   *B.*

Than they wold at his concernyng that eleccyon.
950 They chase Sedycyon, as yt is now manyfest,
In spytt of his harte. Than he for ther rebellyon
Exyled them all and toke ther hole possessyon
In to hys owne handes, them sendyng ouer see,
Ther lyuynges to seke in extreme poverte.

955 This custum also he hath, as it is tolde me:
Whan prelates depart—yea, bysshope, abbott or curate—
He entreth theyr landes with owt my lyberte,
Takyng þe profyghtes tyll the nexte be consecrate,
Instytute, stallyd, indeucte or intronyzate.
960 And of þe pyed monkes he entendeth to take a dyme.
All wyll be marryd yf I loke not to yt in tyme.

Diss. Yt is takyn, ser. Þe somme ys un-resonnable— (p. 24[a], fol. 13)
A nynne thowsand marke; to lyve they are not able.
His suggesteon was to subdew the Yrysh men.
965 *Pr. W.* Yea, that same peple doth ease þe church now and then;
For that enterpryse they wold be lokyd vppon.
Us. P. They gett no mony, but they shall haue clene remyssion,
For those Yrysh men are euer good to þe church;
Whan kynges dysobeye yt, than they begynne to worch.
970 *Pr. W.* And all that they do ys for indvlgence and pardon.
Sed. By the messe, and þat is not worth a rottyn wardon!
Us. P. What care we for that? To them yt is venyson.
Pr. W. Than lett them haue yt, a Godes dere benyson!
Us. P. Now, how shall we do for this same wycked kyng?
975 *Sed.* Suspend hym and curse hym, both with yowr word and wrytyng;
Yf that wyll not holpe, than interdyct his land
With extrem cruellnes; and yf þat wyll not stand,
Cawse other prynces to revenge þe churchys wronge.
Yt wyll profytte yow to sett them aworke amonge;
980 For clene remyssyon one kyng wyll subdew another.
Yea, þe chyld sumtyme wyll sle both father and mother.
Us. P. This cownsell ys good; I wyll now folow yt playne.
Tary thow styll here tyll we returne agayne.

957 theyr] ther *A.*   970 Indvlgence] Indvlgensys *A.*
965 then] than *A.**   976 Interdyct] Interdyght *A.**

Her go owt Vsurpid Powr
and Privat Welth and Sedycyon;
Vsurpyd Powr shall drese for þe pope,
Privat Welth for a cardynall,
and Sedycyon for a monke.
Þe cardynall shall bryng in þe crose,
and Stevyn Lavnton þe bocke, bell and candell.

Diss. This Vsurpid Powr, whych now is gon from hence,
985　For the holy church wyll make such ordynance
　　That all men shall be vnder his obedyens.
　　Yea, kynges wyll be glad to geve hym their alegyance,
　　And than shall we pristes lyve here with owt dysturbans.
　　As Godes owne vyker anon ye shall se hym sytt,
990　His flocke to avaunse by his most polytyke wytt.

　　He shall make prelates, both byshopp and Cardynall,　(p. 23, fol. 12)
　　Doctours and prebendes with furde whodes and syde gownes.
　　He wyll also create the orders monastycall,
　　Monkes, chanons and fryers, with gaye coates and shauen crownes,
995　And buylde them places to corrupt cyties and townes.
　　The dead sayntes shall shewe both visyons and myracles;
　　With ymages and rellyckes he shall wurke sterracles.

　　He wyll make mattens, houres, masse and euensonge
　　To drowne the scriptures for doubte of heresye;
1000　He wyll sende pardons to saue mennys sowles amonge,
　　Latyne deuocyons, with the holye rosarye.
　　He wyll apoynt fastynges and plucke downe matrimonye;
　　Holy water and breade shall dryue awaye the deuyll;
　　Blessynges with blacke bedes wyll helpe in euery euyll.

1005　Kynge Iohan of Englande, bycause he hath rebelled
　　Agaynst holy churche, vsynge it wurse than a stable,
　　To gyue vp hys crowne shall shortly be compelled.

983 S.D. for a monke] for stevyn　　　991-1011 *Added in B.*
　　lavnton monke *A.*　　　　　　　995 buylde] byylde *b.*
987 hym　their　alegyance] hym　　997 shall] wyll *b.*
　　alegyance *A.*　　　　　　　　1002 plucke] pull *b.*
988 than shall we] than shall shall
　　we *A.**

And the Albygeanes, lyke heretykes detestable,
Shall be brent bycause agaynst our father they babble;
1010 Through Domynyckes preachynge an .xviij. thousande are slayne
To teache them how they shall holye churche disdayne.

All this to performe he wyll cawle a generall   (p. 24[b], fol. 13)
  cowncell
Of all Cristendom to þe church of Laternense.
His intent shall be for to suprese the Gospell,
1015 Yett wyll he glose yt with a very good pretens:
To subdwe the Turkes by a Cristen vyolens.
Vnder this colovre he shall grownd ther many thynges,
Whych wyll at þe last be Cristen mennys vndoynges.

The popys powr shall be abowe þe powrs all,
1020 And eare confessyon a matere nessessary.
Ceremonys wyll be þe ryghtes ecclesyastycall.
He shall sett vp ther both pardowns and purgatory;
The Gospell prechyng wyll be an heresy.
Be this provyssyon and be soch other kyndes
1025 We shall be full suere all waye to haue owr myndes.

[*Enter Usurped Power as the Pope,*
Private Wealth as a cardinal,
and Sedition as the monk Stephen Langton.]
Pope. Ah, ye are a blabbe! I perseyve ye wyll tell all.
I lefte ye not here to be so lyberall.
Diss. Mea culpa, mea culpa, gravissima mea culpa!   (p. 25, fol. 13ᵛ)
Geve me yowr blyssyng *pro deo et sancta Maria.*
                     Knele and knoke on þi bryst.
1030 *Pope.* Thow hast my blyssyng, aryse now and stond asyde.
Diss. My skyn ys so thyke yt wyll not throw glyde.
Pope. Late vs goo abowȝt owr other materes now.
Diss. ⎫
Card. ⎬ We wayte her vpon þe greate holynes of yow.
S. Lang. ⎭
Pope. For as moch as kyng Iohn doth holy church so handle,
1035 Here I do curse hym wyth crosse, boke, bell and candle:
Lyke as this same roode turneth now from me his face,
So God I requyre to sequester hym of his grace;

1021 ryght*es*] ryghte *A.*
1026 blabbe] blabe *A.*
1028 mea (*second*)] me *A.*

1031 throw glyde] throw me glyde
  *A.**
1035 I do curse] I curse *A.*

As this boke doth speare by my worke maanuall,
I wyll God to close vppe from hym his benyfyttes all;
1040 As this burnyng flame goth from this candle in syght,
I wyll God to put hym from his eternall lyght;
I take hym from Crist, and after þe sownd of þis bell,
Both body and sowle I geve hym to þe devyll of hell.
I take from hym baptym, with the othere sacramentes
1045 And suffrages of þe churche, bothe ember dayes and lentes.
Here I take from hym bothe penonce and confessyon,
Masse of þe .v. wondes, with sensyng and processyon.
Here I take from hym holy water and holy brede,
And neuer wyll them to stande hym in any sted.
1050 This thyng to publyshe I constytute yow thre,
Gevyng yow my powr and my full avtoryte.

Diss.
Card. } With the grace of God we shall performe yt, than.
S. Lang.

Pope. Than gett yow foreward so fast as euer ye can
Vppon a bone vyage; yet late vs syng meryly.
1055 *S. Lang.* Than begyne þe song and we shall folow gladly.

Here they shall syng.

Pope. To colovre this thyng, thow shalte be callyd Pandvlphus;
Thow, Steuyn Langton; thy name shall be Raymundus.
Fyrst thow, Pandolphus, shalt opynly hym suspend
With boke, bell and candle; yf he wyll not so amend,
1060 Interdycte his lande and þe churches all vp speare.
Card. I haue my massage; to do yt I wyll not feare.

Here go owt
and dresse for Nobylyte.

Pope. And thow, Stevyn Langton, cummaund þe bysshoppes all
So many to curse as are to hym benefycyall—
Dwkes, erles and lordes—wherby they may forsake hym.
1065 *S. Lang.* Sur, I wyll do yt, and that, I trow, shall shake hym.

[Exit.]

Pope. Raymundus, go thow forth to þe Crysten princes all;
Byd them in my name þat they vppon hym fall,
Bothe with fyre and sword, þat þe churche may hym conquarre.
Diss. Yowr plesur I wyll no lengar tyme defarre.
1070 *Pope.* Saye this to them also: pope Innocent the thred
Remyssyon of synnes to so many men hath graunted

1057 name] *Collier*; nane *B.*   1059 not so amend] not amend *A.*

[100]

As wyll do ther best to slee hym yf they may.

Diss. Sur, yt shall be don with owt ony lenger delay.

[*Exit.*]

Pope. In the meane season I shall soch gere avaunce　(p. 27[a], fol. 15)

1075　As wyll be to vs a perpetuall furderaunce:
　　　Fyrst eare confessyon, than pardons, than purgatory,
　　　Sayntes worchyppyng than, than sekyng of ymagery,
　　　Than Laten servyce with the cerymonyes many,
　　　Wherby owr bysshoppes and abbottes shall get mony.
1080　I wyll make a law to burne all herytykes,
　　　And kynges to depose whan they are sysmatykes.
　　　I wyll all so reyse vp þe fower beggyng orderes
　　　That they may preche lyes in all þe cristen borderes.
　　　For this and other I wyll call a generall cownsell
1085　To ratyfye them in lyke strength with þe Gospell.

　　　　　Here þe pope go owt. . . .
　　　　　　The interpretour.　　　　(p. 26, fol. 14)

　　　In thys present acte we haue to yow declared,
　　　As in a myrrour, the begynnynge of kynge Iohan,
　　　How he was of God a magistrate appoynted
　　　To the gouernaunce of thys same noble regyon,
1090　To see maynteyned the true faythe and relygyon.
　　　But Satan the Deuyll, whych that tyme was at large,
　　　Had so great a swaye that he coulde it not discharge.

　　　Vpon a goode zele he attempted very farre
　　　For welthe of thys realme to prouyde reformacyon
1095　In the churche therof. But they ded hym debarre
　　　Of that good purpose, for by excommunycacyon
　　　The space of .vij. yeares they interdyct thys nacyon.
　　　These bloudsuppers thus, of crueltie and spyght,
　　　Subdued thys good kynge for executynge ryght.

1100　In the second acte thys wyll apeare more playne,
　　　Wherin Pandulphus shall hym excommunycate
　　　Within thys hys lande, and depose hym from hys reigne.
　　　All other princes they shall moue hym to hate
　　　And to persecute after most cruell rate.
1105　They wyll hym poyson in their malygnyte
　　　And cause yll report of hym alwayes to be.

1086-1120 *Added in B.*　　　　　1097 thys] *Collier*; thy *B.*

[101]

Thys noble kynge Iohan, as a faythfull Moyses,
Withstode proude Pharao for hys poore Israel,
Myndynge to brynge it out of the lande of Darkenesse.
1110 But the Egyptyanes ded agaynst hym so rebell
That hys poore people ded styll in the desart dwell,
Tyll that duke Iosue, whych was our late kynge Henrye,
Clerely brought vs in to the lande of mylke and honye.

As a stronge Dauid at the voyce of verytie,
1115 Great Golye, the pope, he strake downe with hys slynge,
Restorynge agayne to a Christen lybertie
Hys lande and people, lyke a most vyctoryouse kynge,
To hir first bewtye intendynge the churche to brynge,
From ceremonyes dead to the lyuynge wurde of þe lorde.
1120 Thys the seconde acte wyll plenteously recorde.
finit actus primus.

1111 ded] must *b.*   1116 a] the *b.*

... [Sedition as Stephen Langton] and   (p. 27[b], fol. 15)
Nobylyte cum in and say:

Nob. It petyeth my hart to se the controvercye
   That now a dayes reygnethe betwyn þe kyng and þe clargy.
   All Cantorbery monkes are now þe realme exyled,
   The prystes and bysshoppes contyneally revyled;
1125   The Cistean monkes are in soche perplexyte
   That owt of Englond they reken all to flee.
   I lament the chaunce as I wold God shuld me saue.
S. Lang. Yt is gracyously sayd; Godes blyssyng myght ye haue!
   Blyssyd is þat man þat wyll graunte or condyssend
1130   To helpe relygyon or holy churche defend.
Nob. For there mayntenance I haue gevyn londes full fayere
   And haue dysheryted many a lavfull ayere.
S. Lang. Well, yt is yowr owne good; God shall reward yow for ytt,
   And in hevyn full hyghe for soch good workes shall ye sytt.
1135 *Nob.* Yowr habyte showyth ye to be a man of relygeon.
S. Lang. I am no worse, sur; my name is good perfeccyon.
Nob. I am the more glad to be aquented with ye.
S. Lang. Ye show yowr selfe here lyke a noble man, as ye be.
   I perseyve ryght well yowr name ys Nobelyte.
1140 *Nob.* Yowr servont and vmfrey. Of trewthe, father, I am he.
S. Lang. From Innocent þe pope I am cum from Rome evyn now.
   A thowsand tymes, I wene, he commendyth hym vnto yow,
   And sent yow clene remyssyon to take þe chyrches parte.
Nob. I thanke his holynes. I shall do yt with all my harte.
1145   Yf ye wold take paynes for heryng my confessyon,
   I wold owt of hand resayue this cleane remyssyon.
S. Lang. Mary, with all my hart! I wyll be full glad to do ytt.
Nob. Put on yowr stolle, then, and I pray yow in Godes name sytt.
   Here sett down, and
   Nobelyte shall say benedycyte.

   Benedicite.
1150 *S. Lang. Dominus: In nomine domini pape, amen.* Say forth yowr
   mynd, in Godes name.

1121 petyeth] petyth *A.*	1146 this cleane remyssyon] this re-
1124 contyneally] *Collier;* conty-	myssyon *A.*
meally *B.*	1150 domini pape] domini nostri
1126 reken] rekund *A.**	pape *A.*
1135 ye,] ye: *A.**	

Nob. I haue synnyd agaynst God; I knowlege my selfe to blame:
In the vij dedly synnys I haue offendyd sore;
Godes ten commaundymentes I haue brokyn euer   (p. 28, fol. 15ᵛ)
    more;
My .v. boddyly wytes I haue on-godly kepte;
1155   The workes of charyte in maner I haue owt slepte.
S. Lang. I trust ye beleve as holy chyrch doth teache ye,
And from the new lernyng ye are wyllyng for to fle.
Nob. From the new lernyng, mary, God of hevyn saue me!
I never lovyd yt of a chyld, so mote I the.
1160   *S. Lang.* Ye can saye yowr crede and yowr Laten aue Mary?
Nob. Yea, and dyrge also, with sevyn psalmes and letteny.
S. Lang. Do ye not beleve in purgatory and holy bred?
Nob. Yes, and þat good prayers shall stand my sovle in stede.
S. Lang. Well, than, good inowgh; I warant my sovlle for yowr.
1165   *Nob.* Than execute on me the holy fatheres powr.
S. Lang. Naye, whyll I haue yow here vnderneth *benedicite*,
In þe popys behalfe I mvst moue other thynges to ye.
Nob. In þe name of God, saye here what ye wyll to me.

S. Lang. Ye know þat kyng Iohn ys a very wycked man
1170   And to holy chyrch a contynuall adversary.
Þe pope wyllyth yow to do þe best ye canne
To his subduyng, for his cruell tyranny;
And for þat purpose this prevylege gracyously
Of clene remyssyon he hath sent yow this tyme,
1175   Clene to relesse yow of all yowr synne and cryme.

Nob. Yt is clene agenst þe nature of nobelyte
To subdew his kyng with owt Godes autoryte,
For his princely estate and powr ys of God.
I wold gladly do yt, but I fere his ryghtfull rode.
1180   *S. Lang.* Godes holy vycare gaue me his whole avtoryte.
Loo, yt is here, man; beleve yt, I beseche the,
Or elles thow wylte faulle in danger of damnacyon.
Nob. Than I submyt me to the chyrches reformacyon.
S. Lang. I assoyle the here from þe kynges obedyence

1167 moue] show *A.*   1180 whole] hole *A.**
1178 estate] state *A.*   1181 the] þe *A.*
1179 ryghtfull] ryght *A.*

1185 By þe avctoryte of þe popys magnifycence:
Auctoritate romani pontyficis ego absoluo te
From all possessyons gevyn to þe spiritualte,
In nomine domini pape, amen.
Kepe all thynges secrett, I pray yow hartely.

Go owt Nobelyte.

1190 *Nob.* Yes, that I wyll, sur, and cum agayne hether shortly.

Here enter Clargy and Cyuyl order together,
and Sedysyon [as Stephen Langton] shall go
vp and down a praty whyle.

Cler. Ys not yowr fatherhod archebysshope of Canterbery?
S. Lang. I am Stevyn Langton. Why make ye here inquyry?

Knele and say both:

Cler. ⎫
C. Ord. ⎬ Ye are ryght welcum to this same regyon, trewly.

S. Lang. Stond vp, I pray yow. I trow þou art þe clargy.

1195 *Cler.* I am þe same, sur, and this is Cyvyle order.
S. Lang. Yf a man myght axe yow, what make yow   (p. 29, fol. 16)
    in this bordere?
Cler. I herd tell yester daye ye were cum in to the land.
    I thowght for to se yow, sum newes to vnderstand.
S. Lang. In fayth, thow art welcum. Ys Cyuyll order thy frynd?

1200 *Cler.* He is a good man and beryth the chyrch good mynd.
C. Ord. Ryght sory I am of þe great controvarsy
    Betwyn hym and þe kyng. Yf I myght yt remedy—
S. Lang. Well, Cyvyll order, for thy good wyll gramercy;
    Þat mater wyll be of an other facyon shortly.

1205 Fyrst, to begynne with we shall interdyte þe land.
C. Ord. Mary, God forbyde we shuld be in soche band!
    But who shall do yt, I pray yow hartyly?
S. Lang. Pandulphus and I; we haue yt in owr legacy.
    He went to þe kyng for þat cawse yester daye,

1210 And I wyll follow so fast as euer I maye.
    Lo, here ys þe bull of myn avctoryte.
Cler. I pray God to saue the popys holy maieste.
S. Lang. Sytt downe on yowr kneys and ye shall haue absolucyon
    A pena et culpa, with a thowsand dayes of pardon.

1185 magnifycence] *prehemynence*   pape *A.*
    A.   1190 S.D. Cyuyl] sevyll *A.**
1186 romani] *roma A.*   1199 In] A *A.*
1188 domini pape] *domini nostri*   1212 god to saue] god saue *A.*

[105]

1215 Here ys fyrst a bone of the blyssyd trynyte,
A dram of þe tord of swete seynt Barnabe;
Here ys a feddere of good seynt Myhelles wyng,
A toth of seynt Twyde, a pece of Davyds harpe stryng,
Þe good blood of Haylys and owr blyssyd ladys mylke,
1220 A lowse of seynt Fraunces in this same crymsen sylke,
A scabbe of saynt Iob, a nayle of Adams too,
A maggott of Moyses, with a fart of saynt fandigo;
Here is a fygge leafe and a grape of Noes vyneyearde,
A bede of saynt Blythe, with the bracelet of a berewarde,
1225 The Deuyll that was hatcht in maistre Iohan Shornes bote,
That the tree of Iesse ded plucke vp by the roote;
Here ys the lachett of swett seynt Thomas shewe,
A rybbe of seynt Rabart, with the huckyll bone of a Iewe;
Here ys a ioynt of darvell gathyron
1230 Besydes other bonys and relyckes many one.
In nomine domini pape, amen.
Aryse now lyke men and stande vppon yowr fete,
For here ye haue caught an holy and a blyssyd hete.
Ye are now as clene as þat day ye were borne
1235 And lyke to haue increase of chylderne, catell and corne.
C.*Ord.* Chyldryn? He can haue non, for he ys not of þat loade.
S.*Lang.* Tushe, thowgh he hath non at home, he maye haue sume
abroade.
Now Clargy, my frynd, this mvst thow do for þe pope
And for holy chyrch: thow must mennys conscyence grope,
1240 And as thow felyst them so cause them for to wurcke.
Leat them show kyng Iohn no more faver than a Turcke;
Every wher sture them to make an insurreccyon.
Cler. All that shall I do, and to provoke them more,
This interdyccyon I wyll lament very sore
1245 In all my prechynges, and saye throwgh his occacyon

1216 a dram] & a dram *A.**
1218 a toth] & a toth *A.**
1220 a lowse] here ys alowse *A.*
1220 this same crymsen] this crymsen *A.*
1221-26 *Added in B.*
1225 hatcht] hatchst *b.**
1228 a Rybbe] & a Rybe *A.*
1228 the] a *A.*

1231 d*omini* pape] d*omini* n*ostri*
pape *A.*
1233 caught an holy and a] caught
a *A.*
1236 loade] Rode *A.**
1237 hath] haue *A.*
1237 abroade] abrode *A.*
1245 all my prechyng*es*] all prechyng*es* *A.*

All we are vnder the danger of dampnacyon;
And this wyll move peple to helpe to put hym downe,
Or elles compel hym to geue vp septur and crowne.
Yea, and that wyll make those kynges þat shall succede
1250   Of the holy chyrche to stond euer more in drede.
And bysydes all this, the chyrch dores I wyll vpseale,   (p. 30, fol. 16ᵛ)
And closse vp þe belles that they ryng neuer a pele.
I wyll spere vp þe chalyce, crysmatory, crosse and all,
That masse they shall haue non, baptym nor beryall.
1255   And thys I know well wyll make the peple madde.
    S. Lang. Mary, that yt wyll! Soche savce he neuer had.
And what wylte thow do for holy chyrche, Cyvyll ordere?
    C. Ord. For the clargyes sake I wyll in euery border
Provoke the gret men to take þe comonnys parte.
1260   With cavtyllys of the lawe I wyll so tyckle ther hart
They shall thynke all good þat they shall passe vpon,
And so shall we cum to ower full intent anon;
For yf the church thryve than do we lawers thryve,
And yf they decay, ower welth ys not alyve.
1265   Therfor we must helpe yowr state, masters, to vphold,
Or elles owr profyttes wyll cache a wynter colde.
I neuer knew lawer whych had ony crafty lernyng
That euer escapte yow with owt a plentyows levyng;
Therfor we may not leve holy churchys quarell,
1270   But euer helpe yt, for ther fall ys owr parell.
    S. Lang. Godes blyssyng haue ye; this ger than wyll worke, I trust.
    C. Ord. Or elles sum of vs are lyke to lye in the dust.
    S. Lang. Let vs all avoyde! Be þe messe, the kyng cummyth her!
    Cler. I wold hyde my selfe for a tyme yf I wyst where.
1275   *C. Ord.* Gow we hence apace, for I haue spyed a corner.
            Here go owt all, and kyng Iohn cummyth in.
    K. John. For non other cawse God hathe kynges constytute
And gevyn them þe sword but for to correct all vyce.
I haue attempted this thyng to execute
Vppon transgressers accordyng vnto ivstyce,
1280   And be cawse I wyll not be parcyall in myn offyce
For theft and mvrder to persones spirytuall,
I haue ageynst me the pristes and the bysshoppes all.

1248 compel] comple *A.*＊   1260 tyckle] tycle *A.*＊
1255 madde] made *A.*   1262 full] fule *A.*

A lyke dysplesure in my fatheres tyme ded fall
Forty yeres ago for ponnyshment of a clarke.
1285   No cunsell myght them to reformacyon call—
In ther openyon they wer so stordy and starke—
But ageynst ther prynce to þe pope they dyd so barke
That here in Ynglond, in euery cyte and towne,
Excomminycacyons as thonder boltes cam downe.

1290   For this ther captayn had after a pared crowne
And dyed vpon yt, with owt þe kynges consent.
Than interdiccyons wer sent from þe popys renowne,
Whych neuer left hym tyll he was penytent
And fully agreed vnto the popes apoyntment,
1295   In Ynglond to stand with the chyrches lyberte
And suffer the pristes to Rome for appeles to flee.

They bownd hym also to helpe Ierusalem cyte
With ij hundrid men the space of a yere and more,
And thre yere after to maynteyne battell free   (p. 31, fol. 17)
1300   Ageynst the Sarazens, whych vext þe Spannyardes sore.
Synce my fatheres tyme I haue borne them groge therfor,
Consydryng þe pryde and the capcyose dysdayne
That they haue to kynges, whych owȝte ouer them to rayne.

Privat Welth
cum in lyke a cardynall.

Card. God saue yow, sur kyng, in yowr pryncly mageste.
1305   K. John. Frynd, ye be welcum. What is yowr plesur with me?
Card. From the holy father, pope Innocent þe thred,
As a massanger I am to yow dyrectyd
To reforme the peace betwyn holy chyrch and yow.
And in his behalfe I avertyce yow here now
1310   Of the chyrchys goodes to make full restytucyon,
And to accepte also the popys holy constytucyon
For Stevyn Langton, archebysshop of Canturbery,
And so admytt hym to his state and primacy.
The monkes exilyd ye shall restore agayne
1315   To ther placys and londes, and nothyng of theres retayne.
Owr holy fatheres mynde ys þat ye shall agayne restore
All þat ye haue ravyshyd from holy chyrche, with þe more.

1311 holy] *Manly*; hely *B.*

[108]

K. John. I reken yowr father wyll neuer be so harde,
  But he wyll my cawse as well as theres regarde.
1320 I haue done nothyng but þat I may do well;
  And as for ther taxe, I haue for me þe Gospell.
Card. Tushe, Gospell or no ye mvst make a recompens.
K. John. Yowr father is sharpe and very quycke in sentence
  Yf he wayeth the word of God nomor than so.
1325 But I shall tell yow in this what Y shall do:
  I am well content to receyve þe monkes agayne
  Vpon amendement; but as for Stevyn Langton, playne,
  He shall not cum here, for I know his dysposycyon.
  He is moche inclyned to sturdynesse and sedycyon.
1330 Ther shall no man rewle in þe lond wher I am kyng
  With owt my consent, for no mannys plesur lyvyng.
  Neuer þe lesse, yet vpon a newe behaver,
  At þe popys request here aftere I may hym faver
  And graunt hym to haue sum other benyfyce.
1335 *Card.* By thys I perseyve ye bare hym groge and malyce.
  Well, thys wyll I say by cause ye are so blunte:
  A prelate to dyscharge holy chyrche was neuer wonnt,
  But her custome ys to mynyster ponnyshment
  To kynges and princes beyng dyssobedyent.
1340 *K. John.* Avant, pevysh prist! What, dost thow thretten me?
  I defye þe worst, both of þi pope and the!
  The powr of princys ys gevyn from God above,
  And, as sayth Salomon, ther hartes þe lord doth move.
  God spekyth in þer lyppes whan they geve iugement.
1345 The lawys þat they make are by þe lordes appoyntment.
  Christ wylled not his the princes to correcte,   (p. 32, fol. 17ᵛ)
  But to ther precepptes rether to be subiecte.
  The offyce of yow ys not to bere þe sword,
  But to geve cownsell acordyng to Godes word.
1350 He neuer tawght his to weare nowther sword nor sallett,
  But to preche abrode with owt staffe, scrypp or walett;
  Yet are ye becum soche myghty lordes this howr
  That ye are able to subdewe all princes powr.
  I can not perseyve but ye are becum Belles prystes,
1355 Lyvyng by ydolles; yea, the very Anty chrystes.

1322 tushe, gospell] tushe · the gos-   1329 inclyned] *Collier*; in clymed
  pell *A.** *B.*
                   1329 sturdynesse] rumer *A.*

Card. Ye haue sayd yowr mynd, now wyll I say myn also.
Here I cursse yow for þe wronges þat ye haue do
Vnto holy churche, with crosse, bocke, bell and candell;
And by sydes all thys, I mvst yow otherwyse handell.
1360 Of contvmacy the pope hath yow convyt;
From this day forward yowr lond stond interdytt.
The bysshope of Norwyche and þe bysshope of Wynchester
Hath full avtoryte to spred it in Ynglond here;
The bysshope of Salysbery and þe bysshope of Rochester
1365 Shall execute yt in Scotlond euery where;
The bysshope of Landaffe, Seynt Assys and Seynt Davy
In Walles and in Erlond shall puplyshe yt openly.
Throwgh owt all Crystyndom þe bysshoppes shall suspend
All soche as to yow any mayntenance pretend;
1370 And I cursse all them that geue to yow ther harte,
Dewkes, erlles and lordes, so many as take yowr parte;
And I assoyle yowr peple from yowr obedyence,
That they shall owe yow noyther fewte nor reverence.
By the popys awctoryte I charge them with yow to fyght
1375 As with a tyrant agenst holy chyrchys ryght;
And by the popys avctoryte I geve them absolucyon
A pena et culpa, and also clene remyssyon.

Extra locum:

Sed. Alarum! Alarum! Tro ro ro ro ro, tro ro ro ro ro, tro ro ro ro ro!
Thomp, thomp, thomp! Downe, downe, downe! To go, to go, to go!
1380 *K. John.* What a noyse is thys that without the dore is made?
Card. Suche enmyes are vp as wyll your realme inuade.
K. John. Ye cowde do nomor and ye cam from the devyll of hell
Than ye go abowt here to worke by yor wyckyd cownsell.
Ys this the charyte of þat ye call the churche?
1385 God graunt Cristen men not after yowr wayes to worche.
I sett not by yowr curssys þe shakyng of a rod,
For I know they are of the devyll and not of God.
Yowr curssys we haue, þat we neuer yet demaundyd,
But we can not haue þat God hath yow commaundyd.
1390 *Card.* What ye mene by þat I wold ye shuld opynlye tell.
K. John. Why, know ye it not? The prechyng of þe Gospell.
Take to ye yowr traysh, yowr ryngyng, syngyng and pypyng,
So þat we may haue the scryptures openyng.

1363 it] þat *A.*   1378-81 *Added in B.*
1373 noyther] nowther *A.*   1391 ye it not?] ye not? *A.*

But þat we can not haue; yt stondyth not with yowr avantage.

1395 *Card.* Ahe! Now I fell yow for this heretycall langage:

I thynke noyther yow nor ony of yowres, iwys—

We wyll so provyd—shall ware þe crowne after this.

Go owt and dresse for Nobylyte.

K. John. Yt becum not the Godes secret workes to   (p. 33, fol. 18)

deme.

Gett the hence, or elles we shall teche þe to blaspheme!

1400 Oh lord, how wycked ys that same generacyon

That neuer wyll cum to a godly reformacyon.

The prystes report me to be a wyckyd tyrant

Be cause I correct ther actes and lyfe vnplesaunt.

Of thy prince, sayth God, thow shalt report non yll,

1405 But thy selfe applye his plesur to fulfyll.

The byrdes of þe ayer shall speke to ther gret shame—

As sayth Ecclesyastes—þat wyll a prince dyffame.

The powrs are of God—I wot Powle hath soch sentence;

He þat resyst them agenst God maketh resystence.

1410 Mary and Ioseph, at Cyrinus appoyntment,

In þe descripcyon to Cesar wer obedyent.

Crist ded paye trybute, for hymselfe and Peter to,

For a lawe prescrybyng þe same vnto pristes also;

To prophane princes he obeyed vnto dethe.

1415 So ded Iohn baptyst so longe as he had brethe.

Peter, Iohn and Powle, with þe other apostles all,

Ded neuer withstand the powers imperyall.

[*Enter Civil Order.*]

Prystes are so wycked they wyll obeye no powr,

But seke to subdewe ther prynces day and howr,

1420 As they wold do me; but I shall make them smart,

Yf that nobelyte and law wyll take my parte.

C. Ord. Dowȝtles we can not tyll ye be reconcylyd

Vnto holy chyrche, for ye are a man defylyd.

K. John. How am I defylyd? Telme, good gentyll mate.

1425 *C. Ord.* By the popys hye powr ye are excomynycate.

K. John. By the word of God, I pray the, what powr hath he?

C. Ord. I spake not wyth hym, and therfor I can not tell ye.

K. John. With whom spake ye not? Late me know yowr intent.

1396 noyther] nowther *A*.   1397 shall ware] shall ne*uer* ware *A*.

1396 nor ony of yowr*es* Iwys] nor   1419 seke] laber *A*.

    that ony of yowr*es* *A*.

C.Ord. Mary, not with God sens þe latter wecke of lent.
[*Enter Clergy.*]
1430 *K.John.* Oh mercyfull God, what an vnwyse clawse ys this,
Of hym that shuld se þat nothyng ware amys.
That sentence or curse þat scriptur doth not dyrect
In my opynyon shall be of non effecte.
Cler. Ys that yowr beleve? Mary, God saue me from yow!
1435 *K.John.* Prove yt by scriptur, and than wyll I yt alowe.
But this know I well: whan Baalam gaue þe curse
Vppon Godes peple, they war neuer a whyt þe worse.
Cler. I passe not on þe scriptur; that ys inow for me
Whyche þe holy father approvyth by his auctoryte.
1440 *K.John.* Now alas, alas! What wreched peple ye are
And how ygnorant yowr owne wordes doth declare.
Woo ys þat peple whych hath so wycked techeres.
Cler. Naye, wo ys that peple that hathe so cruell rewlars.
Owr holy father, I trow, cowd do no lesse,
1445 Consyderyng the factes of yowr owtragyosnes.
[*Enter Nobility.*]
Nob. Com awaye, for shame, and make no more ado.   (p. 34, fol. 18ᵛ)
Ye are in gret danger for commynnyng with hym so.
He is acursyd; I mervell ye do not waye yt.
Cler. I here by his wordes that he wyll not obeye yt.
1450 *Nob.* Whether he wyll or no, I wyll not with hym talke
Tell he be assoyllyd. Com on, my fryndes, wyll ye walke?
K.John. Oh, this is no tokyn of trew nobelyte,
To flee from yowr kyng in his extremyte.
Nob. I shall dyssyer yow as now to pardone me;
1455 I had moche rather do agaynst God, veryly,
Than to holy chyrche to do any iniurye.
K.John. What blyndnes is this? On this peple, lord, haue mercy!
Ye speke of defylyng, but ye are corrupted all
With pestylent doctryne or leven pharesayycall.
1460 Good and faythfull Susan sayd þat yt was moche bettere
To fall in daunger of men than do þe gretter,
As to leve Godes lawe, whych ys his word most pure.
Cler. Ye haue nothyng, yow, to allege to vs but scripture?

1443 hathe so cruell] hath cruell *A.*
1444 holy] hohy *A.**
1449 word*es*, that he] word*es* · he
       A.

1456 InIurye] InIerye *A.*
1460 Good and faythfull] *Manly*;
       good to faythfull *B*; good
       faythfull *A.**

Ye shall fare the worse for þat, ye may be sure.
1465 *K. John.* What shuld I allege elles, thu wycked pharyse?
To yowr false lernyng no faythfull man wyll agree.
Dothe not þe lord say, *nvnc reges intelligite:*
Þe kynges of þe erthe that worldly cawses iuge,
Seke to the scriptur, late þat be yowr refuge?
1470 *C. Ord.* Haue ye nothyng elles but this? Than God be with ye!
K. John. One questyon more yet ere ye departe from me
I wyll fyrst demaund of yow, Nobelyte:
Why leve ye yowr prince and cleave to the pope so sore?
Nob. For I toke an othe to defend þe chyrche euer more.
1475 *K. John.* Clergy, I am sure than yowr quarell ys not small.
Cler. I am proffessyd to the ryghtes ecclesyastycall.
K. John. And yow, Cyvyle order, oweth her sum offyce of dewtye?
C. Ord. I am hyr feed man; who shuld defend her but I?
K. John. Of all thre partyes yt is spokyn resonably:
1480 Ye may not obeye becawse of þe othe ye mad,
Yowr strong professyon maketh yow of þat same trad,
Yowr fee provokyth yow to do as thes men do.
Grett thynges to cawse men from God to þe devyll to go!
Yowr othe is growndyd, fyrst, vppon folyshenes,
1485 And yowr professyon vppon moche pevyshenes;
Yowr fee, last of all, ryseth owt of covetusnes,
And thes are þe cawses of yowr rebellyosnes.
Cler. Cum, Cyvyll order; lett vs too departe from hence.
K. John. Than are ye at a poynt for yowr obedyence?
1490 *C. Ord.* We wyll in no wysse be partakeres of yowr yll.
      Here go owt Clargy and dresse for Ynglond,
       and Syvyll order for Commynnalte.
K. John. As ye haue bene euer so ye wyll contynew styll.
Thowgh they be gone, tarye yow with me a whyle;
The presence of a prynce to yow shuld neuer be vyle.
Nob. Sir, nothyng grevyth me but yowr   (p. 35, fol. 19)
    excomynycacyon.
1495 *K. John.* That ys but a fantasy in yowr ymagynacyon.
The lord refuse not soch as hath his great cursse,
But call them to grace and fauer them neuer þe worsse.

1464 ye shall fare] ye fare *A.*   1476 ryght*es*] ryght *A.**
1465 thu] yow *A.*   1478 feed] frend *A.*
1467 nvnc] nonc *A.**   1478 defend her but] defend but *A.*
1467 intelligite] *Manly;* intellige *B.*   1480 ye mad] ye haue mad *A.*

[113]

Saynt Pawle wyllyth yow whan ye are among soch sort
Not to abhore them, but geve them wordes of comfort.
1500 Why shuld ye than flee from me, yowr lawfull kyng,
For plesur of soch as owght to do no suche thyng?
The chyrches abusyons, as holy seynt Powle do saye,
By the princes powr owght for to be takyn awaye;
He baryth not þe sword withowt a cawse, sayth he.
1505 In this neyther bysshope nore spirituall man is free;
Offendyng þe lawe, they are vnder þe poweres, all.
Nob. How wyll ye prove me þat the fatheres sprytuall
Were vnder þe princes euer contynewally?
K. John. By the actes of kynges I wyll prove yt by and by:
1510 Dauid and Salomon the pristes ded constitute,
Commandyng þe offyces that they shuld execute.
Iosaphat the kyng the mynysters ded appoynt;
So ded kyng Ezechias, whom God hym selfe ded anoynt.
Dyverse of þe princes for þe pristes ded make decrees,
1515 Lyke as yt is pleyn in the fyrst of Machabees.
Owr pristes are rysyn throwgh lyberte of kynges
By ryches to pryd and other vnlawfull doynges,
And þat is the cawse that they so oft dysobeye.
Nob. Good lord, what a craft haue yow thes thynges to convaye!
1520 *K. John.* Now, alas, þat the false pretence of superstycyon
Shuld cawse yow to be a mayntener of sedycyon.
Sum thynkyth nobelyte in natur to consyst,
Or in parentage; ther thowȝt is but a myst.
Wher habundance is of vertu, fayth and grace,
1525 With knowlage of þe lord, nobelyte is ther in place,
And not wher as is the wylfull contempte of thynges
Pertaynyng to God in the obedyence of kynges.
Beware ye synke not with Dathan and Abiron
For dysobeyng the powr and domynyon.
1530 *Nob.* Nay, byd me be ware I do not synke with yow here;
Beyng acurssyd, of trewth ye put me in fere.
K. John. Why, are ye gone hence, and wyll ye no longar tarrye?
Nob. No, wher as yow are in place, by swete seynt Marye!
Here Nobelyte go owt and dresse for þe cardynall.

1499 of] o *A.*
1505 neyther] nowther *A.*
1505 man] men *A.*
1515 is] sheweth *A.*

1515 machabees] machabevs *A.*
1533 wher as yow] wher yow *A.*
1533 by swete seynt] by seynt *A.*

Here enter Ynglond and Commynalte.

K.*John.* Blessed lorde of heauen, what is the wretchednesse

1535   Of thys wycked worlde! An euyll of all euyls, doubtlesse.
Perceyue ye not here how the clergye hath reiecte
Their true allegeaunce to maynteyne the popysh secte?
See ye not how lyghte the lawers sett the poure,
Whome God commaundeth them to obeye yche daye and howre?

1540   Nobylyte also, whych ought hys prynce to assyste,
Is vanyshed awaye, as it were a wynter myste.
All they are from me; I am now left alone,
And, God wote, knowe not to whome to make my mone.
Oh, yet wolde I fayne knowe the mynde of my commynnalte,

1545   Whether he wyll go with them or abyde with me.

Eng. He is here at hond, a symple creatur as may be.

K.*John.* Cum hether, my frynde; stand nere. Ys þi selfe he?

Com. Yf it lyke yowr grace, I am yowr pore commynnalte.

K.*John.* Thow art poore inowgh; yf þat be good,   (p. 36, fol. 19ᵛ)
       God helpe the!

1550   Me thynke thow art blynd. Tell me, frynde, canst þou not see?

Eng. He is blynd in dede; yt is the more rewth and pytte.

K.*John.* How cummyst thow so blynd? I pray þe, good fellow, tell me.

Com. For want of knowlage in Christes lyuely veryte.

Eng. This spirituall blyndnes bryngeth men owt of þe waye

1555   And cause them oft tymys ther kynges to dyssobaye.

K.*John.* How sayst thow, Commynnalte? Wylt not þou take my
       parte?

Com. To þat I cowd be contented with all my hart,
But, alas, in me are two great impedymentes.

K.*John.* I pray þe, shew me what are those impedymentes.

1560 *Com.* The fyrst is blyndnes, wherby I myght take with þe pope
Soner than with yow; for, alas, I can but grope,
And ye know full well ther are many nowghty gydes.
The nexte is poverte, whych cleve so hard to my sydes
And ponych me so sore þat my powr ys lytyll or non.

1565 K.*John.* In Godes name, tell me how cummyth þi substance gone?

1534-43 *Added in B.*   1547 my] good *A.*
1541 were] *Collier*; we *B.*   1553 lyuely] owne *A.*
1544 Oh . . . commynnalte] now   1557 contented] content *A.*
     wold I fayne know · þe   1558 two] to *A.*
     mynd of my commynnalte *A.**

Com. By pristes, channons and monkes, which do but fyll þer bely
 With my swett and labour for þer popych purgatory.
Eng. Yowr grace promysed me that I shuld haue remedy
 In þat same mater whan I was last here, trewly.
1570 *K. John.* Dowȝtles I ded so; but, alas, yt wyll not be.
 In hart I lament this great infelycyte.
Eng. Late me haue my spowse and my londes at lyberte,
 And I promyse yow my sonne here, yowr commynallte,
 I wyll make able to do ye dewtyfull servyce.
1575 *K. John.* I wold I ware able to do to the that offyce,
 But, alas, I am not, for why my nobelyte,
 My lawers and clargy hath cowardly forsake me.
 And now last of all, to my most anguysh of mynd,
 My commynnalte here I fynd both poore and blynd.
1580 *Eng.* Rest vpon this, ser, for my governor ye shall be
 So long as ye lyve; God hath so apoynted me.
 His owtward blyndnes ys but a syngnyficacyon
 Of blyndnes in sowle for lacke of informacyon
 In the word of God, which is the orygynall grownd
1585 Of dyssobedyence, which all realmies doth confund.
 Yf yowr grace wold cawse Godes word to be tawȝt syncerly
 And subdew those pristes that wyll not preche yt trewly,
 The peple shuld know to ther prynce þer lawfull dewty;
 But yf ye permytt contynvance of ypocresye
1590 In monkes, chanons and pristes, and mynysters of the clargy,
 Yowr realme shall neuer be withowt moch traytery.
K. John. All þat I perceyve and therfor I kepe owt fryers,
 Lest they shuld bryng the moch farder into þe bryers.
 They haue mad labur to inhabytt this same regyon;
1595 They shall for my tym not enter my domynyon.
 We haue to many of soch vayne lowȝtes all redy.
 I beshrew ther hartes! They haue made yow .ij. full nedy.
  Here enter Pandwlfus, þe cardynall, and sayth:
Card. What, Commynalte, ys this þe connaunt (p. 37, fol. 20)
  kepyng?
 Thow toldyst me þou woldest take hym no more for þi kyng.
1600 *Com.* *Peccaui, mea culpa!* I submyt me to yowr holynes.
Card. Gett the hence than shortly and go abowt þi besynes.

1575 do to the] do the *A.*   1596 we] whe *A.**
1581 apoynted me] apoynted *A.* 1597 they haue made] they made *A.*
1590 monkes] *Collier;* monke *B.* 1597 S.D. Pandwlfus] pandwlfus *A.*

Wayet on thy capttaynes, Nobelyte and þe clargy,
With Cyvyll Order and the other company.
Blow owt yowr tromppettes and sett forth manfully,
1605   The frenche kyng Phelype by sea doth hether apply
With the powr of Fraunce to subdew this herytyke.
K. John. I defye both hym and the, lewde scysmatyke!
Why wylt þou forsake þi prince or þi prince leve the?
Com. I mvst nedes obbay whan holy chirch commandyth me.

                                     Go owt Commynulte.
1610   *Eng.* Yf thow leve thy kyng, take me neuer for thy mother.
Card. Tush, care not þou for that, I shall provyd þe another.
Yt ware fytter for yow to be in another place.
Eng. Yt shall becum me to wayte vpon his grace
And do hym servyce where as he ys resydente,
1615   For I was gevyn hym of þe lord omnypotente.
Card. Thow mayst not abyde here, for whye we haue hym curssyd.
Eng. I beshrow yowr hartes, so haue ye me onpursed.
Yf he be acurssed than are we a mete cuppell,
For I am interdyct. No salue that sore can suppell.
1620   *Card.* I say, gett the hence and make me no more pratyng.
Eng. I wyll not awaye from myn owne lawfull kyng,
Appoyntyd of God tyll deth shall vs departe.
Card. Wyll ye not in dede? Well than, ye are lyke to smarte.
Eng. I smarte all redy throw yowr most suttell practyse,
1625   And am clene ondone by yowr false merchandyce—
Yowr pardons, yowr bulles, yowr purgatory pyckepurse,
Yowr lent fastes, yowr schryftes—that I pray God geve yow his
        cursse!
Card. Þou shalt smart better or we haue done with the,
For we haue this howr great navyes vpon þe see
1630   In euery quarter, with this loller here to fyght
And to conquarre hym for the holy chyrchis ryght.
We haue vn þe northe Alexander, þe kyng of Scottes,
With an armye of men þat for their townnes cast lottes;
On the sowthe syde we haue þe french kyng with his powr,

1605 sea] se *A.*
1616 abyde here, for whye, we]
    abyde thowght · for we *A.*
1617 so haue ye me] so ye haue me
    A.
1619 interdyct] *Collier;* interdyet *B.*

1619 salue] saue *A.**
1619 sore] sone *A.**
1631 for the holy] for holy *A.*
1633 their townn*es* cast] þe townn*es*
    they cast *A.*

[117]

1635   Which wyll sle and burne tyll he cum to Londen towr;
       In þe west partes we haue kyng Alphonse with the Spanyardes,
       With sheppes full of gonepowder now cummyng hether towardes;
       And on þe est syde we haue Esterlynges, Danes and Norwayes,
       With soch powr landynge as can be resystyd nowayes.

1640   *K. John.* All that is not true that yow haue here expressed.
       Card. By the messe, so true as I haue now confessed.
       K. John. And what do ye meane by such an hurly burlye?
       Card. For the churches ryght to subdue ye manfullye.

                    [*Enter Sedition.*]

       Sed. To all that wyll fyght I proclame a Iubyle
1645   Of cleane remyssyon, thys tyraunt here to slee.
       Destroye hys people, burne vp both cytie and towne,
       That the pope of Rome maye haue hys scepture and crowne.
       In the churches cause to dye thys daye be bolde;
       Your sowles shall to heauen ere your fleshe and bones be colde.

1650   *K. John.* Most mercyfull God, as my trust is in the,
       So comforte me now in this extremyte;
       As thow holpyst Dauid in his most hevynes,
       So helpe me this hour of thy grace, mercye and goodnes.

       Card. This owtward remorse þat ye show here evydent
1655   Ys a grett lykelyhod and token of amendment.
       How say ye, kyng Iohn? Can ye fynd now in   (p. 38[a], fol. 20ᵛ)
          yowr hart
       To obaye holy chyrch and geve ower yowr froward part?
       K. John. Were yt so possyble to hold thes enmyes backe,
       That my swete Ynglond perysh not in this sheppwracke?

1660   *Card.* Possyble, quoth he? Yea, they shuld go bake in dede,
       And ther gret armyse to some other quarteres leede,
       Or elles they haue not so many good blyssynges now,
       But as many cursynges they shall haue, I make God avowe.
       I promyse yow, sur, ye shall haue specyall faver
1665   Yf ye wyll submyt yowr sylfe to holye chyrch here.
       K. John. I trust than ye wyll graunt some delyberacyon   (p. 39, fol. 23)

1635 tyll] tell *A*.	1653 hour] owr *A*.
1636 part*es* we haue, kyng] part*es* kyng *A*.	1653 grace, mercye,] great grace *A*.
1638 danes] danyes *A*.	1661 quarter*es* leede] quarter*es* *A*.
1639 landynge,] co*m*myng · *A*.	1666-1724 *Added in B*.
1640-49 *Added in B*.	1666 I trust than ye wyll, grau*n*t some delyberacyon] I trust,
1643 manfullye] *Collier*; mafullye *B*.	therupon, ye wyll grau*n*t delyberacyon *b*.

To haue an answere of thys your protestacyon.

Sed. Tush, gyue vpp the crowne and make nomore a do.

K. John. Your spirytuall charyte wyll be better to me than so.

1670   The crowne of a realme is a matter of great wayght;

In gyuynge it vpp we maye not be to slayght.

Sed. I saye, gyue it vp! Lete vs haue nomore a do.

Card. Yea, and in our warres we wyll no farder go.

K. John. Ye wyll gyue me leaue to talke first with my clergye?

1675   *Sed.* With them ye nede not; they are at a poynt alreadye.

K. John. Than with my lawers, to heare what they wyll tell?

Sed. Ye shall euer haue them as the clergye gyue them counsell.

K. John. Then wyll I commen with my nobylyte.

Sed. We haue hym so iugled he wyll not to yow agree.

1680   *K. John.* Yet shall I be content to do as he counsell me.

Card. Than be not to longe from hence, I wyll aduyse ye.

                           [*Exeunt King John and England.*]

Sed. Is not thys a sport? By the messe, it is, I trowe.

What welthe and pleasure wyll now to our kyngedom growe!

Englande is our owne, whych is the most plesaunt grounde

1685   In all the rounde worlde; now maye we realmes confounde.

Our holye father maye now lyue at hys pleasure

And haue habundaunce of wenches, wynes and treasure.

He is now able to kepe downe Christe and hys gospell,

True fayth to exyle and all vertues to expell.

1690   Now shall we ruffle it, in veluattes, golde and sylke,

With shauen crownes, syde gownes, and rochettes whyte as mylke.

By the messe, Pandulphus, now maye we synge *Cantate,*

And crowe *Confitebor,* with a ioyfull *Iubilate!*

Holde me, or els for laughynge I must burste!

1695   *Card.* Holde thy peace, whorson! I wene thu art accurst.

Kepe a sadde countenaunce. A very vengeaunce take the!

Sed. I can not do it, by the messe, and thu shuldest hange me.

If Solon were here I recken that he woulde laugh,

Whych neuer laught yet; yea, lyke a whelpe he woulde waugh.

1700   Ha, ha, ha! Laugh, quoth he! Yea, laugh and laugh agayne!

We had neuer cause to laugh more free, I am playne.

Card. I praye the, nomore, for here come the   (p. 40[a], fol. 23ᵛ)

    kynge agayne.

              [*Enter King John and England.*]

Ye are at a poynt wherto ye intende to stande?

1671 In gyuynge] In the gyuynge *b.*

Sed. Yea, hardely sir; gyue vp the crowne of Englande.

1705 *K.John.* I haue cast in mynde the great displeasures of warre,
The daungers, the losses, the decayes both nere and farre,
The burnynge of townes, the throwynge downe of buyldynges,
Destructyon of corne and cattell, with other thynges,
Defylynge of maydes and shedynge of Christen blood,

1710 With suche lyke outrages, neyther honest, true nor good.
These thynges consydered, I am compelled thys houre
To resigne vp here both crowne and regall poure.

Eng. For the loue of God, yet take some better aduysement!

Sed. Holde your tunge, ye whore, or by þe messe ye shall repent!

1715 Downe on your mary bones and make nomore a do.

Eng. If ye loue me, sir, for Gods sake do neuer so.

K.John. O Englande, Englande, shewe now thyselfe a mother;
Thy people wyll els be slayne here without nomber.
As God shall iudge me, I do not thys of cowardnesse

1720 But of compassyon, in thys extreme heauynesse.
Shall my people shedde their bloude in suche habundaunce?
Naye, I shall rather gyue vpp my whole gouernaunce.

Sed. Come of apace, than, and make an ende of it shortly.

Eng. The most pytiefull chaunce þat hath bene hytherto, surely.

1725 *K.John.* Here I submytt me to pope Innocent   (p. 38[b], fol. 20ᵛ)
the thred,
Dyssyering mercy of hys holy fatherhed.

Card. Geve vp þe crowne, than; yt shalbe the better for ye.
He wyll vnto yow the more fauorable be.

> *Here þe kyng delevyr þe*
> *crowne to þe cardynall.*

K.John. To hym I resygne here the septer and þe crowne

1730 Of Ynglond and Yrelond, with þe powr and renowne,
And put me wholly to his mercyfull ordynance.

Card. I may say this day þe chyrch hath a full gret chaunce.
Thes .v. dayes I wyll kepe this crowne in myn owne hande,
In the popes behalfe vpseasyng Ynglond and Yerlond.

1735 In the meane season ye shall make an oblygacyon
For yow and yowr ayers, in this synyficacyon:
To recayve yowr crowne of þe pope for euer more

1716 *Assigned to* k. Iohan *in b.*   1730 þe powr] þe hole powr *A.*
1727 crowne · than, yt] crowne · yt   1731 wholly] wholl *A.*
    A.   1733 this] thes *A.*
1729 here] wpe *A.*   1733 myn] my *A.*

In maner of fefarme; and for a tokyn therfor
Ye shall euery yere paye hym a thowsand marke
1740   With the peter pens, and not agenst yt barke.
Ye shall also geve to the bysshoppe of Cantorbery
A thre thowsand marke for his gret iniury.
To þe chyrch besydes, for the great scathe ye haue done,
Forty thowsand marke ye shall delyver sone.
1745 *K. John.* Ser, the taxe þat I had of the hole realme of Ynglond
Amownted to no more but vnto .xxx^ti. thowsand.
Why shuld I than paye so moche vnto þe clargy?
Card. Ye shall geve yt them; ther is no remedy.
K. John. Shall they paye no tribute yf þe realme stond in rerage?
1750 *Card.* Sir, they shall paye none; we wyll haue no soch bondage.
K. John. The pope had at once thre hundred thowsand marke.
Card. What is that to yow? Ah, styll ye wyll be starke.
Ye shall paye yt, sir; ther is no remedy.
K. John. Yt shall be performed as ye wyll haue yt, trewly.
1755 *Eng.* So noble a realme to stande tributarye, Alas,   (p. 40[b], fol. 23^v)
To the Deuyls vycar! Suche fortune neuer was.
Sed. Out with thys harlot! Cockes sowle, she hath lete a fart!
Eng. Lyke a wretche thu lyest; thy report is lyke as thu art.
[*Exit Sedition.*]
Card. Ye shall suffer the monkes and channons to   (p. 38[c], fol. 20^v)
make reentry
1760   In to ther abbayes and to dwell ther peacebly.
Ye shall se also to my great labur and charge.
For other thynges elles we shall commen more at large.
K. John. Ser, in euery poynt I shall fulfyll yowr plesur.
Card. Than plye yt apace and lett vs haue þe tresur.
1765 *Eng.* Alacke for pyte that euer ye grantyd this.   (p. *1[a], fol. 21)
For me, pore Ynglond, ye haue done sore amys;
Of a fre woman ye haue now mad a bonde mayd.
Yowr selfe and heyres ye haue for euer decayd.
Alas, I had rether be vnderneth the Turke
1770   Than vnder the wynges of soch a thefe to lurke.

1740 with] In *A.*
1743 the great scathe] the scathe *A.*
1745 the (*first*)] ye *A.*
1755-58 *Added in B.*
1762 we shall commen] I wyll show
  yow *A.*

1765-72 *Omitted in Collier, Manly,*
  Farmer.
1767 bonde] hand *A.*
1768 decayd] decaye *A.*
1770 soch a thefe] soch thefe *A.*

K. John. Content the, Ynglond, for ther ys no remedy.

Eng. Yf yow be plesyd, than I mvst consent gladly.

K. John. If I shoulde not graunt, here woulde be a   (p. 40[c], fol. 23ʳ)
    wondrefull spoyle;

  Euery where the enemyes woulde ruffle and turmoyle.

1775   The losse of people stycketh most vnto my harte.

Eng. Do as ye thynke best; yche waye is to my smarte.

Card. Are ye at a poynt with þe same oblygacyon?   (p. *1[b], fol. 21)

K. John. Yt is here redye at yowr interrogacyon.

     Here kyng Iohn shall delevyr þe oblygacyon.

Card. Wher is the mony for yowr full restytucyon?

1780 *K. John.* Here, ser, accordyng to yowr last constytucyon.

Card. Cum hether, my lorde. By the popys autoryte
  Assoyll this man here of irregularyte.

                      Here þe bysshop Stevyn Langton cum in.

K. John. Me thynke this bysshope resembleth moch Sedycyon.

Card. I cownsell yow yet to be ware of wrong suspycyon.

1785 This is Stevyn Langton, yowr meteropolytan.

K. John. Than do the offyce of þe good samarytan
  And pore oyle and wyne in my old festerd wownd.
  Releace me of synne þat yt doth not me confownd.

  Confiteor domino pape et omnibus cardinalibus eius et vobis,

1790 *quia peccaui nimis exigendo ab ecclesia tributum, mea culpa.*
  Ideo precor sanctissimum dominum papam et omnes prelatos
  eius et vos, orare pro me.

S. Lang. Misereatur tui omnipotens papa, et dimittat tibi omnes
  erratus tuos, liberetque te a suspencione, excominicacione et

1795 *interdicto, et restituat te in regnum tuum.*

K. John. Amen.

S. Lang. Dominus papa noster te absoluat, et ego absoluo te
  auctoritate eius, et apostolorum Petri et Pauli in hac parte
  mihi comissa, ab omnibus impietatibus tuis, et restituo te

1800 *corone et regno, in nomine domini pape, amen.*

Card. Ye are well content to take this man for yowr primate?

1773-76 *Added in B.*

1777-1803 *Omitted in Collier, Man-*
    ly, Farmer.

1779 restytucyon] *ed.*; restyticyon *B.*

1782 assoyll] & assoyll *A.*

1783 resembleth] resemble *A.*

1791 sanctissimum] sanctissimi *A.*

1791 dominum] domini *A.*

1791 omnes] omnis *A.**

1792 et] e *A.*

1793 Misereatur] Miseriatur *A.*

1795 restituat te] restituatte *A.*

1798 hac] ac *A.*

1799 mihi] wee *A.**

1799 comissa] commissa *A.*

1800 domini pape] domini nostri
    pape *A.*

K. John. Yea, and to vse hym accordyng to his estate.

I am ryght sory that euer I yow offended.

S. Lang. And I am full gladde that ye are so welle   (p. 41, fol. 24)

  amended.

1805 Vnto holy churche ye are now an obedyent chylde,

Where ye were afore with heresye muche defyelde.

Eng. Sir, yonder is a clarke whych is condempned for treason.

The shryues woulde fayne knowe what to do with hym thys season.

[*Enter Treason.*]

K. John. Come hyther, fellawe. What? Me thynke thu art a pryste.

1810 *Tr.* He hath ofter gessed that of the truthe haue myste.

K. John. A pryste and a traytour? How maye that wele agree?

Tr. Yes, yes, wele ynough vnderneth *Benedicite.*

Myself hath played it, and therfor I knowe it the better.

Amonge craftye cloyners there hath not bene a gretter.

1815 *K. John.* Tell some of thy feates; thu mayest the better escape.

S. Lang. Hem! Not to bolde yet; for a mowse the catte wyll gape.

Tr. Twenty thousande traytour I haue made in my tyme

Vndre *Benedicite* betwyn hygh masse and pryme.

I made Nobylyte to be obedyent

1820 To the churche of Rome, whych most kynges maye repent.

I haue so conuayed that neyther priest nor lawer

Wyll obeye Gods wurde, nor yet the Gospell fauer.

In the place of Christe I haue sett vp supersticyons;

For preachynges, ceremonyes; for Gods wurde, mennys tradicyons.

1825 Come to the temple and there Christe hath no place;

Moyses and the paganes doth vtterly hym deface.

Eng. Marke wele, sir. Tell what we haue of Moyses.

Tr. All your Ceremonyes, your copes and your sensers, doubtlesse,

Your fyers, your waters, your oyles, your aulters, your ashes,

1830 Your candlestyckes, your cruettes, your salte, with suche lyke

  trashes.

Ye lacke but the bloude of a goate or els a calfe.

Eng. Lete vs heare sumwhat also in the paganes behalfe.

Tr. Of the paganes ye haue your gylded ymages all,

In your necessytees vpon them for to call

1835 With crowchynges, with kyssynges and settynge vp of lyghtes,

Bearynge them in processyon and fastynges vpon their nyghtes;

Some for the tothe ake, some for þe pestylence and poxe,

1804 *Cf. A1.*   1807-08 *Cf. A2-3.*
1805-06 *Added in B.*   1809-70 *Added in B.*

With ymages of waxe to brynge moneye to the boxe.
Eng. What haue they of Christe in the churche, I praye the tell.

1840   *Tr.* Marry, nothynge at all but the epystle and the Gospell,
And that is in Latyne that no man shoulde it knowe.
S. Lang. Peace, noughty whoreson, peace! Thu playest (p. 42, fol. 24ᵛ)
    the knaue, I trowe.
K. John. Hast thu knowne suche wayes and sought no reformacyon?
[*Tr.*] It is the lyuynge of our whole congregacyon.

1845   If supersticyons and ceremonyes from vs fall,
Farwele monke and chanon, priest, fryer, byshopp and all.
Our conueyaunce is suche þat we haue both moneye and ware.
S. Lang. Our occupacyon thu wylt marre! God gyue the care.
Eng. Very fewe of ye wyll peters offyce take?

1850   *Tr.* Yes, the more part of vs our maistre hath forsake.
Eng. I meane for preachynge. I praye God thu be curste!
Tr. No, no, with Iudas we loue wele to be purste.
We selle our maker so sone as we haue hym made,
And as for preachynge, we meddle not with that trade

1855   Least Annas, Cayphas and the lawers shulde vs blame,
Callynge vs to a reckenynge for preachynge in that name.
K. John. But tell to me, person, whie wert thu cast in preson?
[*Tr.*] For no great matter, but a lyttle petye treason:
For coniurynge, calkynge, and coynynge of newe grotes,

1860   For clippynge of nobles, with suche lyke pratye motes.
Eng. Thys is hygh treason, and hath bene euermore.
K. John. It is suche treason as he shall sure hange fore.
Tr. I haue holy orders. By þe messe, I defye your wurst!
Ye can not towche me but ye must be accurst.

1865   *K. John.* We wyll not towche the, the halter shall do yt alone.
Curse the rope, therfor, whan thu begynnest to grone.
Tr. And sett ye nomore by the holy ordre of prestehode?
Ye wyll proue your selfe an heretyke, by the rode.
K. John. Come hyther, Englande, and here what I saye to the.

1870   *Eng.* I am all readye to do as ye commaunde me.
K. John. For so much as he hath falsefyed our coyne,
As he is worthie lete hym with an halter ioyne.
Thu shalt hange no priest nor yet none honest man,
But a traytour, a thefe, and one þat lyttle good can.

1875   *Card.* What, yet agaynst the churche? Gett me boke, belle and candle;

1871-72 *Cf. A4-5.*   1875-76 *Cf. A6-7.*
1873-74 *Added in B.*

As I am true priest, I shall ye yett better handle.
Ye neyther regarde hys crowne nor anoynted fyngers,
The offyce of a priest nor the grace that therin lyngers.
S. Lang. Sir, pacyent yourselfe and all thynge shall   (p. 43, fol. 25)
   be well.
1880   Fygh, man! To the churche that ye shulde be styll a rebell!
Eng. I accompt hym no priest that worke such haynouse treason.
S. Lang. It is a worlde to heare a folysh woman reason!
Card. After thys maner ye vsed Peter Pomfrete,
   A good symple man, and as they saye, a profete.
1885   *K. John.* Sir, I ded proue hym a very supersticyouse wretche
   And blasphemouse lyar; therfor ded the lawe hym vpstretche.
   He prophecyed first I shulde reigne but .xiiij. years,
   Makynge the people to beleue he coulde bynde bears;
   And I haue reigned a seuentene yeares and more.
1890   And anon after he grudged at me very sore,
   And sayde I shulde be exylded out of my realme
   Before the ascencyon—whych was turned to a fantastycall dreame—
   Saynge he woulde hange if hys prophecye were not true.
   Thus hys owne decaye hys folyshnesse ded brue.
1895   *Card.* Ye shoulde not hange hym whych is a frynde to the churche.
   K. John. Alac, that ye shoulde counte them fryndes of the churche
   That agaynst all truthe so hypocritycally lurche;
   An yll churche is it that hath suche fryndes in dede.
Eng. Of maister Morres suche an other fable we reade,
1900   That in Morgans fyelde þe sowle of a knyght made verses,
   Apearynge vnto hym; and thys one he rehearces:
   Destruet hoc regnum rex regum duplici plaga—
   Whych is true as God spake with the Ape at Praga.
   The sowles departed from thys heauye mortall payne
1905   To the handes of God returneth neuer agayne.
   A maruelouse thynge that ye thus delyght in lyes!
S. Lang. Thys queane doth not els but mocke our blessed storyes.
   That Peter Angred ye whan he called ye a deuyll incarnate.
K. John. He is now full sure nomore so vncomely to prate.
1910   Well, as for thys man, because that he is a priste
   I gyue hym to ye; do with hym what ye lyste.

1877-82 *Added in B.*   *lier*; whych was turned a to
1883-89 *Cf. A8-13.*   *B*; whych turned to *b.*
1890-1909 *Added in B.*   1907 our] the *b.**
1892 whych was turned to a] *Col-*   1910-15 *Cf. A14-17.*

Card. In the popes behalfe I wyll sumwhat take vpon me.
Here I delyuer hym by the churches lyberte,
In spyght of your hart. Make of it what ye lyste.

1915 *K. John.* I am pleased, I saye, because he ys a pryste.
Card. Whether ye be or no it shall not greatly force.
Lete me see those cheanes. Go thy waye and haue remorce.
Tr. God saue your lordeshypps. I trust I shall amende
And do nomore so, or els, sir, God defende.

[*Exit Treason.*]

1920 *S. Lang.* I shall make the, I trowe, to kepe thy   (p. 44, fol. 25ᵛ)
    benefyce.
By the Marye Messe, the knaue wyll neuer be wyse!
Eng. Lyke lorde, lyke chaplayne; neyther barrell better herynge.
S. Lang. Styll she must trattle; that tunge is alwayes sterynge.
A wurde or two, sir, I must tell yow in your eare.

1925 *Card.* Of some aduauntage I woulde very gladly heare.
S. Lang. Releace not Englande of the generall interdictyon
Tyll the kynge hath graunted the dowrye and the pencyon
Of Iulyane, the wyfe of kynge Richarde Cour de Lyon.
Ye knowe very well she beareth the churche good mynde.

1930 Tush, we must haue all, Manne, that she shall leaue behynde.
As the saynge is, he fyndeth that surely bynde.
It were but folye suche louce endes for to lose.
The lande and the monye wyll make well for our purpose.
Tush, laye yokes vpon hym, more than he is able to beare;

1935 Of holye churche so he wyll stande euer in feare.
Suche a shrewe as he it is good to kepe vndre awe.
Eng. Woo is that persone whych is vndreneth your lawe!
Ye maye see, good poeple, what these same merchauntes are;
Their secrete knaueryes their open factes declare.

1940 *S. Lang.* Holde thy peace, callet! God gyue the sorowe and care!
Card. Ere I releace yow of the interdyctyon heare,
In the whych your realme contynued hath thys seuen yeare,
Ye shall make Iulyane, your syster in lawe, thys bande,
To gyue hir the thirde part of Englande and of Irelande.

1945 *K. John.* All the worlde knoweth, sir, I owe hir no suche dewtye.
Card. Ye shall gyue it to hir; there is no remedye.

1915 a] *ed.*
1916-40 *Added in B.*
1918-19 *Assigned to* Sedicyon (*i.e.,*
    Stephen Langton) *in b.*

1935 wyll] shall *b.**
1941-44 *Cf. A18-21.*
1942 realme] hame *b.*
1945-48 *Added in B.*

[126]

Wyll ye styll withstande our holy fathers precepte?

S. Lang. In peyne of dampnacyon hys commaundement must be kepte.

K. John. Oh, ye vndo me, consyderynge my great paymentes.

1950 *Eng.* Sir, disconfort not, for God hath sent debatementes;
Your mercyfull maker hath shewed vpon ye hys powere,
From thys heauye yoke delyuerynge yow thys howre.
The woman is dead; suche newes are hyther brought.

K. John. For me, a synnar, thys myracle hath God wrought.

1955 In most hygh paryls he euer me preserued,
And in thys daunger he hath not from me swerued.
In genua procumbens Deum adorat, dicens:
As Dauid sayth, Lorde, thu dost not leaue thy seruaunt
That wyll trust in the and in thy blessyd couenaunt.

S. Lang. A vengeaunce take it! By the messe, it is   (p. 45, fol. 26)
vnhappye

1960 She is dead so sone. Now is it past remedye.
So must we lose all now that she is clerely gone.
If that praye had bene ours, oh, it had bene alone!
The chaunce beynge suche, by my trouth, euen lete it go:
No grote no Pater noster, no penye no *placebo*.

1965 The deuyll go with it, seynge it wyll be no better.

Eng. Their myndes are all sett vpon the fylthie luker.

Card. Than here I releace yow of your interdictyons all,
And strayghtly commaunde yow vpon daungers þat maye fall
Nomore to meddle with the churches reformacyon,

1970 Nor holde men from Rome whan they make appellacyon,
By God and by all the contentes of thys boke.

K. John. Agaynst holy churche I wyll nomore speake nor loke.

S. Lang. Go, open the churche dores and lete the belles be ronge,
And through out the realme see that *Te Deum* be songe.

1975 Pryck vpp your candels before saynt Loe and saynt Legearde,
Lete saynt Antonyes hogge be had in some regarde.
If your ale be sower and your breade moulde, certayne,
Now wyll they waxe swete, for þe pope hath blest ye agayne.

Eng. Than within a whyle I trust ye wyll preache the Gospell?

1980 *S. Lang.* That shall I tell the, kepe thu it in secrete counsell:

1949-50 *Cf. A22-23.*   1958 thy] thys *b.*
1951-52 *Added in B.*   1959-66 *Added in B.*
1953-54 *Cf. A24-25.*   1967-74 *Cf. A28-35.*
1955-56 and S.D. *Added in B.* 1970 men] them *b.*
1957-58 *Cf. A26-27.*   1975-81 *Added in B.*

[127]

It shall neyther come in churche nor yet in chauncell.
Card. Goo your wayes a pace and see our pleasure be done.
K. John. As ye haue commaunded all shall be perfourmed sone.

                              [Exeunt King John and England.]

Card. By the messe, I laugh to see thys cleane conueyaunce!
1985   He is now full glad as our pype goeth to daunce.
By cockes sowle, he is now become a good parrysh clarke.
S. Lang. Ha, ha, wylye whoreson, dost that so busyly marke?
I hope in a whyle we wyll make hym so to raue
That he shall become vnto vs a commen slaue
1990   And shall do nothynge but as we byd hym do.
If we byd hym slea, I trowe he wyll do so;
If we bydde hym burne suche as beleue in Christe,
He shall not saye naye to the byddynge of a priste.
But yet it is harde to trust what he wyll be,
1995   He is so crabbed, by the holye Trinyte.
To saue all thynges vp I holde best we make hym more sure
And gyue hym a sawce that he no longar endure.
Now that I remembre, we shall not leaue hym thus.
Card. Whye, what shall we do to hym els, in the name of Iesus?
2000 *S. Lang.* Marry, fatche in Lewes, kynge Phylyppes   (p. 46, fol. 26ᵛ)
           sonne of fraunce,
To fall vpon hym with hys menne and ordynaunce,
With wyldefyer, gunpouder, and suche lyke myrye tryckes,
To dryue hym to holde and searche hym in the quyckes.
I wyll not leaue hym tyll I brynge hym to hys yende.
2005 *Card.* Well, farwele Sedicyon; do as shall lye in thy myende.

                                   [Exit Cardinal.]

S. Lang. I maruele greatly where dissymulacyon is.
Diss. I wyll come anon if thu tarry tyll I pysse.

                      [Enter Dissimulation.]

S. Lang. I beshrewe your hart! Where haue ye bene so longe?
Diss. In the gardene, man, the herbes and wedes amonge,
2010   And there haue I gote the poyson of a toade.
I hope in a whyle to wurke some feate abroade.
S. Lang. I was wonte sumtyme of thy preuye counsell to be.
Am I now adayes become a straunger to the?

1982-85 *Cf. A36-39.*   1998-2001 *Cf. A40-43.*
1986-97 *Added in B.*   2002-03 *Added in B.*
1988 so to] suche ans *b.*   2004-25 *Cf. A44-65.*
1996 hy*m* more sure] hy*m* sure *b.*   2010 a] *ed.* (*cf. A50*).

Diss. I wyll tell the all vndreneth *Benedicite*,

2015 What I mynde to do in case thu wylte assoyle me.

S. Lang. Thu shalt be assoyled by the most holy fathers auctoryte.

Diss. Shall I so in dede? By the masse, than, now haue at the!
Benedicite.

S. Lang. In nomine Papę, Amen.

2020 *Diss.* Sir, thys is my mynde: I wyll gyue kynge Iohan thys poyson,

So makynge hym sure that he shall neuer haue foyson.

And thys must thu saye to colour with the thynge,

That a penye lofe he wolde haue brought to a shyllynge.

S. Lang. Naye, that is suche a lye as easely wyll be felte.

2025 *Diss.* Tush, man, amonge fooles it neuer wyll be out smelte,

Though it be a great lye. Set vpon it a good face,

And that wyll cause men beleue it in euery place.

S. Lang. I am sure, than, thu wylt geue it hym in a drynke.

Diss. Marry, that I wyll, and the one half with hym swynke

2030 To encourage hym to drynke the botome off.

S. Lang. If thu drynke the halfe thu shalt fynde it no scoff;

Of terryble deathe thu wyllt stacker in the plashes.

Diss. Tush, though I dye, man, there wyll ryse more of my ashes.

I am sure the monkes wyll praye for me so bytterlye

2035 That I shall not come in helle nor in purgatorye.

In the popes kychyne the scullyons shall not brawle

Nor fyght for my grese. If the priestes woulde for me yewle

And grunt a good pace *placebo* with Requiem Masse,

Without muche tarryaunce I shulde to paradyse passe,

2040 Where I myght be sure to make good cheare and be myrye,

For I can not awaye with that whoreson purgatorye.

S. Lang. To kepe the from thens thu shalt haue fyue   (p. 47, fol. 27)
         monkes syngynge

In Swynsett abbeye so longe as the worlde is durynge;

They wyll daylye praye for the sowle of father Symon,

2045 A Cisteane monke whych poysened kynge Iohn.

Diss. Whan the worlde is done what helpe shall I haue than?

S. Lang. Than shyft for thy self so wele as euer thu can.

Diss. Cockes sowle, he cometh here! Assoyle me þat I were gone then.

S. Lang. Ego absoluo te in nomine papę, Amen.

[*Exeunt Dissimulation and Stephen Langton.*]

2026-27 *Added in B.*	2042-43 *Cf. A74-75.*
2026 great] foule *b.**	2044-45 *Added in B.*
2028-35 *Cf. A66-73.*	2046-67 *Cf. A76-97.*
2036-41 *Added in B.*	

[*Enter King John and England.*]

2050   *K. John.* No prynce in the worlde in suche captiuyte
As I am this houre, and all for ryghteousnesse.
Agaynst me I haue both the lordes and commynalte,
Byshoppes and lawers, whych in their cruell madnesse
Hath brought in hyther the frenche kynges eldest sonne, Lewes.
2055   The chaunce vnto me is not so dolourrouse,
But my lyfe thys daye is muche more tedyouse.

More of compassyon for shedynge of Christen blood
Than any thynge els, my sceptre I gaue vp latelye
To the pope of Rome, whych hath no tytle good
2060   Of iurisdyctyon, but of vsurpacyon onlye.
And now to the, lorde, I woulde resygne vp gladlye
                                              Flectit Genua.
Both my crowne and lyfe; for thyne owne ryght it is,
If it woulde please the, to take my sowle to thy blys.

Eng. Sir, discomfort ye not; in the honour of Christe Iesu
2065   God wyll neuer fayle yow, intendynge not els but vertu.
  K. John. The anguysh of sprete so pangeth me euery where
That incessauntly I thyrst tyll I be there.
  Eng. Sir, be of good chere, for the pope hath sent a legate
Whose name is Gualo, your foes to excommunycate;
2070   Not only Lewes, whych hath wonne Rochestre,
Wynsore and London, Readynge and wynchestre,
But so manye els as agaynst ye haue rebelled
He hath suspended and openly accursed.
  K. John. They are all false knaues; all men of them be ware.
2075   They neuer left me tyll they had me in their snare.
Now haue they Otto the emproure so wele as me,
And the french kynge, Phylypp, vndre their captiuyte.
All Christen princes they wyll haue in their bandes.
The pope and hys priestes are poyseners of all landes.
2080   All Christen people be ware of trayterouse pristes,
For of truthe they are the pernicyouse Antichristes.

2060 iurisdyctyon] *ed.*; iurisdycton   2068-85 *Added in B.*
    B.   2075 neuer left] neuer yet left *b.*
2062 Both my crowne] If it woulde
    b.

Eng. Thys same Gualo, sir, in your cause doth stoughtly barke.

K. John. They are all nought, Englande, so many as weare that Marke.

From thys habytacyon, swete lorde, delyuer me,

2085   And preserue thys realme, of thy benygnyte.

Diss. Wassayle, wassayle, out of the mylke payle,   (p. 48, fol. 27ᵛ)

Wassayle, wassayle, as whyte as my nayle,

Wassayle, wassayle, in snowe, froste and hayle,

Wassayle, wassayle, with partriche and rayle.

2090   Wassayle, wassayle, that muche doth auayle,

Wassayle, wassayle, that neuer wyll fayle.

K. John. Who is that, Englande? I praye the stepp fourth and see.

Eng. He doth seme a farre some relygyouse man to be.

                [Enter Dissimulation.]

Diss. Now Iesus preserue your worthye and excellent grace,

2095   For doubtlesse there is a very Angelyck face.

Now forsoth and God, I woulde thynke my self in heauen

If I myght remayne with yow but yeares aleuyn;

I would couete here none other felicyte.

K. John. A louynge persone thu mayest seme for to be.

2100 *Diss.* I am as gentle a worme as euer ye see.

K. John. But what is thy name, good frynde? I praye the tell me.

Diss. Simon of Swynsett my very name is, per dee.

I am taken of men for monastycall deuocyon,

And here haue I brought yow a maruelouse good pocyon,

2105   For I hearde ye saye that ye were very drye.

K. John. In dede I wolde gladly drynke. I praye the come nye.

Diss. The dayes of your lyfe neuer felt ye suche a cuppe,

So good and so holsome if ye woulde drynke it vpp.

It passeth malmesaye, capryck, tyre or ypocras.

2110   By my faythe, I thynke a better drynke neuer was.

K. John. Begynne, gentle monke; I praye the drynke half to me.

Diss. If ye dronke all vp it were the better for ye.

It woulde slake your thirst and also quycken your brayne.

A better drynke is not in Portyngale nor Spayne.

2115   Therfor suppe it of and make an ende of it quycklye.

K. John. Naye, thu shalte drynke half. There is no remedye.

Diss. Good lucke to ye than; haue at it by and bye.

2086-2101 *Cf. A98-110.*   2116-17 *Cf. A121-122.*
2102 *Added in B.*   2116 drynke half, there] drynke,
2103-12 *Cf. A111-120.*   there *b.*
2113-15 *Added in B.*

Halfe wyll I consume if there be no remedye.

K. John. God saynt the, good monke, with all my very harte.

2120 *Diss.* I haue brought ye half; conueye me that for your parte.

Where art thu, Sedicyon? By the masse, I dye, I dye!

Helpe now at a pynche. Alas, man, cum awaye shortlye!

[*Enter Sedition.*]

Sed. Come hyther apace and gett the to the farmerye.

I haue prouyded for the, by swete saynt Powle,

2125 Fyue monkes þat shall synge contynually for thy sowle,

That I warande the thu shalt not come in helle.   (p. 49, fol. 28)

Diss. To sende me to heauen goo rynge the holye belle

And synge for my sowle a masse of *Scala Celi*,

That I maye clyme vp aloft with Enoch and Heli.

2130 I do not doubte it but I shall be a saynt;

Prouyde a gyldar, myne Image for to paynt.

I dye for the churche with Thomas of Canterberye;

Ye shall fast my vigyll and vpon my daye be merye.

No doubt but I shall do myracles in a whyle,

2135 And therfor lete me be shryned in the north yle.

Sed. To the than wyll offer both crypple, halte and blynde,

Mad men and mesels, with suche as are woo behynde.

Exeunt.

K. John. My bodye me vexeth; I doubt muche of a tympanye.

Eng. Now alas, alas, your grace is betrayed cowardlye!

2140 *K. John.* Where became the monke that was here with me latelye?

Eng. He is poysened, sir, and lyeth a dyenge, surelye.

K. John. It can not be so, for he was here euen now.

Eng. Doubtlesse, sir, it is so true as I haue tolde yow.

A false Iudas kysse he hath gyuen yow and is gone.

2145 The halte, sore and lame thys pitiefull case wyll mone.

Neuer prynce was there that made to poore peoples vses

So many masendewes, hospytals and spyttle howses

As your grace hath done yet sens the worlde began.

K. John. Of priestes and of monkes I am counted a wycked man

2150 For that I neuer buylte churche nor monasterye,

But my pleasure was to helpe suche as were nedye.

2118 *Added in B.*

2119-21 *Cf. A123-125.*

2120 conueye me that] now dry*n*ke

  out that *b.*

2122 *Added in B.*

2123-27 *Cf. A126-130.*

2128-37 *Added in B.*

2138-43 *Cf. A131-136.*

2144-57 *Added in B.*

Eng. The more grace was yours, for at the day of iudgement
    Christe wyll rewarde them whych hath done hys commaundement.
    There is no promyse for voluntarye wurkes,
2155   Nomore than there is for sacrifyce of the Turkes.
    K. John. Doubtlesse I do fele muche greuaunce in my bodye.
    Eng. As the lorde wele knoweth, for that I am full sorye.
    K. John. There is no malyce to the malyce of the clergye.
    Well, the lorde God of heauen on me and them haue mercye.

2160   For doynge iustyce they haue euer hated me.
    They caused my lande to be excommunycate
    And me to resygne both crowne and princely dygnyte,
    From my obedyence assoylynge euery estate,
    And now, last of all, they haue me intoxycate.
2165   I perceyue ryght wele their malyce hath none ende.
    I desyre not els but that they maye sone amende.

    I haue sore hungred and thirsted ryghteousnesse   (p. 50, fol. 28ᵛ)
    For the offyce sake that God hath me appoynted;
    But now I perceyue that synne and wyckednesse
2170   In thys wretched worlde, lyke as Christe prophecyed,
    Haue the ouerhande; in me is it verefyed.
    Praye for me, good people, I besych yow hartely,
    That the lorde aboue on my poore sowle haue mercy.

    Farwell, noble men, with the clergye spirytuall;
2175   Farwell, men of lawe, with the whole commynnalte.
    Your disobedyence I do forgyue yow all
    And desyre God to perdon your iniquyte.
    Farwell, swete Englande, now last of all to the;
    I am ryght sorye I coulde do for the nomore.
2180   Farwele ones agayne, yea, farwell for euermore.

    Eng. With the leaue of God I wyll not leaue ye thus,
    But styll be with ye tyll he do take yow from vs,
    And than wyll I kepe your bodye for a memoryall.
    K. John. Than plye it, Englande, and prouyde for my buryall.
2185   A wydowes offyce it is to burye the deade.

2158-61 *Cf. A137-140.*   2170 In thys wretched worlde,]
2159 lorde God of] lorde of *b.*   Haue the ouerhande *b.*
2164 of all, they] of, they *b.*

[133]

Eng. Alas, swete maistre, ye waye so heauy as leade.
 Oh horryble case, that euer so noble a kynge
 Shoulde thus be destroyed and lost for ryghteouse doynge
 By a cruell sort of disguysed bloud souppers—
2190 Vnmercyfull murtherers, all dronke in þe bloude of marters!
 Report what they wyll in their most furyouse madnesse,
 Of thys noble kynge muche was the godlynesse.   *Exeunt.*

[*Enter Verity.*]

Ver. I assure ye, fryndes, lete men wryte what they wyll,
 Kynge Iohan was a man both valeaunt and godlye.
2195 What though Polydorus reporteth hym very yll
 At the suggestyons of the malicyouse clergye?
 Thynke yow a Romane with the Romanes can not lye?
 Yes! Therfor, Leylonde, out of thy slumbre awake,
 And wytnesse a trewthe for thyne owne contrayes sake.

2200 For hys valeauntnesse many excellent writers make,
 As Sigebertus, Vincentius and also Nauclerus;
 Giraldus and Mathu Parys with hys noble vertues take—
 Yea, Paulus Phrigio, Iohan Maior and Hector Boethius.
 Nothynge is allowed in his lyfe of Polydorus
2205 Whych discommendeth hys ponnyshmentes for trayterye,
 Aduauncynge very sore hygh treason in the clergye.

 Of hys godlynesse thus muche report wyll I:
 Gracyouse prouysyon for sore, sycke, halte and lame
 He made in hys tyme, he made both in towne and cytie,
2210 Grauntynge great lyberties for mayntenaunce of þe same
 By markettes and fayers in places of notable name.
 Great monymentes are in Yppeswych, Donwych   (p. 51, fol. 29)
   and Berye,
 Whych noteth hym to be a man of notable mercye.
       [*Enter Nobility, Clergy and Civil Order.*]
 The cytie of London through hys mere graunt and premye
2215 Was first priuyleged to haue both mayer and shryue,
 Where before hys tyme it had but baylyues onlye.
 In hys dayes the brydge the cytiezens ded contryue.

2198 out of thy slumbre awake]   *contrayes* s *b.*
    Collier; out of thy su*m*bre 2203 Phrigio, Iohan Maior] Phri-
    awake *B*; for thyne owne   gio, Maior *b.*

Though he now be dead hys noble actes are alyue.
Hys zele is declared as towchynge Christes religyon
2220 In that he exyled the Iewes out of thys regyon.

Nob. Whome speake ye of, sir? I besyche ye hartelye.
Ver. I talke of kynge Iohan, of late your prynce most worthye.
Nob. Sir, he was a man of a very wycked sorte.
Ver. Ye are muche to blame your prynce so to reporte.
2225 How can ye presume to be called nobilyte,
Diffamynge a prynce in your malygnyte?
Ecclesiastes sayth, If thu with an hatefull harte
Misnamest a kynge, thu playest suche a wycked parte
As byrdes of ayer to God wyll represent
2230 To thy great parell and excedynge ponnyshment.
Saynt Hierome sayth also that he is of no renowne
But a vyle traytour that rebelleth agaynst the crowne.
Cler. He speaketh not agaynst the crowne but the man, per dee.
Ver. Oh, where is the sprete whych ought to reigne in the!
2235 The crowne of it selfe without the man is nothynge.
Learne of the scriptures to haue better vndrestandynge.
The harte of a kynge is in the handes of the lorde,
And he directeth it—wyse Salomon to recorde.
They are abhomynable that vse hym wyckedlye.
2240 *Cler.* He was neuer good to vs, the sanctifyed clergye.
Ver. Wyll ye knowe the cause before thys worshypfull cumpanye?
Your conuersacyon and lyues are very vngodlye.
Kynge Salomon sayth, Who hath a pure mynde,
Therin delyghtynge, shall haue a kynge to frynde.
2245 On thys wurde *Cleros*, whych signyfieth a lott
Or a sortynge out into a most godly knott,
Ye do take your name, for that ye are the lordes
Select, of hys wurde to be the specyall recordes,
As of saynt Mathias we haue a syngular mencyon,
2250 That they chose hym out anon after Christes ascencyon.
Thus do ye recken. But I feare ye come of *Clerus*,
A very noyfull worme, As Aristotle sheweth vs,
By whome are destroyed the honycombes of bees;
For poore wydowes ye robbe, as ded the pharysees.
2255 *C. Ord.* I promyse yow it is vncharytably spoken.   (p. 52, fol. 29ᵛ)

2228 playest suche a] playest a *b.*   2254 for poore wydowes] for wyd-
2234 Oh, Where] Where *b.*   owes *b.*

Ver. Trouthe ingendereth hate; ye shewe therof a token.
Ye are suche a man as ought euery where to see
A godly order, but ye loose mare commynalte.
Plato thought alwayes that no hyghar loue could be
2260 Than a man to peyne hymself for hys own countreye.
Dauid for their sake the proude Phelistyan slewe,
Aioth mad Eglon hys wyckednesse to rewe,
Esdras from Persye for his owne contreys sake
Came to hierusalem, their stronge holdes vp to make;
2265 But yow, lyke wretches, cast ouer both contreye and kynge.
All manhode shameth to see your vnnaturall doynge.
Ye wycked rulers, God doth abhorre ye all.
As Mantuan reporteth in hys Egloges pastorall,
Ye fede not the shepe, but euer ye pylle the flocke
2270 And clyppe them so nygh that scarsely ye leaue one locke.
Your iugementes are suche that ye call to God in vayne
So longe as ye haue your prynces in disdayne.
Chrysostome reporteth that Nobylyte of fryndes
Auayleth nothynge, except ye haue godly myndes.
2275 What profiteth it yow to be called spirytuall
Whyls yow for lucre from all good vertues fall?
What prayse is it to yow to be called cyuylyte
If yow from obedyence and godly order flee?
Anneus Seneca hath thys most prouable sentence:
2280 The gentyll free hart goeth neuer from obedyence.
C. Ord. Sir, my bretherne and I woulde gladly knowe your name.
Ver. I am Veritas, that come hyther yow to blame
For castynge awaye of our most lawfull kynge.
Both God and the worlde detesteth your dampnable doynge.
2285 How haue ye vsed kynge Iohan here now of late?
I shame to rehearce the corruptyons of your state.
Ye were neuer wele tyll ye had hym cruelly slayne,
And now, beynge dead, ye haue hym styll in disdayne.
Ye haue raysed vp of hym most shamelesse lyes,
2290 Both by your reportes and by your written storyes.
He that slewe Saul through fearcenesse vyolent
Was slayne sone after at Dauids iust commaundement,
For bycause that Saul was anoynted of the lorde.

2256 ye shewe therof a] *in* yow perceyue I the *b.*
2258 mare] yche *b.*＊

2259 thought alwayes that no] ded
  esteme, no *b.*＊
2268 Mantuan] mantuan *b.*

The seconde of kynges of thys beareth plenteouse recorde.
2295 He was in those dayes estemed wurthie to dye
On a noynted kynge that layed handes violentlye.
Ye are not ashamed to fynde fyue priestes to synge   (p. 53, fol. 30)
For that same traytour that slewe your naturall kynge.
A trayterouse knaue ye can set vpp for a saynte,
2300 And a ryghteouse kynge lyke an hatefull tyraunt paynte.
I coulde shewe the place where yow most spyghtfullye
Put out your torches vpon hys physnomye.
In your glasse wyndowes ye whyppe your naturall kynges.
As I sayde afore, I abhorre to shewe your doynges.
2305 The Turkes, I dare saye, are a thousande tymes better than yow.
Nob. For Gods loue, nomore! Alas, ye haue sayde ynough.
Cler. All the worlde doth knowe that we haue done sore amys.
C. Ord. Forgyue it vs, so that we neuer heare more of thys.
Ver. But are ye sorye for thys vngodly wurke?
2310 *Nob.* I praye to God! Els I be dampned lyke a Turke!
Ver. And make true promyse ye wyll neuer more do so?
Cler. Sir, neuer more shall I from true obedyence goo.
Ver. What saye yow, brother? I must haue also your sentence.
C. Ord. I wyll euer gyue to my prynce due reuerence.
2315 *Ver.* Well, than, I doubt not but the lorde wyll condescende
To forgyue yow all, so that ye mynde to amende.
Adewe to ye all, for now I must be gone.
[Enter Imperial Majesty.]
I. Maj. Abyde, Veryte; ye shall not depart so sone.
Haue ye done all thynges as we commaunded yow?
2320 *Ver.* Yea, most gracyouse prynce, I concluded the whole euen now.
I. Maj. And how do they lyke the customs they haue vsed
With our predecessours, whome they haue so abused,
Specyally kynge Iohan? Thynke they they haue done well?
Ver. They repent that euer they folowed sedicyouse counsell
2325 And haue made promes they wyll amende all faultes.
I. Maj. And forsake the pope with all hys cruell assaultes?
Ver. Whie do ye not bowe to imperyall maieste?
Knele and axe pardon for your great enormyte.
Nob. Most godly gouernour, we axe your gracyouse pardon,
2330 Promysynge neuermore to maynteyne false sedicyon.
Cler. Neyther pryuate welthe nor yet vsurped poure
Shall cause me disobeye my prynce from thys same houre.

2300 hatefull] odyouse *b.**

[137]

[*C. Ord.*] False dissymulacyon shall neuer me begyle;
Where I shall mete hym I wyll euer hym reuyle.

2335 *I. Maj.* I perceyue, Veryte, ye haue done wele your   (p. 54, fol. 30ᵛ)
    part,
Refourmynge these men. Gramercyes with all my hart!
I praye yow take paynes to call our commynalte
To true obedyence, as ye are Gods Veryte.

Ver. I wyll do it, sir; yet shall I haue muche a doo
2340 With your Popish prelates. They wyll hunte me to and fro.

I. Maj. So longe as I lyue they shall do yow no wronge.

Ver. Than wyll I go preache Gods wurde your commens amonge.
But first I desyre yow their stubberne factes to remytt.

I. Maj. I forgyue yow all and perdon your frowarde wytt.

Nob.
2345 *Cler.* } The heauenly gouernour rewarde your goodnesse for it.
C. Ord.

Ver. For Gods sake obeye lyke as doth yow befall,
For in hys owne realme a kynge is iudge ouer all
By Gods appoyntment, and none maye hym iudge agayne
But the lorde hymself. In thys the scripture is playne.
2350 He that condempneth a kynge condempneth God without dought;
He that harmeth a kynge to harme God goeth abought;
He that a prynce resisteth doth dampne Gods ordynaunce
And resisteth God in withdrawynge hys affyaunce.
All subiectes offendynge are vndre the kynges iudgement;
2355 A kynge is reserued to the lorde omnypotent.
He is a mynyster immedyate vndre God,
Of hys ryghteousnesse to execute the rod.
I charge yow, therfor, as God hath charged me,
To gyue to your kynge hys due supremyte
2360 And exyle the pope thys realme for euermore.

Nob.
Cler. } We shall gladly doo accordynge to your loore.
C. Ord.

Ver. Your grace is content I shewe your people the same?

I. Maj. Yea, gentle veryte, shewe them their dewtye, in Gods name.
                                  [*Exit Verity.*]

To confyrme the tale that veryte had now
2365 The seconde of kynges is euydent to yow.

2358 charged] *Manly conj.*; *Farmer*; charge *B*.

The yonge man that brought the crowne and bracelett
Of Saul to Dauid, saynge that he had hym slayne,
Dauid commaunded as though he had done þat forfett
Strayght waye to be slayne. Gods sprete ded hym constrayne
2370 To shewe what it is a kynges bloude to distayne.
So ded he those two that in the fyelde hym mett
And vnto hym brought the heade of Isboset.

Consydre that Christe was vndre the obedyence
Of worldly prynces so longe as he was here,
2375 And always vsed them with a lowly reuerence,
Paynge them tribute, All hys true seruauntes to stere
To obeye them, loue them, and haue them in   (p. 55, fol. 31)
  reuerent feare.
Dampnacyon it is to hym that an ordre breake
Appoynted of God, lyke as the Apostle speake.

2380 No man is exempt from thys, Gods ordynaunce—
Bishopp, monke, chanon, priest, Cardynall nor pope.
All they by Gods lawe to kynges owe their allegeaunce.
Thys wyll be wele knowne in thys same realme, I hope.
Of Verytees wurdes the syncere meanynge I grope;
2385 He sayth that a kynge is of God immedyatlye.
Than shall neuer pope rule more in thys monarchie.

Cler. If it be your pleasure, we wyll exyle hym cleane,
That he in thys realme shall neuermore be seane,
And your grace shall be þe supreme head of þe churche.
2390 To brynge thys to passe ye shall see how we wyll wurche.
I. Maj. Here is a nyce tale! He sayth, if it be my pleasure
He wyll do thys acte to the popes most hygh displeasure,
As who sayth I woulde for pleasure of my persone
And not for Gods truthe haue suche an enterpryse done.
2395 Full wysely conuayed! The crowe wyll not chaunge her hewe.
It is maruele to me and euer ye be trewe.
I wyll the auctoryte of Gods holy wurde to do it
And it not to aryse of your vayne slypper wytt.
That scripture doth not is but a lyght fantasye.
2400 Cler. Both Daniel and Paule calleth hym Gods aduersarye,
And therfor ye ought as a Deuyll hym to expell.

2398 And it not] And not b.

[139]

I. Maj. Knewe ye thys afore and woulde it neuer tell?
Ye shoulde repent it had we not now forgyuen ye.
Nobylyte, what saye yow? Wyll ye to thys agree?
2405 *Nob.* I can no lesse, sir, for he is wurse than the Turke,
Whych none other wayes but by tyrannye doth wurke.
Thys bloudy bocher with hys pernycyouse bayte
Oppresse Christen princes by frawde, crafte and dissayte,
Tyll he compell them to kysse hys pestylent fete,
2410 Lyke a leuyathan syttynge in Moyses sete.
I thynke we can do vnto God no sacrifyce
That is more accept nor more agreynge to iustyce
Than to slea that Beaste and slauterman of the deuyll,
That Babylon boore whych hath done so muche euyll.
2415 *I. Maj.* It is a clere sygne of a true Nobilyte
To the wurde of God whan your conscyence doth agree.
For as Christe ded saye to Peter, *Caro et sanguis*
Non reuelauit tibi, sed pater meus celestis:
Ye haue not thys gyfte of carnall generacyon,   (p. 56, fol. 31ᵛ)
2420 Nor of noble bloude, but by Gods owne demonstracyon.
Of yow, Cyuyle order, one sentence woulde I heare.
C. Ord. I rewe it that euer any harte I ded hym beare.
I thynke he hath spronge out of the bottomlesse pytt
And in mennys conscyence in þe stede of God doth sytt,
2425 Blowynge fourth a swarme of grassopers and flyes—
Monkes, fryers and priestes—that all truthe putrifyes.
Of the Christen faythe playe now the true defendar;
Exyle thys monster and rauenouse deuourar
With hys venym wormes, hys adders, whelpes and snakes,
2430 Hys cuculled vermyne, that vnto all myschiefe wakes.
I. Maj. Than in thys purpose ye are all of one mynde?
Cler. We detest the pope and abhorre hym to the fynde.
I. Maj. And are wele content to disobeye hys pryde?
Nob. Yea, and hys lowsye lawes and decrees to sett asyde.
2435 *I. Maj.* Than must ye be sworne to take me for your heade.
C. Ord. We wyll obeye yow as our gouernour in Gods steade.
I. Maj. Now that ye are sworne vnto me, your pryncypall,
I charge ye to regarde the wurde of God ouer all,

2408 Oppresse Christen] Oppresse   2419 generacyon] *ed.*; generacon *B.*
    all Christen *b.*   2434 hys . . . decrees] all his de-
2410 Lyke a] I thyn *b.*   crees, and his lawes *b.*
2415 of a true] of true *b.*

And in that alone to rule, to speake and to iudge,
2440 As ye wyll haue me your socour and refuge.
Cler. If ye wyll make sure ye must exyle sedicyon,
False dyssymulacyon, with all vayne superstycyon,
And put priuate welthe out of the monasteryes;
Than vsurped power maye goo a birdynge for flyes.
2445 *I. Maj.* Take yow it in hande and do your true dilygence,
Iche man for hys part; ye shall wante no assystence.
Cler. I promyse yow here to exyle vsurped powre
And your supremyte to defende yche daye and howre.
Nob. I promyse also out of the monasteryes
2450 To put priuate welthe and detect hys mysteryes.
C. Ord. False dissymulacyon I wyll hange vp in Smythfylde,
With suche supersticion as your people hath begylde.
I. Maj. Than I trust we are at a very good conclusyon,
Vertu to haue place and vyce to haue confusyon.
2455 Take veryte wyth ye for euery acte ye doo;   (p. 57, fol. 32)
So shall ye be sure not out of the waye to goo.

Sedicyon intrat.

[*Sed.*] [*Sing*] Pepe, I see ye! I am glad I haue spyed ye.
Nob. There is Sedicyon. Stande yow asyde a whyle;
Ye shall see how we shall catche hym by a wyle.
2460 *Sed.* No noyse amonge ye? Where is the mery chere
That was wont to be, with quassynge of double bere?
The worlde is not yet as some men woulde it haue.
I haue bene abroade, and I thynke I haue playde þe knaue.
C. Ord. Thu canyst do none other, except thu change thy wunte.
2465 *Sed.* What myschiefe ayle ye that ye are to me so blunte?
I haue sene the daye ye haue fauoured me, perfectyon.
Cler. Thy selfe is not he; thu art of an other complectyon.
Sir, thys is the thiefe that first subdued kynge Iohn,
Vexynge other prynces that sens haue ruled thys regyon;
2470 And now he doth prate he hath so played the knaue
That the worlde is not yet as some men woulde it haue.
It woulde be knowne, sir, what he hath done of late.
I. Maj. What is thy name, frynde? To vs here intymate.
Sed. A sayntwary, a sayntwary! For Gods dere passyon, a sayntwarye!
2475 Is there none wyll holde me, and I haue made so manye?
I. Maj. Tell me what thy name is; thu playest þe knaue, I trowe.

2452 supersticion] *Collier*; supersti-   2468 the] that *b.*
  con B.   2470 prate] saye *b.**

[141]

Sed. I am wyndelesse, good man; I haue muche peyne to blowe.

I. Maj. I saye tell thy name or the racke shall the constrayne.

Sed. Holy perfectyon my godmother called me playne.

2480 *Nob.* It is Sedicyon. God gyue hym a very myschiefe!

C. Ord. Vndre heauen is not a more detestable thiefe.

Sed. By the messe, ye lye! I see wele ye do not knowe me.

I. Maj. Ah, Brother, art thu come? I am ryght glad we haue the.

Sed. By bodye, bloude, bones and sowle, I am not he! (p. 58, fol. 32ᵛ)

2485 *Cler.* If swearynge myghte helpe, he woulde do wele ynough.

I. Maj. He scape not our handes so lyghtly, I waraunde yow.

Cler. Thys is that thiefe, sir, that all Christendome hath troubled,
And the pope of Rome agaynst all kynges maynteyned.

Nob. Now that ye haue hym nomore but hange hym vppe.

2490 *C. Ord.* If ye so be content, it shall be done ere I suppe.

I. Maj. Loo, the clergye accuseth the, Nobylyte condempneth the,
And the lawe wyll hange the. What sayst now to me?

Sed. I woulde I were now at Rome at the sygne of the cuppe,
For heauynesse is drye. Alas, must I nedes clymbe vppe?

2495 Perdon my lyfe and I shall tell ye all,
Both that is past and that wyll herafter fall.

I. Maj. Aryse; I perdon the, so that thu tell the trewthe.

Sed. I wyll tell to yow suche treason as ensewthe;
Yet a ghostly father ought not to bewraye confessyon.

2500 *I. Maj.* No confessyon is but ought to discouer treason.

Sed. I thynke it maye kepe all thynge saue heresye.

I. Maj. It maye holde no treason, I tell the verelye,
And therfor tell the whole matter by and bye.
Thu saydest now of late that thu haddest played þe knaue

2505 And that þe worlde was not as some men woulde it haue.

Sed. I coulde playe Pasquyll but I feare to haue rebuke.

I. Maj. For vtterynge the truthe feare neyther byshopp nor duke.

Sed. Ye gaue iniunctyons that Gods wurde myghte be taught,
But who obserue them? Full manye a tyme haue I laught

2510 To see the conueyaunce that prelates and priestes can fynde.

I. Maj. And whie do they beare Gods wurde no better mynde?

Sed. For if that were knowne than woulde the people regarde
No heade but their prynce; with the churche than were it harde.
Than shoulde I lacke helpe to maynteyne their estate,

2515 As I attempted in the Northe but now of late,

2485 wele] *Collier*; we *B.*   2505 worlde] worde *b.*
2486 our] my *b.*

And sens that same tyme in other places besyde
Tyll my setters on were of their purpose wyde.
A vengeaunce take it! It was neuer well with me
Sens the cummynge hyther of that same veryte.
2520 Yet do the byshoppes for my sake vexe hym amonge.
I. Maj. Do they so in dede? Well, they shall not (p. 59, fol. 33)
do so longe.
Sed. In your parlement commaunde yow what ye wyll,
The popes ceremonyes shall drowne the Gospell styll.
Some of the byshoppes at your iniunctyons slepe,
2525 Some laugh and go bye and some can playe boo pepe;
Some of them do nought but searche for heretykes,
Whyls their priestes abroade do playe the scysmatykes.
Tell me in London how manye their othes discharge
Of the curates there; yet is it muche wurse at large.
2530 If your true subiectes impugne their trecheryes,
They can fatche them in anon for sacramentaryes
Or Anabaptystes; thus fynde they a subtyle shyfte.
To proppe vp their kyngedome suche is their wyly dryfte.
Get they false wytnesses, they force not of whens they be,
2535 Be they of Newgate or be they of the marshall see.
Parauenture a thousande are in one byshoppes boke,
And agaynst a daye are readye to the hooke.
I. Maj. Are those matters true that thu hast spoken here?
Sed. What can in the worlde more euydent wytnesse bere?
2540 First of all consydre the prelates do not preache,
But persecute those that the holye scriptures teache;
And marke me thys wele, they neuer ponnysh for popery,
But the Gospell readers they handle very coursely,
For on them they laye by hondred poundes of yron
2545 And wyll suffer none with them ones for to common.
Sytt they neuer so longe, nothynge by them cometh fourthe
To the truthes furtheraunce that any thynge ys wourthe.
In some byshoppes howse ye shall not fynde a testament,
But yche man readye to deuoure the innocent.

2523 the Gospell] *Collier*; the þe
Gospell *B.*
2531 in, anon for] in, for *b.*
2533 proppe vp] helpe *b.**
2535 marshall] mass *b.**
2543 handle very coursely] exam-

yne very strayghtly *b.*
2548 ye shall not fynde] *Collier*;
ye shall not shall not fynde
B.
2549 deuoure] deuorre *b.*

2550   We lyngar a tyme and loke but for a daye
      To sett vpp the pope, if the Gospell woulde decaye.
      Cler. Of that he hath tolde hys selfe is the very grounde.
      I.Maj. Art thu of counsell in thys that thu hast spoken?
      Sed. Yea, and in more than that if all secretes myght be broken;
2555   For the pope I make so muche as euer I maye do.
      I.Maj. I praye the hartely, tell me why thu doest so.
      Sed. For I perceyue wele the pope is a Iolye fellawe,
      A trymme fellawe, a ryche fellawe, yea, and a myry fellawe.
      I.Maj. A Iolye fellawe how dost thu proue the pope?
2560   *Sed.* For he hath crosse keyes, with a tryple crowne and a cope,
      Trymme as a trencher, hauynge hys shoes of golde,   (p. 60, fol. 33ᵛ)
      Ryche in hys ryalte and Angelyck to beholde.
      I.Maj. How dost thu proue hym to be a fellawe myrye?
      Sed. He hath pypes and belles, with kyrye, kyrye, kyrye.
2565   Of hym ye maye bye both salt, creame, oyle and waxe,
      And after hygh masse ye maye learne to beare þe paxe.
      I.Maj. Yea, and nothynge heare of the Pystle and the Gospell?
      Sed. No, sir, by the Masse! He wyll gyue no suche counsell.
      I.Maj. Whan thu art a broade, where doest thy lodgynge take?
2570   *Sed.* Amonge suche people as God ded neuer make:
      Not only cuckoldes, but suche as folowe the popes lawes
      In disgysed coates, with balde crownes lyke Iacke dawes.
      I.Maj. Than euery where thu art the popes altogyther?
      Sed. Ye had proued it ere thys If I had not chaunced hyther.
2575   I sought to haue serued yow lyke as I ded kynge Iohn,
      But that veryte stopte me. The deuyll hym poyson!
      Nob. He is wurthie to dye and there were men nomore!
      C.Ord. Hange vp the vyle knaue and kepe hym no longar in store!
      I.Maj. Drawe hym to Tyburne; lete hym be hanged and quartered.
2580   *Sed.* Whye, of late dayes ye sayde I shoulde not so be martyred.
      Where is the pardon that ye ded promyse me?
      I.Maj. For doynge more harme thu shalt sone pardoned be.
      Haue hym fourth, Cyuyle ordre, and hange hym tyll he be dead,
      And on London brydge loke ye bestowe hys head.
2585   *C.Ord.* I shall see it done and returne to yow agayne.
      Sed. I beshrewe your hart for takynge so muche payne!
      Some man tell the pope, I besyche ye with all my harte,
      How I am ordered for takynge the churches parte,
      That I maye be put in the holye letanye
2590   With Thomas Beckett, for I thynke I am as wurthye.

Praye to me with candels, for I am a saynt alreadye.
O blessed saynt Partryck, I see the, I verylye!
[*Exeunt Civil Order and Sedition.*]
I. Maj. I see by thys wretche there hath bene muche faulte in ye;
Shewe your selues herafter more sober and wyse to be.

2595   Kynge Iohan ye subdued for that he ponnyshed treason,
Rape, theft and murther in the holye spirytualte.
But Thomas Becket ye exalted without reason
Because that he dyed for the churches wanton lyberte,
That the priestes myght do all kyndes of inyquyte   (p. 61, fol. 34)
2600   And be vnponnyshed. Marke now the iudgement
Of your ydle braynes, and for Gods loue repent.

Nob. As God shall iudge me, I repent me of my rudenesse.
Cler. I am ashamed of my most vayne folyshenesse.

Nob. I consydre now that God hath for Sedicyon
2605   Sent ponnyshmentes great. Examples we haue in Brute,
In Catilyne, in Cassius and fayer Absolon,
Whome of their purpose God alwayes destytute,
And terryble plages on them ded execute
For their rebellyon. And therfor I wyll be ware,
2610   Least hys great vengeaunce trappe me in suche lyke snare.
[*Enter Civil Order.*]
Cler. I pondre also that sens the tyme of Adam
The lorde euermore the gouernours preserued.
Examples we fynde in Noe and in Abraham,
In Moyses and Dauid, from whome God neuer swerued.
2615   I wyll therfor obeye least he be with me displeased.
Homerus doth saye that God putteth fourth hys shyelde,
The prynce to defende whan he is in the fyelde.

C. Ord. Thys also I marke: whan the priestes had gouernaunce
Ouer the Hebrues, the sectes ded first aryse,
2620   As Pharisees, Sadducees and Essees, whych wrought muche
        greuaunce
Amonge the people by their most deuylysh practyse,
Tyll destructyons the prynces ded deuyse,
To the quyetnesse of their faythfull commens all,
As your grace hath done with the sectes papistycall.

[145]

2625 *I. Maj.* That poynt hath in tyme fallen to your memoryes.
The Anabaptystes, a secte newe rysen of late,
The scriptures poyseneth with their subtle allegoryes,
The heades to subdue after a sedicyouse rate.
The cytie of Mynster was lost through their debate.
2630 They haue here begonne their pestilent sedes to sowe,
But we trust in God to increace they shall not growe.

Cler. God forbyd they shoulde, for they myght do muche harme.
C. Ord. We shall cut them short if they do hyther swarme.
I. Maj. The adminystracyon of a princes gouernaunce
2635 Is the gifte of God and hys hygh ordynaunce,
Whome with all your power yow thre ought to support
In the lawes of God, to all hys peoples comfort.
First yow, the clergye, in preachynge of Gods worde;
Than yow, Nobilyte, defendynge with the sworde;
2640 Yow, Cyuyle order, in executynge iustyce.   (p. 62, fol. 34ʳ)
Thus I trust we shall seclude all maner of vyce,
And after we haue establyshed our kyngedome
In peace of the lorde and in hys godly fredome,
We wyll confirme it with wholesom lawes and decrees,
2645 To the full suppressynge of Antichristes vanytees.
              Hic omnes rex osculatur.
Farwele to ye all; first to yow, Nobilyte,
Than to yow, Clergye, than to yow, Cyuylyte.
And aboue all thynges, remembre our iniunctyon.
Nob.   ⎫
Cler.   ⎬ By the helpe of God, yche shall do hys functyon.
C. Ord.   ⎭

                              [*Exit Imperial Majesty.*]
2650 *Nob.* By thys example ye maye see with your eyes
How Antichristes whelpes haue noble princes vsed.
Agayne ye maye see how they with prodigyouse lyes
And craftes vncomely their myschiefes haue excused.
Both nature, Manhode and grace they haue abused,
2655 Defylynge the lawe and blyndynge Nobilyte—
No Christen regyon from their abusyons free.

Cler. Marke wele the dampnable bestowynge of their masses,
With their foundacyons for poysenynge of their kynge.

2629 Mynster] mynster *b*.   2632 they (*first*)] *Collier*; the *B*.

Their confessyon driftes all other traytery passes.
2660 A saynt they can make of þe most knaue thys daye lyuynge,
Helpynge their market. And to promote the thynge
He shall do myracles. But he that blemysh their glorye
Shall be sent to helle without anye remedye.

C. Ord. Here was to be seane what ryseth of Sedicyon,
2665 And howe he doth take hys mayntenaunce and grounde
Of ydle persones brought vpp in supersticyon,
Whose daylye practyse is alwayes to confounde
Such as myndeth vertu and to them wyll not be bounde.
Expedyent it is to knowe their pestylent wayes,
2670 Consyderynge they were so busye now of late dayes.

Nob. Englande hath a quene—Thankes to the lorde aboue—
Whych maye be a lyghte to other princes all
For the godly wayes whome she doth dayly moue
To hir liege people, through Gods wurde specyall.
2675 She is that Angell, as saynt Iohan doth hym call,
That with the lordes seale doth marke out hys true seruauntes,
Pryntynge in their hartes hys holy wourdes and Covenauntes.

Cler. In Danyels sprete she hath subdued the Papistes,
With all the ofsprynge of Antichristes generacyon;
2680 And now of late dayes the secte of Anabaptistes
She seketh to suppresse for their pestiferouse facyon. (p. 63, fol. 35)
She vanquysheth also the great abhomynacyon
Of supersticyons, witchecraftes and hydolatrye,
Restorynge Gods honoure to hys first force and bewtye.

2685 C. Ord. Praye vnto the lorde that hir grace maye contynewe
The dayes of Nestor to our sowles consolacyon;
And that hir ofsprynge maye lyue also to subdewe
The great Antichriste, with hys whole generacyon,
In Helias sprete to the confort of thys nacyon;
2690 Also to preserue hir most honourable counsell,
To the prayse of God and glorye of the Gospell.
        Thus endeth the .ij. playes of kynge Iohan.

2660 they] *Collier*; the *B.*   2684 honoure] honorre *b.*
2667 alwayes] order *b.*   2690 hir] the qu *b.*

NOTES

Dramatis Personae

King John: the play's only consistently literal, historical character.

England: conceptually the play's most complex personage. Although God's "widow" (ll. 108-109, 113), her actions are better understood in terms of her relationships with Commonalty and John. As the "mother" of Commonalty (ll. 1573, 1610), she is at times the most comprehensive personification of England considered as a social and political entity (see especially ll. 62-63, 527, 1568-69), and in this respect she may be considered the "central figure" (see Intro., pp. 61-63, and cf. Irving Ribner, *The English History Play in the Age of Shakespeare* [Princeton, 1957], p. 37). (According to this view, she is logically the "mother" of Nobility, Clergy, and Civil Order, as well as Commonalty, but see ll. 68-69.) On the other hand, by virtue of her close association with John (see especially ll. 1615-22, where the echo of the marriage ceremony is very marked), she is more a personification of abstract sovereignty.

Nobility: like Temporality in Lindsay's *Satyre of the Thrie Estaits*, more a generalized type comprehending a social class than a personification of abstract nobility. According to Imperial Majesty, his special function in the body politic is to defend his prince with the sword (l. 2639).

Clergy: a representative type of the English clergy, whose special function is to preach God's word (l. 2638). He corresponds roughly to Lindsay's Spirituality.

Civil Order: referred to as Civility (ll. 2277 and 2647) and Law (ll. 1421, 2492), but usually treated as a type of a social group—specifically lawyers (ll. 288, 1263, 1538, etc.)—rather than the personification of an abstraction. His principal function is executing justice and thus preserving social harmony (see ll. 381-387, 2640).

Commonalty: the blind son of England (ll. 1550, 1573, 1610); like Lindsay's John Commonweal, a type of the common people and a victim of the social injustice associated with the ruling classes.

Sedition: as the principal tempter and chief comic figure, the Vice of the play. The distinction between his "real" and disguised or historical personality is for the most part carefully maintained, but see ll. 2000-01, 2499 and notes. In his undisguised condition he occasionally claims the alias Good or Holy Perfection, or simply Perfection (see note to l. 1136). He is a Roman by birth (ll. 181-183) and claims to be the pope's ambassador (l. 213).

Dissimulation: dubbed Raymundus at one point (see l. 1057 and

[148]

note), but otherwise in his disguised condition identified as a Cistercian monk, Simon of Swynsett. He also claims the abstract alias Monastical Devotion (see l. 2103 and note to l. 1136).

Usurped Power: a cant term for the papacy in sixteenth-century anti-Catholic writings.

Private Wealth: associated particularly with the English monastic establishments (see ll. 2443, 2449-50).

Treason: a type of the treasonous man rather than a personification of treason in the abstract.

Verity: referred to also as God's Verity (l. 2338); a personification of Reformation doctrine generally, with particular reference to preaching (see l. 2342). Kirchmeyer's Veritas (who, unlike Bale's Verity, is a female) is less narrowly conceived. For example, when forced into hiding by Pammachius, she considers returning to Asia, her "former home" (*Pammachius*, ll. 2876-79). The Verity of Lindsay's *Satyre* serves as adviser to Rex Humanitas, while Bale's Verity is Imperial Majesty's agent (see especially ll. 2319, 2337-38).

Imperial Majesty: as "þe supreme head of þe churche" (l. 2389) and "the true defendar" of the Christian faith (l. 2427), an obvious representation of Henry VIII.

The Interpreter: the author as commentator (see Intro., p. 45).

[Scene i (ll. 1-626)]

This scene is laid at some unspecified place in England (see ll. 181-182, 312, etc.). Historical time is treated only vaguely and without much attention to consistency: the action supposedly takes place after John's loss of his French possessions in 1202 (see ll. 569-570) but before the publication of the interdict in 1208 (dramatized in the third scene). The references in ll. 16 and 571 to John's control over Scotland, Ireland, and Wales, however, would seem to apply to a period during or after the summer of 1210, although the medieval chroniclers whom Bale knew frequently disagree about the dates of John's early conquests: see, e.g., *Ann. mon.*, I, 209 (Burton annals), Ireland subdued in 1208; II, 262 (Waverley annals), Wales and Ireland under John's control in 1209; I, 59 (Tewkesbury annals), John's conquest of all Ireland and much of Wales in 1210; Roger of Wendover, II, 58, John's successful campaign against the Welsh in 1211.

For the first 555 lines John dominates the situation; the other characters enter to him, and Nobility, Clergy, and Civil Order (already corrupted in varying degrees by seditious doctrine) eventually make formal acknowledgment of his supremacy. The lines of conflict are drawn in Sedition's exchange with the king and developed more fully in Clergy's brief debate with Nobility (ll. 557-626). The first stage clearance occurs at l. 626.

1 Because the manuscript contains no list of characters, act division, or notice of entrances, Collier (p. 105) suspected that the beginning of the play had been lost. The physical makeup of the manuscript, however, proves that no leaves have been lost at the beginning; at the same time it is possible that an original prologue was excluded from the text as we have it (see Intro., pp. 4 and 21-22).

7 *was*. The alteration from *were* is probably by Bale, although both ink and forms are somewhat doubtful. The different inks on p. 1 are generally more difficult to identify than those in any other part of the manuscript, but there seems to be no example of the ink of scribal revision.

10-11 John's father was Henry II, but neither of his grandfathers was an emperor. His paternal grandmother, Matilda, however, had been married to Henry V, the Holy Roman Emperor, before she married Geoffrey Plantagenet, father to Henry II and grandfather to John.

12 *kyng my*: deletion of *to* possibly scribal.

14 *fortynable*: a common sixteenth-century spelling of *fortunable*, i.e., 'fortunate.'

20 *To reforme the lawes*. According to Roger of Wendover, I, 287, part of the triple oath sworn by John at his coronation bound him to establish and maintain justice (". . . quod, perversis legibus destructis, bonas substitueret et rectam justitiam in regno Angliæ exerceret"). A similar oath is recorded by Roger of Hoveden, describing John's investiture as Duke of Normandy (*Chronica*, ed. William Stubbs, Rolls Series 51, IV [London, 1871], 88).

22 The point of England's entrance is uncertain, but her first words indicate that she has been onstage during at least part of John's speech.

23 *vsyd, as*. Bale has deleted the scribal *as* and rewritten the word above the line.

24 *swer*: Farmer modernizes to *swear*, but the word is really a common scribal spelling of Modern English *sure*. See ll. 141, 191, 409, and rhymes.

33-34 Matt. xiii.13-14, cited by Bale in a similar context in his *Apology*, fol. 116.

43 First assigned to *ynglond*; the correction is in the ink of the original scribal draft.

44 *s[e y]ow*: *e* and tail of *y* worn away.

45 *vngodlye*: *v* altered from *o* in ambiguous ink, probably by Bale.

50 *I am no spycer*. Sedition catches up and distorts John's words in the manner of the morality Vice: he takes *powder* in the preceding line as 'spice,' ignoring the biblical allusion. See ll. 74 and 769, where he does much the same thing. Examples of the same use of equivocation in other sixteenth-century plays are cited in L. W. Cushman, *The Devil and the Vice in the English Dramatic Literature before Shakespeare* (Halle, 1900), pp. 107-108.

55 Col. iv.6. The King James and Rheims versions read *seasoned* where Tyndale, the Great Bible, Geneva, and the Bishops' Bible read *powdred* (as in ll. 49, etc.).

60 *wat*: 'person,' 'fellow.' *Wyly watte* as a general term of abuse appears again in Bale's *Apology*, fol. 73. It is difficult to say how much opprobrium attaches to the noun alone (see *OED* citations).

65 *grosse vp: engross*, in the sense 'acquire,' 'appropriate,' or as in the usual English translation of the biblical verses Bale has in mind (Mark xii.38-40 and Luke xx.46-47) 'devour.'

86 *aper de sylua*: Ps. lxxix.14 (Vulgate).

95 *wedred*: an obsolete form of *withered*.

96 See Tilley, M49.

97 *Quodcumque ligaueris*. See Matt. xvi.19: "And I wyll geve vnto the the keyes of the kyngdom of heven: and what soever thou byndest vpon erth, shall be bounde in heven: and what soever thou lowsest on erthe, shalbe lowsed in heven" (Tyndale's translation). This verse was traditionally cited in support of the Catholic doctrine of penance, with particular reference to the priestly powers to forgive or retain sin (see John xx.23). Tyndale objects to this interpretation in the *Obedience*, foll. 143-145ᵛ; he also discusses this verse and its application to the pope's "temporale power above kynge and Emperoure" (*Obedience*, fol. 101), which is Bale's immediate concern here (see below, ll. 240-241, and the reference to the *keyes*, ll. 620-622). In the *Pammachius*, ll. 2050-53, the power of loosing and binding ("solvendi atque ligandi") has particular reference to the primacy of Peter and his successors over the other bishops of Christendom (see especially ll. 2109-11).

100 *common*: "to confer, converse, talk . . ." (*OED*, 6b); cf. ll. 872, 1447, 1678, etc.

103-104 Cf. *Obedience*, fol. 44ᵛ: "Heedes and governers are ordened off God and are even the gyft of God / whether thei be good or bad. And what so ever is done vnto vs by them / that doeth God / be it good or bad. Yf they be evill whi are yᵉ evil? verely for oure wekednesse sake are the evyll. Because that when they were good we wolde

not receave that goodnesse of the hande of God and be thankefull. . . .
Therfore doeth God make his scorge of them. . . ."

108-109 The allegorical implications of England's marriage to God
are not developed; see ll. 1618-22, where England speaks as if she were
married to John.

131-132 Isa. i.17.

135 Perhaps spoken in an aside to the audience, as Creeth notes. See
Intro., p. 51.

136 *vndyscuste*: *v* altered from *o* by the scribe in revision.

154 S.D. The entire direction was added by the scribe in revision.

166 *lytyll*. Bale's reason for altering scribal *lytyll* to the meaningless
lysyl is not apparent.

169-170 First written at the foot of p. 4 (after l. 166) as *say thow
what þou wylte her mater shall not perysh / yt is Ioye of hym þat
women so can cherysh*. The anticipation is a clear sign of transcription.
In rewriting these lines in their proper place, the scribe accidentally
omitted the first pronoun, which Bale has supplied in the form *thu*.

173-175 See J[ames] H[owell], "English Proverbs or Old Sayed-
Sawes," in παροιμιοτραφια: *Proverbs, or, Old Sayed Sawes & Adages*
(London, 1659), p. 16, for the proverb "Ther's no more pitty to be taken
of a woman weeping than of a Goose going bare-foot," and cf. "He
may shoe the goose," a proverbial expression for wasting time on
trifles (Tilley, G354). Sedition's sarcasm, then, may be paraphrased
thus: One should waste no more time on a weeping woman than on a
creeping *dodman* 'snail' or—to use a trite comparison that you (John)
would appreciate—a barefoot goose.

177-178 Collier (followed by Manly and Farmer) places the comma
after *vnnaturall* and the colon after *chyld*. The passage makes better
sense, however, if the antithesis in l. 178 is treated as an amplification of
vnnaturall.

184 *vn*: *v* altered from *o*, perhaps by the scribe in revision.

189 *facyon*: as in ll. 247 and 337, a variant of *faction* in the sense
'sect' or 'group.' In l. 2681 the word has the more abstract sense of 'dis-
sension.' Cf. l. 583, where the related word *fashion* is spelled *fassyon*.

205 *This cumpany*: perhaps the audience (see l. 770 and note), but
more likely the various religious sects and types cataloged above.

morttmayne: "the condition of lands or tenements held inalienably
by an ecclesiastical or other corporation" (*OED*, citing this passage
from *King Johan*).

215 *Sprvse and Beine*: i.e., Prussia and Bohemia.

238 *sawce bothe swet and sowr*: cf. Tilley, M839: "Sweet meat must

have a sour sauce." Bale has the two sauces refer to the twofold power of the clergy to *saue and lose* (l. 240).

239 *howre*: abbreviation of final *e* smudged, doubtful.

240 *saue and lose*: i.e., to save or condemn, equivalent to the power of loosing and binding in its spiritual sense (see l. 97 and note). In the following line John takes the formula in its secular sense and understands the "sour sauce" of l. 238 as deposition.

244-252 Cf. *Obedience*, fol. 111^{r-v}: "That [viz. auricular confession] is their holde / thereby know they all secrets / there by mocke they all men and all mens wives and begyle knyght and squyer / lorde and kynge / and betraye all realmes. The Bisshopes with the Pope have a certeyne conspiracion and secret treason agenst the whole worlde. And by confession know they what kynges and Emperours thinke. Yf ought be agenst them / doo they never so evyll / then move they their captives to warre & to fight and geve them pardons to sley whom they will have taken out of the waye." Bale includes many of these accusations in this and later passages.

252 The line as first written in the original scribal ink appears in the margin as *I am euer ther gyde and þer advocate*. Bale first altered this by adding the superfluous speech-prefix *Sedicyone* and *And* at the head of the line; he then deleted both words and added *more* to produce the present reading.

253 *checke mate*: 'on a par with,' 'equal in position,' apparently through a misunderstanding of the term as used in chess (see *OED*, *checkmate*, B2b).

261 *skoymose*: 'reluctant,' 'unwilling' (see *OED*, *squeamous*, 4).

264 *Benedicite*: spoken by a penitent as part of the verbal formula of confession. As noted by Miller, p. 806, here and throughout the play Bale uses this word as a metonymy for the practice of confession itself, with particular reference to the seal of secrecy which was associated with the practice.

269 Collier and Farmer omit the comma after *Why*. But the grammatical construction, as Manly realized, is the same as that in l. 279 and requires the comma.

277 *amonge*: an adverb meaning 'meanwhile,' 'at the same time,' or 'occasionally,' 'now and then.' Cf. ll. 471, 979, 1000, etc.

282 *tache*: an aphetic form of *attach*, here in the sense of 'arrest' (see *OED*, *tache*, v.^{2} 2).

300 Collier and Farmer omit the comma after *Why*. See l. 269 and note.

304-305 Sedition's verbal slip, like Clergy's in l. 512, resembles the

[153]

"truth-revealing jest" characteristic of the morality Vice (see the examples cited in Spivack, pp. 168-170). A similar device, usually employed with a sharper satiric edge, is common in Tudor religious polemic; see, e.g., *Obedience*, fol. 128ᵛ: ". . . heretikes / I wolde saye heremytes. . . ."

312 S.D. *Sedwsion . . . ordere*: added by the scribe in revision; the doubling called for is impossible and probably represents the scribe's own invention (see Intro., pp. 10 and 44).

314 *dyssolute*. Bale has superimposed *u* on the *a* of the A-text *dyso-late* and interlined another character (apparently another form of *u*) above the same letter; he has also added a second *s*. Cf. Pafford and Greg, l. 315 and note.

316 *ther*: *r* (superior) added by the scribe in revision.
in: macron added to *ĩ* by the scribe in revision.
commynnalte: here equivalent to *commonwealth* (*OED, commonalty*, 1); elsewhere, as in l. 534 and the name of the character who enters with England at l. 1534, a term applied to the common people considered collectively (*OED, commonalty*, 3).

317 First written after l. 314 with *dalyaunce* for *dallyaunce*. The anticipation indicates transcription.

320 *mervell at*: original *yow* deleted in ambiguous ink, but probably by Bale.

323 Collier and Creeth end this line with a question mark, evidently taking *intymate* as an adjective modifying *love*. The evidence of the *OED* citations, however, suggests that *intymate* is the imperative of the verb meaning "to make known formally, to notify, announce, state." The punctuation of Manly and Farmer (query after *of*, exclamation after *intymate*) is also possible.

326 Collier omits the question mark; Manly and Farmer omit the question mark and place a comma after *not*.

330 *both*. Bale seems to have touched up the *at* of *hath* before deleting the A-text *I hath* and substituting *both*.

331 S.D. Clergy's entrance is not marked in the manuscript. Collier and Farmer place it after l. 337, but his first words seem to be spoken in response to John's comments in ll. 334-337 and thus indicate that he is on stage somewhat earlier.

350 *pestelens*: second *e* smudged, perhaps *oo*; no sign of alteration (cf. Pafford and Greg).

354-358 Probably Bale is alluding to the fourteenth-century statutes of *praemunire* as revived by Henry in the early 1530's for the purpose of bringing the English clergy more closely under his control. See A. G.

Dickens, *The English Reformation* (London, 1964), pp. 87-88, 103-104.

361 *Yes*: *e* inserted by Bale, crowded; *y* perhaps touched up by Bale but not altered.

370 *vyle*: *r* of original *vyler* deleted in ambiguous ink, possibly by the scribe.

375 *Cyuyle*: first two letters of original *sevyll* altered to *Ci*, probably by Bale, who has rewritten the entire word in the margin as *Cyuyle*. Cf. ll. 1180, 1190 S.D., and notes.

377 Something seems to have been erased at the end of this line.

381-387 The erratic punctuation of the original makes the syntax of these lines particularly confusing. Apparently the four *for* phrases in l. 384 should be read as parallel to *For yowr common welth* (l. 383); and *þat in euery border* is thus a parenthetical interrupter, with *þat* used as a loose demonstrative rather than as a conjunction dependent on *know* (l. 381). Presumably *penalte* (l. 385) has the same meaning as in Modern English, in which case a full stop is demanded after l. 384 (Civil Order appoints the penalty for transgressors, not for offices, lands, law, and liberty). Note that the following rhyme-royal stanza is constructed in the same way—i.e., with a break after l. 4. The punctuation of none of the previous editions succeeds in making sense of this passage.

395 *resounable*. Collier reads *resonnable*, evidently taking the two minims preceded by *o* with macron as *nn*. Similarly he reads *rebonnyth* for *rebounyth* in l. 399, which Manly has successfully emended. See also Farmer's note on p. 321, where the issue is somewhat confused by a misprint.

397-398 *together*: *consyder*. See Moser, pp. 14-15, for other examples of Bale's use of this kind of rhyme.

408 *knowe*. The A-text reading is possibly *knowth* (rather than *knoweth*), but certainly not *knowd* (cf. Pafford and Greg).

409 *affyrme*: A- and B-text readings both doubtful.

422 *iwelles*: second letter possibly *u*.

423 *scalacely messys*: masses carrying a special indulgence associated with St. Bernard's vision of souls going to heaven by a ladder. See l. 2128 for the more common spelling *Scala Celi*. Cf. *Obedience*, fol. 82: "His fatherhode [i.e., the pope] sendeth them to heaven with scala celi: y^t is / with a ladder / to scale ye walles. For by the dore christ / will they not let them come in." Cf. also *Pammachius*, l. 2301 (Porphyrius on the value of pilgrimages): "Et magnis caelum meritis liceat scandere."

434-435 Ps. xliv.10 (Vulgate). I adopt the line division of the modern Vulgate; in the manuscript the break comes after *vestitu*.

439 *thorow all*: original *owt* deleted in ambiguous ink, but probably by Bale.

440 *deckyd*. Collier's edition, in its corrected state (see Intro., p. 18, n. 23), reads *deckyd* for the manuscript *dectyd*. Manly, working from an uncorrected copy of Collier, reads *dectyd*, while recording in a note Kittredge's suggested emendation to *deccyd*. It is difficult to imagine what meaning Manly attached to *dectyd*: the word is not recorded in the *OED*, while the verb *deck* meaning 'clothe' or 'adorn' is listed as having been introduced into English in the sixteenth century and is used in this sense by Bale in his *Three Laws*, l. 620. See also the *Apology*, fol. 112ʳ⁻ᵛ: "Are not they (thinke yow) plesaunt gentylmen, whych stande afore god, all trapped, dysguysed, and decked in their owne stynkynge dyrte, as are monkes in theyr cowles, fryres in theyr coates, and shauen prestes in theyr dysguysynges?"

relygyons: equivalent to the Modern English noun *religious*, i.e., member(s) of a religious order. See *OED, religion*, 2c, and cf. *religious*, B 1a. See also l. 684 and text. note.

441-458 Cf. a similar catalog of religious orders and types in "The Image of Ipocrysy," included in *The Poetical Works of John Skelton*, ed. Alexander Dyce (London, 1843), II, 441-442. Bale's list includes some of the well-known religious orders, such as the *Mynors* (or Franciscans), *Whyght Carmes* (or Carmelites, Bale's own order), *Augustynis, Cluniackes, Carthusyans*, and *Iesuytes*, as well as a number of more obscure groups, some of which have been identified by Farmer, pp. 333-337. Farmer's list, however, should be corrected and supplemented by reference to Oliver L. Kapsner, *Catholic Religious Orders* (Collegeville, Minn., 1957), pp. 5 (*Ambrosyanes*), 229 (*Ensifers, Paulynes*), and 290 (*Crucifers*).

The following have not been satisfactorily identified, and no doubt most of them are fictitious: *Stellifers, Sophyanes, Indianes, Ioannytes, Clarimontensers, Columbynes, newe Niniuytes, Rufyanes, Lorytes, Lazarytes, Hungaryes, Honofrynes, Solauons, Fulygynes, flamynes, Dimysynes, Canons of S. Mark*. Many of these are duplicated in Foxe (1563), fol. (70)ᵛ, as well as in the Skeltonic poem mentioned above. The *monkes of Iosaphathes valleye* (cf. Foxe, "The vale of Iosaphates order") and *bretherne of the black alleye* may have been suggested by the following lines from the same poem: "Some daunte and daly / In Sophathes valley / And in the blak alley" (II, 441).

Bale's list includes some general types as well as specific religious orders and societies: for *Sanbonites* and *Vestals* see Farmer, pp. 334 and 337; for *purgatoryanes* see *Catholic Encyclopedia*, "Purgatorial Societies"; *Monyals* is evidently derived from the Latin generic term for a nun.

455 *monkes*: *k* perhaps altered.

456 *Fulygynes*: first two letters blotted.

457 *Mark*: a final *e* perhaps lost through deterioration of the manuscript.

468 In the *Pammachius*, ll. 2130-35, Porphyrius proposes as one of the chief articles of faith that the pope has the exclusive authority to interpret Scripture.

expownd. *OED* records only one example of B-text *expond*, and that from the fifteenth century. The rhyme with *grownd* and *confownd* also suggests that the manuscript reading is faulty.

473 *pycke strawes*: 'triflers' (see *OED*, *pick*-, and cf. *EDD*, *pick*, 15).

490 Cf. Tyndale, *Obedience*, foll. 149ᵛ-150: "Serve God as he hath appoynted the and not with thy good entente and good zele. . . . God requyreth obedyence vnto his worde and abhoreth all good ententes and good zeles which are without Gods worde."

497 *decaye*. The transitive use of this verb, as here and in ll. 649 and 1768, was common in the sixteenth century (see *OED* citations).

500 Collier omits the comma, apparently taking *vndowtted* as an adjective modifying *God*; the adverbial sense (meaning 'undoubtedly') was common during the sixteenth century and seems to fit the sense of this passage better.

503 *we*: *e* (superior) added by the scribe in revision.

506 S.D. The kneeling called for at three strategic points in the play underlines its basic structural design by presenting visually the principal points in the moral progress of the tripartite protagonist (see Intro., pp. 62-63). Here Clergy (perhaps together with Nobility and Civil Order) kneels to John; at l. 1148 Nobility kneels to Sedition (Stephen Langton), as do Clergy and Civil Order at l. 1192; at l. 2329 all three kneel to Imperial Majesty.

512 See ll. 304-305 and note.

516 *suer*: indistinct tick over *r* possibly meant to indicate a final *e*.

521 *perforne*: the two minims between *r* and *e* perhaps touched up, but evidently not altered to *m*.

Something has been erased after *hand*, probably a raised point.

526 The bracket joining the speakers' names was added by the scribe in revision.

534 First begun after l. 531. The anticipation indicates transcription.

538 *neyther*: *o* of A-text reading doubtful.

556 S.D. *and Syvile order drese hym for Sedewsyon*: added by the scribe in revision, with *dyssymalacyon* first written for *Sedewsyon*; the doubling called for is impossible and probably represents the scribe's own invention (see Intro., pp. 11 and 44).

557-558 The rhyme *wytt* : *wytt* is one of the few examples of identical rhyme (i.e., the rhyming on the same word and not just a homonym) in the play. Others occur in ll. 1558-59, 1700-02 (the first and third lines of a triplet), 1895-96, and 2557-58.

572 *Crystmes songes are mery tales*: evidently a proverb, although not recorded by Tilley. Cf. the "Crystemes songe" sung by New-Guise, Now-a-Days, and Nought in *Mankind*, ll. 328-336 (*The Macro Plays*, ed. F. J. Furnivall and Alfred W. Pollard, EETS, ES 91 [London, 1904]).

576 *tall*. Cf. l. 582, where Bale has altered the scribal *talle* to the more common *tale*, apparently to reinforce the rhyme with *male*.

579 *Artur his nevy*: the only reference to Arthur in the play. Bale significantly avoids the issue of Arthur's claim to the English throne, an issue treated at length in both the *Tr. Reign* and Shakespeare's *King John*. John's granting of Anjou to his nephew seems to be Bale's invention.

580 *an abbeye turneth to a graunge*: a proverbial expression for the effects of prodigality (see Tilley, A3).

582 Collier conjectured that this line should be read as part of the preceding speech by Clergy, and Farmer introduced the suggested change into his text. There is no need for emendation, however, if we assume that Nobility is here quoting a proverbial expression and applying it to John's situation relative to the clergy. Nobility is thus saying in effect that Clergy, who has no love for the king, cannot be trusted to present a reliable account of John's activities. Cf. Tilley, T52: "Believe no tales from an enemy's tongue."

585-589 Nobility here reflects the sentiments of Tyndale as expressed in his *Obedience* (quoted in Intro., p. 25).

585 *Chronycles*: altered by Bale, probably from *crownnycles*, although the first four letters of the A-text reading are doubtful.

593 *tenth parte of owr lyvyng*. Further details about this tax are supplied elsewhere in the play: the *tenth* or *dyme* (l. 960), which amounts to *nynne thowsand marke* (l. 963), is levied by John in his *parlament* (l. 904); it is exacted of the clergy (ll. 904, 960) for the purpose of financing the king's *warres* (l. 905) or specifically his Irish campaign (l. 964). Medieval chroniclers record numerous examples of John's

burdensome financial demands, but the historical event underlying Bale's account is evidently the famous "thirteenth" levied by John at a great council in London early in 1207. The chroniclers differ among themselves in some details of this event, and none agrees completely with Bale. According to Roger of Wendover (II, 35), for example, the thirteenth was imposed on the movables of clergy and laity alike; the Waverley annalist (*Ann. mon.*, II, 258) comes closer to historical truth when he explains that the thirteenth was levied against the laity after the clergy had refused to comply with an earlier proposal by the king (see Norgate, p. 126, n. 4). Variations on these versions are found in the anonymous Canterbury Chronicle (ed. William Stubbs in *The Historical Works of Gervase of Canterbury*, Rolls Series 73, II [London, 1880], lvii-lviii) and in Gaufridus de Coldingham's *Liber . . . de statu ecclesiæ Dunhelmensis*, in *Historiae Dunelmensis Scriptores Tres*, ed. James Raine (London, 1839), p. 23. None of these specifies the amount of tax as a tenth; in fact, John seems never to have levied a tenth (see Sydney Knox Mitchell, *Studies in Taxation under John and Henry III* [New Haven, 1914], Index, under "Tenth"). Bale evidently derived this, as well as some other unhistorical details of the affair, from the English prose Brut (ed. Brie, I, 154): "þo lete he assemble byfore him at London, Erchebisshoppis, bisshoppus, Abbotes & Pryours, Erles & barons, and helde þere a grete Parlement, & axede þere of þe clergye þe tenþe of euery cherche of Engeland, forto conquere & gete aзeyne Normandy & Angoy þat he hade loste. and þai wolde nouзt graunt þat þing; wherfore he was wonder wroþ." The *nynne thowsand marke* and the Irish expedition (ll. 963-964) were probably suggested to Bale by another passage from the Brut dealing with John's taxations (see ll. 1125-26 and note).

607-608 The rhyme *warre* : *debarre* indicates that late ME *a* had not yet rounded under the influence of *w*. For similar rhymes in *King Johan* see ll. 1223-24, 1269-70, 1350-51, 1705-06, 2632-33; and for examples from Bale's other plays see Moser, p. 17.

609 See Matt. xvii.24-26, and Tyndale's exposition of these verses in *Obedience*, fol. 40^{r-v}.

trybytt: a rare form of *tribute*, obsolete in the sixteenth century.

620 *The keyes of þe church.* See note to l. 97.

626 S.D. *Nobylyte and Clar*[gy]: added by the scribe in revision, with *privat welth* first written for *Clar*[gy]. The original *Go owt* direction was placed after l. 624, where it applied to Nobility alone; this arrangement became illogical when the names of Nobility and

[159]

Clergy were added. I follow Collier in locating the direction after Clergy's couplet.

The last two letters of *Clargy* have been almost completely lost through deterioration of the manuscript; only the tail of *g* is still visible.

[Scene ii (ll. 627-1120)]

Most of the action of this scene is localized at Rome: in the previous scene Sedition has revealed his intention of leaving England (l. 310), and in the following scene he tells Nobility that he has just returned from Rome (l. 1141). Dissimulation is represented as having traveled as a messenger from the English clergy (l. 874), and subsequently the pope dispatches Sedition (alias Stephen Langton) and Private Wealth (alias Cardinal Pandulphus) to England. The treatment of place is not consistent, however, for Dissimulation speaks in ll. 758-759 as if he were still in England. See also ll. 717 and 987-988, which may reflect the same inconsistency. The excommunication referred to in ll. 661-663 and 930-934 as having been effected *of late* took place in November 1209; the exile of the English clergy following the dispute over the election of Stephen Langton as Archbishop of Canterbury (ll. 937-939, 948-954) occurred some two years earlier. Bale has characteristically treated the sequence of events with no great attention to historical detail.

The major purpose of this scene is to explain and expose the nature of the forces of evil which oppose King John. This is done largely through direct admission or "confession" on the part of the evil characters (see Spivack, pp. 106-108), but also through the allegorical action of ll. 760 ff. and other more indirect means.

630 *women*: A- and B-text readings both doubtful.

Two symbols for marking the point of an insertion were added by the scribe in revision after this line, but the insertion has not been preserved.

632 *ere they resorte*: original *hether* deleted in ambiguous ink, but probably by Bale; the alteration of *or* to *ere* is definitely his. Collier and Manly retain *hether* (Farmer *hither*), apparently for metrical reasons; but the manuscript punctuation (a comma after *is*) indicates that the B-text line is metrically regular. See Intro., pp. 49-51.

638 S.D. *Dyssymvlacyon*. The final *s* of the manuscript reading is obviously a slip; the form is remarkably close to the scribe's customary *o* with macron.

640 The mocking echo is characteristic of the morality Vice (see Cushman, p. 104). The apparent loss of point of view in Sedition's

parody of a specifically Roman institution is an extension of the homiletic technique of self-exposure common in the traditional English morality and employed extensively by Bale throughout *King Johan*. See Spivack, pp. 106-108, and Rainer Pineas, "The English Morality Play as a Weapon of Religious Controversy," *Studies in English Literature, 1500-1900*, II (1962), 175 and n. 35.

644 *vengeable*: interlined by Bale above *horeble*, which has not been deleted. The meter would be disturbed if both words were retained (see Intro., pp. 17 and 49-51).

647 *nose*. A-text *fas* is peculiar: there is clearly no final *e*, although the scribe uses the nonfinal form of *s*.

657 *tryumphant*: B-text reading possibly *tryumphut*.

664 *scelpe*: 'a blow.'

666 *dane*: an obsolete form of *dan*, the title of respect used especially in addressing religious.

667 *aquentaunce*: letter after *t* carelessly formed, perhaps *e*; no sign of alteration.

668 Manly and Farmer supply *suis* after *ie*. The grammatical slip, however, may have been deliberate on Bale's part.

673-678 This genealogy of evil is obviously not meant to represent any very precise theological doctrine, although the position of Infidelity is perhaps a significant reflection of Bale's Lutheran sympathies. The importance of faith as the *sine qua non* of salvation is treated more fully in the *Three Laws*, which has as its chief representative of evil Infidelitas, the root of all vice.

680 *bysshope Benno*: identified by Farmer (p. 305) and Creeth as an eleventh-century Bavarian churchman.

684 *relygyons*: A-text reading possibly *Relygyows*.

689 *froyter*: a variant of *freitour* 'refectory' (see Walter W. Skeat's note to William Langland, *The Vision of William concerning Piers the Plowman*, VI, 174, 176, C-text).

690 *dorter*: a 'dormitory,' particularly one in a monastery.

691 *senyes*. The meaning of the word is not clear. Farmer (p. 338) explains it as a form of *signs*, "referring to the system the monks had of talking with their fingers." It may also be a form of *synod* (see *OED, sene*), used in the present passage for 'communities.'

693 *menyes*. Farmer (p. 338) glosses this tentatively as either 'means' or 'men.' It may also be a variant of the collective noun *meinie* 'company,' with the unusual plural form dictated by the rhyme.

701 *heades*: alteration from *head* possibly scribal.

706 *drawth*. The manuscript *draw^t* may represent *drawet* (or

drawyt) rather than *drawth*, but the latter is the more common form. See Mary McDonald Long, *The English Strong Verb from Chaucer to Caxton* (Menasha, Wisconsin, 1949), p. 184.

712 *neyther*: A-text reading possibly *nother*.

723 *alone*: A-text reading doubtful except for *b*.

743 *celerer*: a 'steward' or 'butler,' especially one in a monastery. Elsewhere Bale uses the term contemptuously: "Ye apere . . . a moche better cellerer than scripturer. A more expert rent gatherer, than gospell preacher" (*Apology*, fol. 117).

749 *ower*: a letter (or perhaps a tail on *r*) erased at the end of this word.

750 *Vsurpyd*: first *u* of B-text reading possibly *n*.

757 Here Sedition seems to be aware that Usurped Power and the pope are the same person while in ll. 837-839 he registers surprise at this fact.

763 S.D. The entire direction was added by the scribe in revision, with *after* written as *ofter*; Bale has altered *o* to *a* and touched up the stem of *f*. This is the only example of Bale's altering matter introduced by the scribe in revision.

764-765 Cf. Ps. cxxxvi.1-4 (Vulgate). Pineas, p. 176, notes that Bale has substituted *canticum bonum* for the *canticum Domini* of the Vulgate, and by rendering *canticum bonum* as "the song of our goods" he finds a satiric thrust at the Roman clergy. The syntax of the Latin argues against such an interpretation.

766 *placebo*: one of the usual designations of the office of the dead in English service books. See William Maskell, *Monumenta ritualia ecclesiae Anglicanae*, 2nd ed. (Oxford, 1882), III, 115-118.

767 Cf. Gen. xlv.28 (Jacob preparing to visit Joseph in Egypt): ". . . vadam et videbo illum antequam moriar."

770 *Sures*: like *fryndes* below (l. 777), a direct nondramatic address to the audience. See also ll. 1938, 2172, and 2193, as well as the epilogue spoken by Nobility, Clergy, and Civil Order (ll. 2650-91). In all these cases the audience is simply addressed and not conceived of as contributing in any way to the dramatic action or situation. Cf. *Three Laws*, ll. 1672 ff. and 1718 ff., where the audience serves as a congregation of worshippers, first for Evangelium and then for Infidelitas, who concludes his sermon by offering to sell some of his relics. In Bale's *Temptation of Christ*, ed. Paul Schwemmer (Nürnberg, 1919), l. 381 S.D. and l. 386, the role of the audience is ambiguous. See Spivack, pp. 119-120, for a discussion of the use of this convention in homiletic drama generally.

773 *decayve*. Collier emends to *decaye*, but the manuscript reading is actually a form of *deceive* in the sense "to prove false to; to frustrate (a purpose, etc.), . . . to disappoint (hope, expectation, etc.) . . ." (*OED, deceive,* 3b).

786 *howr*. The A-text reading is somewhat obscured by the alteration: Bale has crowded in *h* and perhaps retraced the scribal *o*.

798 *mak þe fort*. The meaning is obscure, whether *þe* is taken as the personal pronoun (with *fort* as an adjective meaning 'strong' or 'powerful') or as the definite article (with *fort* as a noun). Cf. the expression *made þe fort* (*Three Laws,* l. 797), which seems to be equivalent to 'enjoyed yourself.'

800 *be*: interlined by the scribe in revision.

by: altered from *be* by the scribe in revision.

802 S.D. Added by the scribe in revision.

807 *nor*: A-text reading doubtful, perhaps *nor*.

828 S.D. The songs referred to here and at l. 1055 are not preserved; two other songs are included in the manuscript, one with musical notations (see ll. 2086-91, and 2457 and note). In each case singing is associated with the figures of evil and represents the perverse joy they take in anticipation of their vicious activities (see Spivack, p. 121). In his *Three Laws* (ll. 693-695 and 1243 S.D.) Bale uses song in much the same way: Infidelitas first instructs his agents in the art of corrupting the laws and then before dispatching them to their business calls for a song.

831-838 Pafford and Greg, p. xxx, introduce an unnecessary difficulty when they say that "it seems likely that the Pope is really to be identified with Usurped Power, though on the face of it the evidence is of doubling only." Actually the evidence of these lines points unmistakably to a disguise situation (or, in Pafford and Greg's terms, an "identification") rather than a theatrical doubling. Cf. Craik, pp. 88-89.

833 *apparaunt*: 'evidently,' 'manifestly' (cf. *OED, apparent,* A 7).

850 *here*. Farmer modernizes as *hear*, which is probably correct: Dissimulation fears that Sedition's interruptions prevent Usurped Power from hearing his request for absolution. The alternative is much less likely: Dissimulation fears that the pope cannot administer absolution *here*, i.e., under the prevailing circumstances.

852 *stere*: "disturb, trouble, molest, . . . upset" (*OED, stir,* 4, citing this passage).

853 *desyre*: doubtful, perhaps *desire* (altered from A-text *dyssyre*).

861 ff. "Assoilings" or absolutions of various kinds more or less closely associated with sacramental confession recur at key points

[163]

throughout the play and illustrate the various senses of *Quodcumque ligaueris* (see l. 97 and note). For example, Nobility and then the English people generally are assoiled from their obedience to the king (ll. 1184-86, 1372); John is assoiled from the sentence of excommunication (ll. 1797-1800); Dissimulation is absolved before poisoning the king (l. 2049). Cf. the pardon or forgiveness granted by Verity and Imperial Majesty (ll. 2315-16, 2344).

867 *depraue*: 'defame,' 'disparage' (*OED*, s.v. 4).

882 *coffars*: *a* doubtful, perhaps altered by Bale.

884 *hose*. Bale has deleted the A-text reading and written his substitute complete. He has followed the same procedure with three other words on this page: *lose* (l. 885), *horryble* (l. 889), and *ceremony* (l. 891).

889 *horryble*. Bale seems to have added *h* and retraced the A-text *o* before deleting the entire word and interlining his substitute.

890 S.D. Added by the scribe in revision.

891 After this line there is a space in the manuscript for a stage direction which was never supplied (see Intro., p. 9). The stage business intended is obviously some gesture of excessive deference such as might prompt Sedition's comment in l. 893.

904-905 See l. 593 and note.

907 Cf. the proverb quoted in a similar context by Tyndale (*Obedience*, fol. 76): "What cometh once in / maye never moare out."

909 *thus*. Bale has added his tick to the scribal *u*.

931-934 Apparently this is the same excommunication alluded to above (ll. 661-663). The unhistorical list of four bishops is derived from the English prose Brut (ed. Brie, I, 155), which represents these bishops as executing the interdict rather than the excommunication (see Intro., p. 36). Historically William of Ste. Mère-l'Église was bishop of London from 1199 to 1221; Eustace was bishop of Ely from 1198 to 1215; Giles de Braose was bishop of Hereford from 1200 to 1215. The bishop of Winchester in 1208 and 1209 was not *Water* or Walter but Peter des Roches, who was elected in 1205 and served in this post until 1235; far from executing the interdict or the excommunication, he was one of the few English churchmen who sided with the king during his struggle with the pope.

943 John de Gray, Bishop of Norwich and John's choice to succeed Hubert Walter as Archbishop of Canterbury (see ll. 948-954 and note), was one of those who supported the king. Why Bale should have him *flater* Stephen Langton is not clear (cf. l. 251, where *flater* seems to be equivalent to Modern English *flatter*).

[164]

948-954 The death of Hubert Walter, Archbishop of Canterbury, on July 13, 1205, touched off a series of events that led directly to the extended conflict between John and Innocent III. The monks of Canterbury elected as successor to Hugh first Reginald, their subprior, and then, at the king's request, John de Gray, Bishop of Norwich. Both elections were nullified by Innocent, and a delegation of Canterbury monks, under some pressure from the pope, finally chose Stephen Langton. Langton was consecrated at Viterbo on June 17, 1207, and John's refusal to accept him brought about the sentence of interdict the following year. See William Stubbs' Introduction to his edition of the *Memoriale* of Walter of Coventry, II, xlix-lv; and for some important corrections of Stubbs see M. D. Knowles, "The Canterbury Election of 1205-6," *EHR*, LIII (1938), 211-220. See also C. R. Cheney, "A Neglected Record of the Canterbury Election of 1205-6," *Bulletin of the Institute of Historical Research*, XXI (1948), 234, n. 1. According to Roger of Wendover (II, 39), the monks of Canterbury were expelled on July 14, 1207, shortly after John received word of Langton's consecration.

960-964 See l. 593 and note.

965 *then*. The third letter of both A- and B-text readings has been obscured by a blot in what is probably Bale's ink.

966 *that*: *a* altered by Bale, probably from the scribal form of the same letter.

976 *interdyct*: *c* interlined (probably by Bale) above *gh*, which has not been deleted.

983 S.D. The verb *drese for*, usually indicative of a doubling situation, is here used to specify the disguises adopted by Usurped Power, Private Wealth, and Sedition (cf. ll. 831-838 and note). Although it is difficult to distinguish between the real and the assumed personalities of these characters, the purpose of the satirical allegory implied in the costume change is clear: ". . . its purpose is to show that Sedition and his fellows can exist in many shapes and also that the seditious archbishop is sedition personified" (Craik, p. 89).

984-1025 The *generall cowncell* (l. 1012) described in this speech and again, more briefly, in the Pope's speech below (ll. 1074-85) is clearly the Fourth Lateran Council of 1215. Most medieval English chroniclers mention this council in their accounts of John's reign, but none is at all detailed; see, e.g., Roger of Wendover, I, 122-123; II, 138, 155-159 (recording the condemnation of Joachim of Flora's Trinitarian heresies, the date of the council, and Innocent's speech on the Crusade). The Brut is silent on the subject. Bale's version, although highly colored by

[165]

anti-Romanist feelings, is obviously based on a knowledge of the seventy canons approved at the council: see Edward H. Landon, *A Manual of Councils of the Holy Catholic Church*, new and rev. ed. (Edinburgh, 1909), I, 328-333.

988 *than shall we*: deletion of extra *shall* possibly scribal.

991-997 Cf. the *Pammachius*, ll. 2437 ff., where Pope Pammachius vies with God as creator: "Creaturas ego creabo novas, / Creare ne soli relinquatur deo. / Exoriantur cito mei regni cardines!" He then proceeds to bring into existence

> monachorum ordines
> Tonsos et intonsos, pullos et candidos
> Mixtique coloris, pauperes et divites,
> Cinctos et discinctos, pellicios, laneos
> Et lineos, Epicuraeos et Stoicos!

997 *sterracles*: 'spectacle shows' (see *OED, steracle*).

1005-07 Actually John had resigned the crown to Pandulf more than two years before the council convened. In fact, Ralph of Coggeshall (p. 179, *sub anno* 1216) reports that one of Innocent's proposals at the council called for a sentence of excommunication against John's enemies: "His diebus facta fuit denunciatio excommunicationis quam dominus papa in concilio Lateranensi publice fecit in omnes infestantes Johannem regem Angliæ."

1008-11 Cf. Foxe (1576), I, 745: "At which tyme [during the pontificate of Innocent III] also began the first persecution by the Church of Rome, agaynst the Albingenses or Waldenses. . . . Of whom xvij. thousand the same tyme were slayne, by the Popes crossed souldiours. Among whom Frier Dominicke was then the chiefest doer."

1015-17 Cf. Foxe (1563), p. (66) (relative to Innocent's convoking the Fourth Lateran Council): "And to colour those mischiefes whiche he then went about, he caused it by his Legates and Cardinals, very crafty marchauntes, to be noysed abrode, yᵗ his entent was therin only, to haue yᵉ church vniuersally reformed, & the holy lande from the Turkes handes recouered."

1029 S.D. The direction is written in three lines in the left-hand margin opposite Dissimulation's speech. No other stage direction in the manuscript takes this form.

1031 *throw glyde*: deletion of original *me* possibly scribal.

1034-49 The ritual dramatized here represents the personal excommunication of the king which was published on the Continent by exiled English bishops in November 1209. The arrangement of events within the play is somewhat confused, for the excommunication has already been referred to as an accomplished fact (ll. 661-663, 930-934) and is dramatized again in Act II (ll. 1357 ff.). Apparently Bale had in mind three closely related historical events: the sentence of excommunication emanating from Rome, the actual publication of this sentence in 1209, and a subsequent publication which may have been performed at Northampton in 1211.

There is added confusion in the present passage, which seems to mix details appropriate to the general interdict with those of the personal excommunication of the king (see especially the reference to baptism in l. 1044). Theoretically these two actions were quite distinct kinds of ecclesiastical censure, although the two were often confused, even in official documents. See Edward Krehbiel, *The Interdict: Its History and Its Operation* (Washington, D.C., 1909), p. 9 and passim. In the case of Innocent's dealings with John and England, however, the two were carefully distinguished, both in the documents and in the chronicles: the excommunication, which deprived the king of personal benefits as a member of the Church, was imposed somewhat more than a year after the local general interdict had been laid on England. The two are confused elsewhere in the play (see ll. 1096-97 and note at l. 1357) and also in *Tr. Reign*, II.ii.119-120.

Miller, pp. 817-818, compares this passage with the instructions for the pronouncement of major excommunication found in medieval service books and concludes that "the lines and business are approximately authentic."

1038 *speare*: 'to close' or 'shut,' frequently used by Bale with an intensifying *up* (see ll. 1060, 1253, and *OED* citations).

1053 The speech-prefix (*þe pope*) was added by the scribe in revision.

1055 S.D. Added by the scribe in revision. The song is not preserved (see l. 828 S.D. and note).

1056 *Pandvlphus*. The papal legate who served Innocent in the dispute with John and later became bishop of Norwich was frequently confused with Pandulfus Masca; the latter was a cardinal, but not the former. The confusion appears also in *Tr. Reign* and Shakespeare's *King John*. Its origin is obscure (see *DNB*).

1057 *thy ... Raymundus*: addressed to Dissimulation. The alias Raymundus is subsequently ignored, and Dissimulation in his continuous disguise as a Cistercian monk assumes the name Simon of Swynsett (see ll. 2044, 2102). Hardin Craig, *English Religious Drama of the Middle Ages* (Oxford, 1955), p. 371, seems to think that Bale is here identifying Dissimulation with Raymond of Toulouse. This is quite unlikely, since Bale must have known that Raymond, like John his brother-in-law, had been excommunicated by Innocent (see *Selected Letters of Pope Innocent III concerning England (1198-1216)*, ed. C. R. Cheney and W. H. Semple [London, 1953], p. 132 and n. 11). Creeth suggests that Bale may have had Raymund of Pennaforte in mind.

1061 S.D. Added by the scribe in revision. The last two letters of *Nobylyte* have been covered by the paper strip used for mounting.

1074-85 See ll. 984-1025 and note.

1085 S.D. In the original scribal draft the full direction reads *Here þe pope go owt and nobylyte cum in and say*. In revising his draft, the A-text scribe interlined *and dyssymvlacyon* before *and nobylyte*, although the entrance he meant to mark, as revealed by the dialogue which follows, was not Dissimulation's but Sedition's. Craik (p. 33, n. 17), however, argues that the added words mark an exit rather than an entrance—that *dyssymvlacyon* is to be read with *go owt* rather than *cum in*. This interpretation not only puts an unnecessary strain on the syntax of the passage but also ignores the pattern of scribal errors discussed in the Introduction, pp. 9-11.

Bale retained in his B-text the stage direction from the A-text, even though he inserted after l. 1085 a separate leaf containing the Interpreter's speech (ll. 1086-1120) and the rubric *finit actus primus*. The action of B, then, does not agree with the direction from A, for the entrance of the two characters which begins Act II must be delayed until after the Interpreter's speech. I have transferred the second part of the stage direction to its logical place, after l. 1120.

1086-1120 The Interpreter's speech is a nondramatic commentary on Act I and an anticipatory summary of Act II. Although l. 1097 seems to imply a break of seven years between the two acts, this is misleading: the duration of the interdict was in fact close to seven years, but dramatically this time is compressed within the bounds of Act II.

1095 *But*: B written over a stain; no sign of alteration (cf. Pafford and Greg).

1096-97 *by excommunycacyon / . . . they interdyct thys nacyon*. See note to ll. 1034-49.

1107-08 Cf. the following address to Henry from a work attributed to Richard Morrison and printed by Sydney Anglo, "An Early Tudor Programme for Plays and Other Demonstrations against the Pope," *Journal of the Warburg and Courtauld Institutes*, XX (1957), 178: "Is it not convenyant and most meete that yerely for ever, in memorye that our savyour christe, by his Moses, your magestie, hath delyvered us out of the bondage of the most wicked pharao of all pharaos, the bysshop of Rome . . . ?" Anglo dates this work as no later than 1538.

1112 *duke Iosue, whych was our late kynge Henrye.* Cf. *Three Laws*, epilogue: "Who hath restored, these same three lawes agayne? / But your late Josias, *and* valeau*n*t kynge Henrye."

1114-17 For the parallel with *Tr. Reign*, see Intro., pp. 55-56. David's slaying of Goliath is later cited by Verity (l. 2261) as an example of patriotism.

[Scene iii (ll. 1121-2005)]

The historical setting of this scene is for the most part England during the period of the general interdict (1208-1214), although many details relate specifically to an interview between John and Pandulf at Northampton in 1211.

The action develops through three fairly distinct movements to the climactic surrender of the crown to Pandulphus: (*a*) Nobility, Clergy, and Civil Order are corrupted by Sedition (ll. 1121-1275); (*b*) John is threatened and cursed by Pandulphus (ll. 1276-1421); (*c*) John is deserted by Nobility, Clergy, Civil Order, and Commonalty, and as a result his resistance to papel usurpation is overcome (ll. 1422-1597). He then submits to Pandulphus and is further humiliated in the affair with Treason (ll. 1598-1983). Pandulphus and Stephen Langton exult over their victory, and the latter reveals his plans to promote a military conquest of England by the French (ll. 1984-2005).

1120 S.D. See note to l. 1085 S.D.

1122 *betwyn*. The scribe first wrote *betwyll*, but then noticed his error, deleted the last five letters and wrote *twyn* before putting down the next word.

1125-26 The animosity between John and the Cistercians, as explained by Ralph of Coggeshall (p. 102), began in 1200 when the monks refused to pay a tax demanded by the king; when the English monastic houses later refused to contribute to the support of the king's Irish expedition (1210), John imposed an especially heavy burden ("gravissimam . . . mulctam") on all of them but particularly on the Cistercians (p. 163). Bale seems to have drawn on the English prose Brut, although he has transferred some details to an earlier passage which treats the general taxation of 1207 (see l. 593 and note). Chapter 149 of the Brut, "How Kyng Iohn destroyed þe ordre of Cisteaux," begins as follows (ed. Brie, I, 158):

> And in þe same tyme þe Irisshe-me*n* bigon to werr oppon Kyng Iohn; and Kyng Iohn ordeynede hi*m* forto wende into Yrland, and lete arere an huge tax þrouȝ-out al Engel*and*, þat is to *seyn*, xxxv Ml

marʒ; & sent þrouʒ-out al Engel*and* to þe monkes of þe ordre of Cisteaux, þat þai shulde helpe him of vj M̄ᵗ marc of Siluer; and þai ansuerede & saide þat þai derst noþing done wiþoute*n* her chief Abbot of Cisteaux. Wherfore Kyng Iohn, when he come aʒeyne fram Irland, he dede ham so miche sorwe & care, þat þai nist wher forto abide; for he toke so miche ransoun of eu*er*y hous of ham, þe so*m*me amountede ix M̄ᵗ & iij C ma*r*ʒ, so þat þai were clene loste and destroyede, & voidede her hous & her landes þrouʒ-out al Engeland.

1125 *Cistean*. Bale first altered some letters of the A-text reading (either *systean* or *crystean*), then rewrote the entire word in the margin. Cf. ll. 375, 1180, 1190 S.D., and notes.

1126 *reḳen*: A-text reading doubtful.

1135 *ye*. Bale first deleted the A-text reading (either *yo* or *ye*), probably because it was crowded on the line, and then interlined *ye*; the A-text colon seems to have been meant to rectify the crowding.

1136 *good perfeccyon*: a temporary alias revived briefly in one later scene (see ll. 2466 and 2479), but otherwise ignored. Cf. ll. 2102-03, where Dissimulation, disguised as Simon of Swynsett, claims another alias, viz. *monastycall deuocyon*. This kind of deception, in which a representative of evil adopts a name signifying a good concept or practice, is frequently exploited in other sixteenth-century plays which make use of morality conventions. See, e.g., *Magnificence* (Courtly Abusion becomes "Pleasure," Cloaked Collusion becomes "Sober Sadness," etc.), *Lusty Juventus* (Hypocrisy becomes "Friendship"), *Respublica* (Avarice becomes "Policy," etc.). The aliases in these plays are essential to the temptation motif and signify the faulty operation of the protagonist's intellect, a necessary prelude to his decisive commitment to evil. In *King Johan* this kind of deception is minimized; where it does occur it is practiced not on the hero, who is incorruptible, but on Nobility, Clergy, and Civil Order (see Intro., pp. 62-63). A second kind of deception, in which the personifications of evil disguise themselves as historical individuals, although largely satiric in intent, does incidentally function in much the same way: it misleads Nobility, Clergy, and Civil Order, but not John (see especially l. 1783).

1140 *vmfrey*. No other occurrence of this word is known; the context here, as Creeth has recognized, requires a meaning such as 'underling.' Perhaps some form of *unfree* 'base,' 'ignoble' was intended, although the *OED* records no example of the use of this word as a substantive.

1149 ff. This is the fullest of several parodies of sacramental confession in the play. See Miller, pp. 809-810, for an analysis of this scene in terms of typical medieval penitential practices.

1149 In the manuscript the speech-prefix *nobelyte* is unnecessarily repeated before this line.

1150 *yowr*: *r* (superior) added by the scribe in revision.

1178 Rom. xiii.1. This and the following verses of Romans are either quoted or paraphrased in ll. 1408-09, 1502-04, and 2350-57. In the *Obedience* Tyndale opens his chapter entitled "The obedience of Subiectes vn to kynges princes and rulers" with a translation of the first ten verses of this chapter (fol. 29ʳ⁻ᵛ).

1180 *whole*: interlined by Bale over the deleted A-text reading and then repeated in the margin. Cf. ll. 375, 1125, 1190 S.D., and notes.

1187 Manly is probably correct in marking this line as an aside.

1190 S.D. *Cyuyl*. Bale first altered the initial two letters of the A-text reading from *se* to *Cy*, then rewrote the entire word in the margin as *Cyuyl*. Cf. ll. 375, 1125, 1180, and notes.

and Sedysyon shall go vp and down a praty whyle: added by the scribe in revision.

1192 S.D. In the manuscript this is written as the speech-prefix to l. 1193.

1216 *A dram*: original & deleted in ambiguous ink, but probably by Bale.

1218 *A toth*: original & deleted in ambiguous ink, but probably by Bale.

1219 *blood of Haylys*. Cf. *Three Laws*, l. 825, where "bloude of hayles" is paralleled by "Berye" and "our lady of grace" in a catalog of objects or places of veneration. As Foxe (1563) explains, p. 1316, the blood preserved as a relic at the Abbey of Hales in Gloucestershire was thought to be invisible to anyone in mortal sin. See also John S. Farmer's note in his edition of *The Dramatic Writings of John Heywood* (London, 1905), pp. 239-240.

1225 *hatcht*: b-reading doubtful.

maistre Iohan Shornes bote. The allusion, which also occurs in Heywood, has not been explained; see Farmer's comment in Heywood's *Dramatic Writings*, pp. 261-262. See also John Studley's preface "To the Reader" in his translation of Bale's *Acta Romanorum Pontificum* (*The Pageant of Popes* [London, 1576], sig. *b4); his long catalog of popish "toyes" includes "bloude of Hailes" and "s. Iohan Shorns boots."

1229 *darvell gathyron*. On April 6, 1538, Elis Price, of St. Assaph's in Wales, wrote to Cromwell about "an image of Darvellgadarn . . . in whome the people have so great confidence, hope, and truste, that they cumme dayly a pillgramage unto hym . . ." (*Original Letters, Illustrative of English History*, ed. Henry Ellis, 1st Ser., II, 2nd ed. [London, 1825], 83). In a second letter to Cromwell, dated April 28, 1538, Price reported that the image had been taken down, although not without some difficulty, and that he planned to appear in person before Cromwell to answer certain complaints raised by the villagers with regard to his actions in the matter (ibid., 3rd Ser., III [London, 1846], 195). The fate of the image is recorded in Edward Hall's *Chronicle* (London, 1809), p. 826; it was burned at the execution of a certain Friar Forest in London on May 30, 1538. See also Foxe (1563), p. 571, and John Stow's *Annales* (London, 1631), p. 575. Bale mentions the image again in his *Dialogue or Familiar Talke betweene Two Neighbours* (Roane, 1554), sig. C4.

Although it is possible that Bale knew of the image even before it arrived in London, it is far more likely that he is here assuming on the part of his audience a familiarity with a recent, local event. If so, the passage could not have been written before (and not very long after) May 1538. Pafford and Greg drew the same conclusion from this evidence, but since they were intent on proving the existence of a 1536 version behind the A-text (see Intro., p. 22), they evidently took this as one of the "allusions to contemporary events" (p. xxiii), introduced by Bale in the course of his first revision of the hypothetical "original" version.

1236 *loade*: perhaps a nonce shortening of *liveload* or *lifload*—i.e., *livelihood*, in the sense "kind or manner of life" (*OED*, sb. 1).

The *o* of the A-text reading is blotted, doubtful.

1248 *compel*: A-text reading doubtful.

1260 *tyckle*: interlined by Bale above A-text *tycle*, which has not been deleted.

1273 *her*: possibly *here*, although the flourish after *r* does not appear to be a deliberate mark of abbreviation.

1284 *Forty yeres ago*. The reference to the pope's response to the murder of Thomas à Becket in December 1170 agrees well enough with the historical setting of this scene (see note at l. 1121).

1290 *after a pared*. Both the formation and spacing of several letters are ambiguous, but the sense of the passage makes this reading preferable to *a ster apared* (Collier, Pollard) or *a ster-apared* (Manly, Farmer). The allusion to Thomas à Becket's death is coupled with a brief exoneration of Henry II for his complicity in this death, and the result is a confused and overburdened syntax. The verb *pare* in *a pared crowne* is to be understood as meaning 'to injure seriously,' and thus

[172]

a pared crowne is a bloody coxcomb, a damaged head, or the like. This meaning is not recorded in the *OED*, but see the related meaning (*pare*, v.¹ 6b) "to cut off" and *Gammer Gurton's Nedle* (V.ii.202) "whiles Chat his crown did pare." See also the poem on the death of Thomas à Becket in MS. Sloane 2593, edited by Thomas Wright in his *Songs and Carols from a Manuscript in the British Museum of the Fifteenth Century* (London, 1856), p. 67:

> Beforn his aunter he kneled adoun,
> Ther they gunne to paryn his crown;
> He sterdyn the braynys up and down,
> *Optans celi gaudia.*

In l. 1291 *vpon* means "of (a cause of death or illness)" (*OED*, s.v. 11d). The two lines may then be paraphrased thus: For this (action described in ll. 1283-89), their captain (Thomas à Becket) received afterwards a seriously injured head and died as a result of it, even though the killing was done without the king's consent.

Although Pollard quoted the stanza from the poem on the death of Thomas, he preferred the reading *a ster apared crowne*, which he defended as follows: "Bale probably wrote these words intending them to mean 'a star-adorned crown.' . . . The prefix a- (= ge-, y-) was not very uncommon in the 15th century in the formation of past participles, and 'ster apared' may thus mean 'star-clipped.'" This explanation is at least grammatically plausible, but it fails to fit the context of the passage. See also the objections to *ster apared* in J. H. P. Pafford, "Two Notes on Bale's *King John*," *MLR*, LVI (1961), 553-554.

1292 *interdiccyons*: *s* perhaps altered from *o* by Bale.

1297-1300 See L. F. Salzmann, *Henry II* (Boston, 1914), p. 122.

1303 S.D. *Privat Welth*: in the manuscript written as the speech-prefix to l. 1304.

1322 *Tushe, Gospell*: deletion of original *the* possibly scribal.

1325 Something apparently erased after *Y*, although the spacing has not been affected.

1326-34 Cf. the English prose Brut (ed. Brie, I, 159): "þo ansuerede þe Kyng [in reply to Pandulfus' demands]; 'as tochyng þe Priour & his monkes of Kaunterbery, al þat ȝe haue saide, y wille gladelyche do, & al þing þat ȝe wille ordeyne. But as tochyng þe Erchebisshop, y shal telle ȝow in myn hert as it liþ, þat þe Erchebisshop lete his bisshopriche, & þat þe Pope þan for him wolde praye, & þan oppon aventure me shulde like some oþere bisshopriche forto ȝeue him in Engeland; and oppon þis condicioun y wil him resceyue and vnderfonge.'" The same proposal is repeated almost verbatim in Foxe (1563), p. (63), from whom Grafton (II, 104) seems to have copied. Cf. Burton annals (*Ann. mon.*, I, 214-215); Waverley annals (*Ann. mon.*, II, 261, 269).

1336-40 Cf. the English prose Brut (ed. Brie, I, 159): "þo saide Pandolf vnto þe Kyng: 'holy cherche was neuer wont to disgrade [*var. lec.* descharg] Erchebisshop wiþouten cause resonable; but euer she was wont to chastice Pry[n]ces þat to God & holy cherche were in-obedient.' 'What! how now?' *quod* þe Kyng, 'manace ȝe me?'" Foxe (1563), p. (63), gives this almost verbatim; Grafton, II, 104-105, evidently derives from Foxe. Substantially the same exchange is found in the Meaux Abbey chronicle, I, 388.

1342-43 Cf. Prov. xvi.10 and ll. 2237-38.

1354 *Belles prystes*: priests of the Babylonian idol Bel (cf. *Lyvyng by ydolles*, l. 1355) and not, as Creeth believes, "priests who attach undue importance to bell ringing." See Dan. xiv.1-22 (in English versions usually included among the Old Testament Apocrypha).

1357-77 Bale here represents three distinct events: (1) the formal excommunication of 1209 (see note to ll. 1034-49); (2) the imposition of the general interdict in 1208; (3) the alleged absolving of John's subjects from fealty to their king (ca. January 1213). As a rule medieval historians treat these events with chronological fidelity, but see Burton annals (*Ann. mon.*, I, 215) and Waverley annals (*Ann. mon.*, II, 268-271), both of which associate the first and third with John's interview with Pandulf at Northampton in 1211.

1360 *contvmacy*: in context a technical term describing a requisite condition for the sentence of excommunication. See Francis Edward Hyland, *Excommunication: Its Nature, Historical Development and Effects*, Catholic University of America Canon Law Studies No. 49 (Washington, D.C., 1928), p. 2: "... it is this element which is proper to censures and serves to distinguish them from all other ecclesiastical punishments; a censure is a medicinal penalty, its primary and immediate purpose being to correct the offender; hence it presupposes contumacy."

1361 *From this day forward.* Contemporary authorities disagree on the dating of the interdict; modern historians have resolved the question in favor of March 23, 1208. See Frederick Maurice Powicke in *The Cambridge Medieval History*, VI (Cambridge, Eng., 1929), 233, and especially C. R. Cheney, "King John and the Papal Interdict," *Bulletin of the John Rylands Library*, XXXI (1948), 295 and n. 2.

1362-67 Cf. the English prose Brut (ed. Brie, I, 160): "And we assoile quyte Erles & barons, knyȝtȝ, & al oþer maner men, of her

homages, *seruices* & *feauteʒ*, þat þai shulde vnto ʒow done. And þis
þing to *conferme*, We ʒeue pleyn power to þe Bisshop of Wynchestre
& to þe Bisshop of Norwich; And þe same power we ʒeue into Scot*land*
to þe Bisshop of Rouchestr*e* & of Salesbery; & in Walys we ʒeue þe same
power to þe Bisshop of seynt Dauid, of Landa & of Assa." Outside of
Bale and the Brut, this list of bishops is found only in Foxe (1563),
p. (63), and Grafton (II, 105), though an almost identical list is included
in the *Eulogium* (III, 99-100), Robert of Gloucester (II, 706), and the
Waverley annals (*Ann. mon.*, II, 270). See also Burton annals (*Ann.
mon.*, I, 215) for an abbreviated list. Only Bale associates these bishops
with the enforcement of the interdict; the Brut is closer to the more
conventional historical view in associating them with the release of
John's subjects from fealty to their king (see note to ll. 1372-73).

1368-69 Cf. the English prose Brut (ed. Brie, I, 160): "'And more-
ou*er* we sende throuʒ al C*r*istendome, þat al þe bisshopis biʒend þe
see, þat þai accurse all þo þat helpeþ ʒow. . . .'"

1372-73 The absolving of a king's subjects from fealty is tantamount
to deposition, and although the evidence provided by the medieval
chroniclers has been thought to prove that Innocent had taken this
step against John by about January 1213, apparently John never was
actually deposed. (His surrender of the crown to Pandulf, dramatized
in ll. 1705 ff., is historical but not precisely a deposition.) The evidence for this conclusion has been thoroughly analyzed by C. R.
Cheney, "The Alleged Deposition of King John," in *Studies in Medieval History Presented to Frederick Maurice Powicke*, ed. R. W. Hunt
et al. (Oxford, 1948), pp. 100-116, who has also analyzed the sources
which Bale would have relied upon (pp. 100-108). According to these
sources, Innocent's sentence was accompanied by an exhortation to
Philip to execute the deposition by force of arms; Philip subsequently
prepared to invade England (see ll. 1604-06 and cf. ll. 1066-68) but was
restrained by the papal legate when John yielded to the pope's demands.

1373 *fewte*. This and *sewte* (as in Collier and Manly) fit the sense of
the passage well enough; *fewte* as a form of *fealty*, *sewte* as a form of
suit (meaning 'attendance on,' describing a feudal relationship). Although the manuscript reading is not perfectly clear, the initial letter
seems to be *f* rather than *s*.

1374-75 Cf. the English prose Brut (ed. Brie, I, 160): "'And we
assoile ham al also, by þe autorite of þe Pope, & *commanden* ham also
wiþ ʒow forto werr, as wiþ him þat is enemy to al holy cherche.'" This
is repeated with only minor variations in Foxe (1563), p. (63), and

Grafton (II, 105); see Foxe (1576), I, 255, for a slightly different version.

1391 Collier and Pollard omit the comma after *Why*. See l. 269 and note.

1395 *fell*. Manly and Farmer emend to *tell*, but see *OED, fell*, v. 1e, for the meaning 'humiliate.'

1397 S.D. *for*: portion of *r* obscured by paper strip used for mounting.

1404-07 Eccles. x.20. Cf. ll. 2227-30.

1408-09 Rom. xiii.2. See l. 1178 and note.

1410-11 See Luke ii.1 ff.

1411 *descripcyon*: 'enrolment' (*OED*, s.v. 1b).

1422 *reconcylyd*. The second *c* has been interlined by Bale, apparently to replace an original *s* which has not been deleted.

1436-37 See Num. xxii-xxiv.

1444 *holy*: second *h* of original *hohy* partly erased to produce *holy*.

1455-56 Elson, p. 193, sees a significant parallel with *Tr. Reign*, I.v.113-115:

> *Iohn* And what say you to our league, if I doo not submit?
> *Philip* What should I say? I must obey the Pope.
> *Iohn* Obey the Pope, and breake your oath to God?

1459 *pharesayycall*: *ayy* crowded, doubtful; no sign of alteration (cf. Pafford and Greg).

1460 *Good and faythfull*. The B-text reading seems to be an authorial carelessness. Farmer has mistakenly attributed the correction *god to faythfull susan* to Collier when in fact no editor has suggested this emendation, probably because it does not agree with the scriptural passage referred to (see Dan. xiii.23) where the speaker is Susanna, not God.

1463 *yow*: Manly emends to *thowgh*.

1467-69 Ps. ii.10.

1467 *nvnc*: A-text reading doubtful.

1476 *ryghtes*: alteration in ambiguous ink, but probably by Bale.

1480 Cf. Tyndale on unlawful oaths (*Obedience*, fol. 55): "Whosoeuer vowe an vnlawfull vowe / promise an vnlawfull promise swere an vnlawfull othe sinneth agenst God: & ought therfore to breake it. ... They therfore that are sworne to be true vnto Cardinals and Bisshopes / y^t is to saye false vnto God ye kinge & the realme / maye breake their othes lawfully without grudge of conscience by the auctorite of Gods worde."

[176]

1488 *too*: first *o* blotted in ambiguous ink; second *o* possibly added in same ink.

1489 *at a poynt*: 'decided,' 'determined,' as in ll. 1675, 1703, 1777.

1491 *contynew styll*. An original *be styll* has been deleted by the scribe and the present reading set down directly after the deletion in the ink of the original scribal draft.

1498-99 See II Cor. ii.6-9.

1502-04 Cf. Rom. xiii.4 and see l. 1178 and note.

1512 *mynysters*: *e* perhaps altered by Bale from scribal *e* or *o* (cf. Pafford and Greg).

1526 *is*. Collier, apparently through carelessness, prints the manuscript *is* as *in*; Manly prints *is* and ascribes the correction to Kittredge. Farmer makes the same correction but attributes the erroneous reading *in* to Kittredge.

1528 *Dathan and Abiron*. See Num. xvi.34. In the *Eulogium* (III, 99) Pandulf warns the excommunicated John that all those who associate with him will be cut off from the sacraments and find themselves with Dathan and Abiron, swallowed alive by the earth.

1533 Manly and Farmer read *No-where as yow are in place* . . . , but John's question in the preceding line demands a yes or no answer from Nobility.

1533 S.D. *Here enter* . . . *Commynalte*: added by the scribe in ink of initial draft. The addition runs beyond the right-hand bar of the "box" regularly used to enclose centered stage directions.

1542 *me*: doubtful, perhaps *mee*.

1544 The A-text line has been repeated by Bale (with variations) at the end of his marginal interpolation to mark his return to the scribal text.

1549 Manly tries to clarify this puzzling line by punctuating *yf that be, good God helpe the*. Kittredge (as recorded by Manly) suggests *yf that be thow, God helpe the*.

1560 *take with*: apparently 'take part with,' 'agree with' (see *OED, take*, v. 75d).

1592-95 John's exclusion of the friars seems to be Bale's invention.

1592 *perceyve*. Bale has interlined *c* above an original *s*, which he has accidentally neglected to delete. Elsewhere (as in ll. 2165, 2169, 2335) Bale spells this word with *c* rather than *sc*.

1596 *We*: A-text reading somewhat doubtful.

1598 *connaunt*: perhaps *counaunt*, but the macron seems to be placed over the *o* rather than over the *o* and following two minims. Either form is a possible variant of *covenant*.

[177]

1604 Collier ends this line with a period, Manly with a semicolon. The relationship between this and the following line, however, is better indicated by a colon (as in Farmer) or a comma.

1605-06 See note to ll. 1372-73. According to Roger of Wendover (II, 69), the fear of an invasion by Philip was one of the four reasons for John's capitulation to the pope.

1609 S.D. Added by the scribe in revision. Creeth relocates this direction after the following line, but the manuscript arrangement is probably the right one: presumably England was to call after the departing Commonalty.

1618-22 See ll. 108-109 and note.

1619 *salue*. Bale seems to have retraced the scribal *e* after inserting *l* and adding his characteristic tick to the scribal *u*.

sore: A-text reading doubtful.

suppell: 'assuage,' 'mollify' (see *OED, supple*).

1621 *lawfull*: *a* and part of *w* perhaps altered by Bale.

1626 *yowr* (third): *r* (superior) added by the scribe in revision.

1632-39 The impending invasion described here is evidently a reference to Philip's plan to conquer England under cover of papal encouragement to the opponents of the excommunicated English king (see ll. 1372-73 and note). Some details, however, are either unhistorical or partly unhistorical. *Alexander, þe kyng of Scottes*, e.g., was not included in Philip's plan, although he did play a part in the subsequent invasion by Louis in 1216 (see Roger of Wendover, II, 193-194; Ralph of Coggeshall, p. 183). The presence of the other invaders—*kyng Alphonse* of Portugal, the *Esterlynges, Danes* and *Norwayes*—seems to be Bale's invention.

1633 *þat for their townnes cast lottes*. The allusion has not been explained.

1648-49 Cf. Tyndale, in a similar context, describing pernicious papal teachings: ". . . we be taught even of very babes / to kyll a turke / to slee a Iewe / to burne an heritike / to fyght for ye liberties & right of ye church as they call it: . . . or yf we be slayne in the quarell that our soules goo / nay flye to heven / and be there yer oure bloude be colde" (*Obedience*, fol. 23^v).

1650-53 For the parallel with *Tr. Reign* see Intro., pp. 55-56.

1652 *holpyst*. The *o* has been altered by Bale, perhaps from the scribal form of the same letter, definitely not from *e* (cf. Pafford and Greg).

1666-1724 This long Bale interpolation is clearly designed to extenuate John's capitulation to Pandulphus. In the A-text, where the king's submission (l. 1725) follows immediately upon the Cardinal's promise to restrain the invaders (ll. 1660-65), there is a strong suggestion of political compromise. In the B-text John's decision is not only delayed, it is reached only after consultation with his advisers. Thus the king is not solely to blame for what follows.

1666 The final version of this line appears immediately below the deleted b-version. There is no crowding.

1674 *leaue*: *a* apparently altered, perhaps from *e*.

1694-1701 Sedition's exuberant laughter links him unmistakably with the Vice of the morality play. See Spivack, p. 163.

1703 *Ye are at a poynt*. Misled by Collier's inadequate description of the manuscript, Manly took these words as Collier's misreading of *Are ye at a poynt* in l. 1777 and relocated ll. 1773-76 immediately before l. 1703. Farmer was similarly misled but placed ll. 1773-76 after l. 1704. Collier's arrangement, however, was the correct one.

1719-22 Cf. Simon Fish, *A Supplication for the Beggars*, ed. Edward Arber (London, 1880), p. 6: "Here were a blissid sort . . . of bloud-suppers that coude . . . make effusion of the bloude of his [John's] people, oneles this good and blissed king of great compassion, more fearing and lamenting the sheding of the bloude of his people then the losse of his crowne and dignite agaynst all right and conscience had submitted him silf vnto theym."

1727-31 Both historically and dramatically the resignation of the crown represents the climax of John's struggle with the pope. From this point on John and his successors rule England *In maner of fefarme* (l. 1738), doing homage to the pope and, incidentally, benefiting from his protection (see ll. 1372-73, 2069, and notes). John may have himself added the act of homage to the agreement whereby the pope's original demands regarding the installation of Stephen Langton were met: see Walter of Coventry, II, 210, but cf. Roger of Wendover, II, 74-77; see also Norgate, p. 180, and Painter, pp. 193-194.

The formula of submission used by Bale is clearly borrowed from the English prose Brut: "Here y resyngn op þe crone of þe reaume of Engeland into þe Popis Hande, Innocent þe þridde, and put me Holliche in his mercy & ordenance" (ed. Brie, I, 162), which was probably Foxe's direct source as well: "Here I resigne vp the crowne of the realme of England to the popes hands Innocent the thyrd, & put me wholly in his mercy & his ordinaunce" ([1576], I, 256). This passage is not in the 1563 edition of Foxe or in Grafton. There is nothing in the charter of submission itself (see *Councils & Synods, with Other Documents Relating to the English Church*, ed. F. M.

Powicke and C. R. Cheney, II, Pt. 1 [Oxford, 1964], 17-19), or in the redactions of this charter in the monastic chronicles (Roger of Wendover, II, 74-76; *Ann. mon.*, I, 222-223 [Burton annals]; and II, 275-276 [Waverley annals]) that would account for this precise wording.

1733-34 Cf. the English prose Brut (ed. Brie, I, 162-163): "þo vnderfonge Pandolf þe crone of Kyng Iohn, and kepte hit v dayes, as for seising-takyng of þo ij reaumes of Engel*and* and of Yrl*and*. . . ." Foxe (1576), I, 256, repeats this almost verbatim; it is absent from the 1563 edition of Foxe and from Grafton.

1735-39 Cf. the English prose Brut (ed. Brie, I, 162): ". . . and þo [John] ӡaf vp þe reaume of Engel*and* & of Irland, for him & for his heires for eu*er*more þat shuld come aft*er* him, so þat Kyng Iohan & his heires shulde tak þo ij reaumes of þe Popis Hand, & shulde holde þo ij reaumes of the Pope as to ferme, paying eu*er*y ӡer to þe court of Rome a þousand marc of siluer." This is repeated almost verbatim in Foxe (1576), I, 256; there is a more condensed presentation of substantially the same matter in Foxe (1563), p. (66), and Grafton (II, 109).

1739-44 With some minor exceptions, Bale agrees with the conventional medieval accounts of the payments demanded of John. The *thowsand marke* to be paid annually to the pope, specified in the charter of submission (*Councils & Synods*, II, Pt. 1, 18), is recorded by the English monastic chroniclers like Roger of Wendover (II, 75), as well as the French *Histoire des Ducs de Normandie et des Rois d'Angleterre*, ed. Francisque Michel (Paris, 1840), p. 124, and the generally less conservative Meaux Abbey chronicle (I, 391). There is less agreement about the other figures, however. The *thre thowsand marke* to be paid to Langton appears in the charter as 2,500 pounds, although the *Eulogium* (III, 106-107), the Meaux Abbey chronicle (I, 393), and Fabyan (p. 320) all agree with Bale in this particular. The *Forty thowsand marke* to be paid to the church (presumably to the English clergy) seems to be Bale's exaggeration, although the figure was in fact a high one (see Painter, pp. 195-199). According to the English prose Brut (ed. Brie, I, 165), "þai ordeynede and saide, þat þe Kyng shulde ӡeue to þe Erchebisshop*e* iij M^l marӡ for þe wronge þat þe Kyng hade done to him, and also to oþ*er* clerkes xv M^l marc, by porcyons."

1758 S.D. Sedition's exit is necessary if he is to "cum in" at l. 1782. There is no difficulty in the A-text, where Sedition leaves the stage at l. 1275 and remains offstage until l. 1782. In preparing the B-text, however, Bale has brought him back at l. 1644, evidently assuming that he would remain onstage right through to the end of the scene. He has ignored the problem of the "cum in" direction at l. 1782—an A-text direction retained in the B-text. See Intro., p. 14.

1765-72 These lines begin the first of the four folio leaves which were detached from the manuscript at the time Collier prepared his text; consequently they appear in none of the printed editions of the play prior to Pafford and Greg's type-facsimile. They were first printed (with many inaccuracies) by Clarence E. Cason in *JEGP*, XXVII (1928), 42-50.

Although Bale canceled part of the page on which they appear, he clearly intended to retain these lines in his revised text. See Intro., p. 13. In the manuscript these lines are followed immediately by ll. 1777-1803, which were also meant to be retained in the B-text.

1782 The *irregularyte* from which John is absolved in the following lines is his personal excommunication; the relaxation of the interdict does not occur until ll. 1967 ff. (The formula in ll. 1794-95 is probably not meant to be taken literally.) Historically the two events were separated by about a year: John was released from the sentence of excommunication in mid-July 1213, shortly after he had given up the crown to Pandulf, and the interdict was lifted in late June or early July 1214.

In dramatizing John's absolution, Bale has ignored the English prose Brut, which presents a vivid picture of the king's throwing himself at Langton's feet, begging forgiveness and offering "a mark of golde" at the archbishop's mass (ed. Brie, I, 165); he has included instead the rite of absolution itself, not in the Brut. For a discussion of the parodic element in Bale's presentation of this rite, see Miller, pp. 812-813. As Miller notes, the medieval formula for absolution from excommunication varied somewhat according to circumstances, but Bale's parody retains many recognizable features of the authentic form. See especially *Monumenta ritualia ecclesiae Anglicanae*, ed. William Maskell, 2nd ed. (Oxford, 1882), II, 339; III, 326-330; *Manuale et processionale ad usum insignis ecclesiae Eboracensis*, ed. William George Henderson (Durham, Eng., 1875), pp. 129, 107*-108*.

1788 After this line there is a space in the manuscript for a stage direction, which was never inserted (see Intro., p. 9). Apparently John was to kneel in saying his *Confiteor*.

1789 In the manuscript the speech-prefix *kyng Iohn* is unnecessarily repeated at the head of this line.

1791 *omnes*: *i* of A-text reading doubtful.

1799 *mihi*. The A-text reading is doubtful: *w* is unmistakable (cf. Pafford and Greg), but the one or two superior letters which follow have been obscured by Bale's interlineation.

1804 From this point to the end of the play the B-text is entirely in Bale's hand. The corresponding section of the A-text was canceled by Bale and replaced by the greatly expanded version printed here. Only 140 lines of the canceled A-text have survived, and these have been printed in Appendix A.

1807-82, 1910-19 (A2-7, A14-17) The Treason episode, dramatized in the B-text and outlined in the A-text (see Intro., pp. 11-12), can be traced to some early accounts of an interview between John and the papal nuncios Pandulf and Durand at Northampton in 1211. Both Roger of Wendover (II, 58) and Matthew Paris (*Historia*, II, 124) record the interview but say nothing of the clerk whom John wished to hang. In the Burton annals (*Ann. mon.*, I, 217), however, the story of the clerk, a *falsarius*, is set forth with all the significant details which appear in Bale's version. The story is repeated almost verbatim in the Waverley annals (*Ann. mon.*, II, 271) and with some minor variations by Robert of Gloucester (II, 708) and in the Meaux Abbey chronicle, I, 389; see also Thomas Duffus Hardy, *Descriptive Catalogue of Materials Relating to the History of Great Britain and Ireland, to the End of the Reign of Henry VII*, Rolls Series 26, III (London, 1871), 44; and *Anchiennes Cronicques d'Engleterre par Jehan de Wavrin*, ed. Mlle. Dupont, I (Paris, 1858), 38. Bale's immediate source was probably Ch. cl of the English prose Brut (ed. Brie, I, 161), entitled "How Pandolf delyuerede a clerc þat hade falsede & contrefetede þe Kyng*us* monye bifore þe Kyng":

> Anon þo commandede þe Kyng to the Shirrif & bailifs of North-ampton þat were in þe Kynges *pre*sence, þat þai shulde bryng forth alle þe prisoners, þat þai my3t bene done to deþe bifore Pandulf. . . . When þe prysoners were comen bifore þe Kyng, þe Kyng com-manded so*m*me to bene honget, & some to bene drawe, & so*m*me to draw out her eyen of her heued. and amonge alle oþer, þere was a clerc þat hade falsede þe Kynges monye; & þe Kyng commaundede þat he shuld bene honged & drawe. And when Pandolf herd þis comm*an*dement of þe Kyng, he stert op smertly, and anone axed a book & candel, and wolde haue cursed alle ham þat sette oppon þe clerc eny honde. And Pandolf him-self went forto seche a croice; and þe Kyng folwede him, and delyu*er*ede him þe clerc by þe honde, þat he shulde do wiþ him what-euer þat he wolde. And þus was the clerc delyu*er*ede, and went þens. . . .

A somewhat garbled version of this episode appears in Foxe (1576), I, 255-256 (not in 1563). Both Grafton, II, 104-105, and Holinshed, II,

302, record the interview but omit the story of the clerk. Bale apparently has the same story in mind when in the *Summarium* (fol. 100ᵛ) and the *Catalogus* (I, 264) he alludes in passing to certain unnamed clerks who were not only guilty of counterfeiting but also killed a woman and committed other unspecified disgraceful acts. The purpose of the allusion is to illustrate the difficulties experienced by John in trying to deal with the wicked clergy.

1814 *cloyners*. Manly emends to *coyners*, apparently because of the description of Treason's activities in ll. 1859-60. Pafford and Greg suggest the same emendation on the strength of l. A4: "For so moch as he hath falsefyed owr coyne." There is no valid objection to *cloyner*, however: see *OED, cloyne*, "to act deceitfully or fraudulently, to cheat, deceive." See also *Three Laws*, "With holye oyle and watter / I can so cloyne and clatter," ll. 439-440, and the *Apology*, "thys croked cloyner," fol. 39, and "our cloynynge papystes, monkes, massing prestes," fol. 153. Oddly enough, Farmer reads *coiner* even though his "Note-Book and Word-List" includes entries for *cloin* and *cloiner*.

1844 Speech-prefix (*Treason*) added in pencil by a later hand. See Appendix C.

1855-56 An allusion to the examination of John and Peter (cf. *peters offyce*, l. 1849) as recounted in Acts iv.5 ff.; Creeth mistakenly refers to the account of Paul before the high priest Ananias in Acts xxiii.2.

1883-94 Cf. A8-13. The fullest of the early accounts of Peter of Pomfret (sometimes referred to as Peter of Wakefield or Peter of York) are to be found in the *Chronicon Thomae Wykes* (*Ann. mon.*, IV, 57-58); Matthew Paris, *Historia*, II, 129; and the *Histoire des Ducs de Normandie*, pp. 122-126. There are briefer accounts in *Ann. mon.*, III, 34 (Dunstable), and IV, 56 (Oseney); Gaufridus de Coldingham's *Liber ... statu ecclesiæ Dunhelmensis*, pp. 27-28; Robert of Gloucester, II, 709, 711; Fabyan, p. 321; etc. See also Josiah Cox Russell, "The Development of the Legend of Peter of Pontefract," *Medievalia et humanistica*, XIII (1960), 21-31.

Peter, a noted prophet in his day, predicted that John would no longer be king after Ascension Day 1213 and offered to forfeit his life if his prediction proved untrue. When the appointed day had passed uneventfully, John took the prophet at his word and ordered him to be drawn through the streets and hanged. But it was generally thought that Peter's prophecy had in fact been fulfilled, for John had resigned the crown of England and Ireland to the pope's legate on May 15, 1213, just eight days before the Ascension, and thus he had in a sense ceased to be king.

[183]

Traditionally the episode had been recounted as an example of how John's habitual cruelty alienated his subjects. As Polydore Vergil noted (*Anglicae historiae libri XXVI* [Basle, 1534], pp. 274-275), Peter was considered a holy man, and his son (who in most versions was said to have shared Peter's fate) was certainly innocent. The prophet's sanctity was fully documented with circumstantial accounts of his marvelous trances, visions, etc., in the late medieval accounts by Higden (VIII, 192-194), the author of the *Eulogium* (III, 112-113), and others. Among sixteenth-century Protestant writers, however, the story took on a new emphasis. Peter was depicted as a "false counterfeited prophet," an "idell gadder about," whose superstitious predictions were calculated to discredit the king and appeal to the seditious inclinations of the ignorant (Foxe [1563], p. (64); adopted by Grafton, II, 118). Bale seems to have been the first to present this interpretation of the story.

A9 *symple*: *s* perhaps touched up by Bale.

1887-94 (cf. A13) In some accounts Peter is said to have allotted John fourteen years as king, while in others he is represented as prophesying in 1212 that John would no longer be king after the following Ascension Day. Both versions come to the same thing: John reckoned his regnal year according to the ecclesiastical calendar, and having been crowned on Ascension Day 1197 (May 27), his fourteenth year concluded on Ascension Eve 1213 (May 22). He seems to have delayed the execution until May 28 to forestall the objections of those who would calculate the fourteen years by the secular calendar. See Waverley annals (*Ann. mon.*, II, 278) and Walter of Coventry (II, 212).

1888 *bynde bears*: a proverbial expression for the power to do the impossible or the very difficult. See the citations in Tilley, B134, and Bale's *Apology* (fol. 52^{r-v}): "Haue ye forgotten your olde sophystycall dystruccyon on potentie et actus, wher with ye were wont to bynde beares at your pleasur?"

1891-92 *realme*: *dreame*. See Henry Cecil Wyld, *Studies in English Rhymes from Surrey to Pope* (London, 1923), p. 129, for examples of this kind of rhyme in sixteenth-century poetry.

1899-1906 The account of the vision seen by Maurice Morganensis (or Morganus) was discovered in Giraldus Cambrensis, *De principis instructione*, ed. George F. Warner, in *Opera*, Rolls Series 21, VIII (London, 1891), 310-311, by J. H. P. Pafford, *MLR*, LVI (1961), 554-555. In Giraldus the "double misfortune" is explained as the loss of both spiritual and temporal goods during the time of the general interdict in England, and John is held responsible for this misfortune. The story is repeated, but without the application to John, by Higden, VIII, 186-187, and by Fabyan, p. 314. Bale's comment on the same story in his *Summarium* (fol. 98^{r-v}) suggests that he was familiar with the earlier version, for he seems to take exception to the interpretation supplied by Giraldus: "Historici plures sunt, qui hunc scribant, [Mauritium] cum mortuo quodam milite nocturnum habuisse colloquium, de Anglici tunc regni ruina. Sed quid mentiendo non fingit ob uentrem hypocrisis?" On Maurice himself, none of whose works has survived, see *DNB*, "Maurice (fl. 1210)." There is no trace of this matter in the A-text.

1903 *Ape at Praga*. The allusion has not been explained.

1907 *our*: interlined above an original *the*, which Bale has accidentally neglected to delete.

1908 This is part of Bale's nineteen-line addition beginning at l. 1890, but cf. l. A12.

A17 Something apparently erased after *full*, probably a raised point.

1922 *Lyke lorde, lyke chaplayne*. Cf. a similar jibe directed against Pandulf and Innocent in Foxe (1576), I, 255 (marginal comment): "Like master lyke man." For the proverb which completes the line, see Tilley, B94: "Neither (Never a) Barrel better herring."

1931 *he fyndeth that surely bynde*. See Tilley, B352.

1935 *wyll*: interlined above *shall*, which Bale has accidentally neglected to delete.

1938 *good poeple*. See l. 770 and note.

1943 (A20) *Iulyane*. See Intro., p. 37.

1950 *debatementes*. *OED* records no other occurrence of this word, which is explained as a form of *abatements*. The context would seem to demand some such meaning, but cf. the corresponding line from the A-text (l. A23), where the verb is *sett* rather than *sent*.

A24 S.D. Added by the scribe in revision, with *dresse* first written as *drysse*. The doubling direction is faulty and probably a scribal invention: see Intro., pp. 10, 44, and note to l. 1966.

1964 Cf. the "commune sayenge" used by Tyndale to characterize unworthy clerics (*Obedience*, fol. 82^v): "no peny no Pater noster."

1966 According to the stage direction in the A-text (at l. A24), England would have left the stage before this point in the dialogue. The authority of the A-text direction is suspect on other grounds as well (see Intro., pp. 10-11, 44).

1967 (A28) *I ... all*. Most early sources assign this duty to the legate Nicolas of Tusculum; none assigns it definitely to Pandulf, although the English prose Brut (ed. Brie, I, 166) does so by implication. Later historians like John Stow in his *Summarie of the Chronicles of England* (London, 1579), p. 115, and Holinshed, II, 316, agree with the medieval tradition rather than with Bale.

1970 *men*. Bale apparently copied *them* from the corresponding line of the A-text (l. A31) before deciding on the alteration to *men*.

A33 After this line there is a space in the manuscript for a stage direction which was never inserted (see Intro., p. 9). Presumably the direction intended would have required John to perform some act of submission, such as kneeling to the Cardinal.

1976 *saynt Antonyes hogge*. See John S. Farmer and W. E. Henley, *Slang and Its Analogues* (London, 1890-1904), s.v. "Antony pig" and "Tantony" for expressions associated with St. Anthony the hermit, the patron saint of swineherds.

1983 S.D. Bale has characteristically failed to indicate the necessary stage business (see Intro., p. 14). Note that the king's exit is marked in the A-text (l. A37 S.D.).

2000-01 (A42-43) Cf. ll. 2054 (A84), 2070-71. Louis' invasion in 1216 was actually instigated by the English barons, who elected him as their king. See Roger of Wendover, II, 172-174; the Tewkesbury, Waverley, and Dunstable annals (*Ann. mon.*, I, 62; II, 283; III, 45); etc. Stephen Langton is here acting more in accordance with his undisguised condition as the embodiment of sedition than as the historical archbishop.

2002 *tryckes*. A blot in the manuscript has obscured some letters of this word; *yende* in l. 2004 has been more seriously damaged and *myende* in l. 2005 almost totally obliterated. See Appendix C.

2003 *searche*: 'to produce pain by piercing or penetrating' (see *EDD*, *search*, 3).

quyckes. *OED* cites this example as an adjective used substantively, referring to the tender, sensitive, or vital parts; Creeth's gloss ("quick grass, fields") fits the context less convincingly.

2005 S.D. (A45 S.D.) The Cardinal's exit is not marked in the B-text, although it is in the A-text. The A-text breaks off before Nobility returns (cf. l. 2213 S.D.). See Intro., p. 6.

[Scene iv (ll. 2006-2192)]

The action of this scene is not localized beyond an implied setting in England. The single event represented is John's poisoning, which according to most of those authorities who mention poisoning at all took place at Swineshead Abbey in October 1216. The references to Louis' invasion (ll. 2054, 2070-71) and the legate Gualo (ll. 2068-69, 2082) harmonize well enough with this historical setting.

John's death represents a distinct departure from the conventions of the English morality. It is not simply an expression of a *memento mori* sentiment, or the inevitable antecedent to judgment, as it is in some traditional moralities. Nor is it in any sense retribution for sin or folly, as it is in some later and degenerate examples of the type (see Willard Farnham, *The Medieval Heritage of Elizabethan Tragedy* [Berkeley, 1936], Ch. vi). It is essentially a martyr's death, only with the emphasis less on eternal reward than on a tragic recognition of human evil (see especially ll. 2167 ff.).

2010 (A50) *poyson of a toade*. The toad is a standard feature of the poisoning narrative in the prose Brut tradition, although in some manuscripts of the *Eulogium* (see III, xi, n. 2) an owl ("bubo") replaces the toad ("bufo"). In the English prose Brut (see Intro., p. 34) the monk apparently stabs the toad with his "broche"; in the *Eulogium* (III, 110) he causes the animal to vomit forth its poison by irritating it with a small knife ("cum cultello suo"). Foxe (1563) includes a woodcut after fol. 68 (reproduced in Pollard after p. 150), which seems to represent the monk with a knife, although his actions are not perfectly clear. The same cut with a slightly different legend appears in the 1576 edition of Foxe, facing I, 260. Cf. Grafton, II, 115-116, and *Tr. Reign*, II.viii.39.

2011 Elson, p. 193, sees a significant parallel with *Tr. Reign*, II.vi.144: "For now my Lord I goe about my worke."

2017-49 In hearing Dissimulation's "confession," Sedition here corresponds to the "historical" abbot of Swineshead (see Intro., p. 34).

2023 Cf. A63 and see Intro., pp. 33-34. The A- and B-text differ in their figures regarding John's inflationary designs, and neither text agrees completely with any of the earlier versions. In the English prose Brut and in John Major's *Historia Maioris Britanniae* ([Paris], 1521), fol. 56ᵛ, John says he will raise the price of a halfpenny loaf of bread to twenty shillings; in the *Eulogium* (II, 109), he says that the price of a one-pound loaf will go up from less than a halfpenny to a pound of silver. According to other accounts he promises to raise the price of a halfpenny loaf either to twelve *denarii* (Higden, VIII, 196) or twelve *oboli* (*The Chronicle of Walter of Guisborough*, ed. Harry Rothwell [London, 1957], p. 155). *An Anonymous Short English Metrical Chronicle*, ed. Ewald Zettl, EETS, OS 196 (London, 1935), p. 41, presents the king's plans in somewhat different terms: John vows "To fede al Engelond with a spaud / & eke with a wyuys lof" (ll. 971-972).

2026 *great*: interlined above an original *foule*, which has not been deleted. Bale's metrical practice indicates that he did not intend both words to stand in the finished text. See Intro., pp. 49-51.

2032 *stacker in the plashes*: literally, 'stagger in the puddles,' or possibly 'in the bushes.'

2037 *yewle*: a form of *yawl* (note the rhyme), related to *waul* 'to cry out.'

2038 *And grunt . . . placebo*. Creeth takes *pace* as the ablative of *pax* and explains *pace placebo* as a confused running together of the liturgical formula *requiescat in pace* and the opening of the office of the dead (*placebo Domino in regione vivorum*). It seems more likely, however, that *pace* is the English noun, and that *a good pace* is an adverbial phrase modifying *grunt* (cf. Modern English *apace* and see *OED, a*, prep. 9, and *pace*, sb. 4, for the analogous formations "a great speed," "a great pas," etc.).

2044 *father Symon*. Cf. l. 2102, and see Intro., p. 35.

A79 S.D. *and kyng Iohn cum in*: added by the scribe in revision. Cf. l. 2049 S.D.

2058 Collier and Farmer place a period after *els* and read ll. 2057-58 with the two preceding lines. Both the verse form and syntax, however, argue for a break after l. 2056.

2062 *Both my crowne*. Bale's slip is a clear sign of transcription (cf. ll. 2063, A93).

A95 *entendyng*: *t* doubtful, but correction of A-text *enbendyng* clearly by Bale.

2069 *Gualo*. Cf. the English prose Brut (ed. Brie, I, 169): "And in þe same tyme þe Pope sent into Englond a legate þat me callede Swalo, and he was prest Cardinal of Rome, forto mayntene Kyng Iohnes cause aʒeynʒ þe barons of Engeland. . . ." The activities of this legate, Guala Bicchieri, are explained more fully in the monastic chronicles. His mission was clearly to support John, the sworn liegeman of the pope, against Louis and the barons. As England reports below (l. 2073), he *openly accursed* the opponents of the king. See the full account in Roger of Wendover, II, 176-179, 181-182, who makes it clear that John actually welcomed the intervention of the legate. See also *Ann. mon.*, I, 62 (Tewkesbury); II, 284 (Waverley); IV, 406 (Worcester); Ralph of Coggeshall, p. 184; and Henry Richards Luard's preface, Paris' *Chronica*, VII, xxi.

2070-71 For Louis' itinerary during the invasion of 1216 see the English prose Brut (ed. Brie, I, 168); the account in Norgate, pp. 269-276, is even more detailed. See also James Clarke Holt, *The Northerners: A Study in the Reign of King John* (Oxford, 1961), pp. 135-142. All these, as well as the majority of monastic chroniclers, agree that Louis took (*inter alia*) Rochester, London, and Winchester, but none includes Reading and Windsor among Louis' conquests. Windsor, in fact, held out quite successfully against the French: see Roger of Wendover, II, 191-193; Dunstable annals (*Ann. mon.*, III, 47); Ralph of Coggeshall, pp. 182-183.

2076 *Otto the emproure.* Otto's excommunication in 1210 is mentioned in virtually all the English monastic chronicles, but only in the Burton annals (*Ann. mon.*, I, 215) is there a significant comparison with John's situation: John says to Pandulf, "Creditis me sic subicere vobis, sicut nepotem meum Othonem imperatorem? Ego enim ab ipso recepi, quod alium fecistis eligere imperatorem in Alemannia," to which Pandulf replies, "Verum est. Et credit dominus Papa, et certus est, se ita istum facere imperatorem, sicut fecit alium; et sic te subicere sibi, ut fecit alium." This passage is omitted from the Waverley annals, which are otherwise very close to the Burton annals.

2077 *Phylypp.* In 1200 the French king suffered ecclesiastical censure not unlike John's, but Bale seems to be referring here to Philip's siding with the pope against the excommunicated English king. See note to ll. 1372-73.

2086-91 (cf. A98-100) Opposite the three lines of Dissimulation's song in the A-text Bale has written *out of the mylke payle / as whyte as my nayle / with partryche and rayle*, with *my* interlined. All six lines were eventually copied into the rewritten B-text.

2089 *rayle*: a kind of small wading bird.

2099 *louynge.* Bale first interlined *gentle* above his original *louynge*, then reconsidered and deleted the interlined word. Cf. l. A108 (*lovyng*).

2103 (A111) *monastycall deuocyon.* See l. 1136 and note.

2105 *hearde*: a smudged, doubtful.

2106 *In dede I wolde gladly drynke.* Elson, p. 194, sees a significant parallel with *Tr. Reign*, II.vi.100 (the king "will to meate"), and II.viii.1 ("the King desires to eate").

2107 (A115) Cf. the English prose Brut (quoted in Intro., p. 34): "Wassaile! for neuer, dayes of ʒour lyue, dranke ʒe of soche a coppe."

2115 *suppe*: *s* perhaps altered from *d*.

2120 *conueye me that.* Bale seems to have copied the uncorrected A-text line (see l. A124 and text. note) before deciding on the present wording.

2123 (cf. A126) *farmerye.* Cf. the English prose Brut (quoted in Intro., p. 34), where the word is *fermory*. The corresponding passage in the *Eulogium* (III, 110) reads "Monachus infirmariæ adiens. . . ."

2128 *a masse of Scala Celi.* See l. 423 and note.

2131 *gyldar*: either a coin or the person to do the gilding.

2132 *Thomas of Canterberye.* Elson, p. 194, suggests that the author of *Tr. Reign* may have derived the name "Thomas" for his poisoner from this comment by Dissimulation. He also sees a significant parallel with Dissimulation in Thomas' desire to be "canonizd for a holy Saint" (II.vi.95).

2138 *tympanye*: any morbid swelling produced by gas or air, especially one in the intestines. Cf. l. A131, where John fears *þe collyck*.

2167 *thirsted ryghteousnesse.* Manly suggests supplying *for*, as in the modern idiom, but cf. the Wyclif translation of Matt. v.6 "Blessid ben thei that hungren and thristen riȝtwisnesse. . . ." See also *OED, thirst,* for numerous sixteenth-century examples of the same locution.

2172 *good people.* See l. 770 and note.

2189-90 Cf. Simon Fish, *A Supplication for the Beggars*, ed. Edward Arber (London, 1880), p. 6 (addressing Henry on the interdict imposed during John's reign): "For the whiche mater your most nobill realme wrongfully (alas for shame) hath stond tributary (not vnto any kind temporall prince, but vnto a cruell deuelisshe bloudsupper dronken in the bloude of the sayntes and marters of christ) euersins." The ultimate source of the image is Apoc. xvii.6, which Tyndale translates "And I sawe the wyfe dronke with the bloud of saynctes, and with the bloud of the witnesses (*martyrum*) of Iesu." Bale and Fish agree in the more common English translation of *martyrum* (μαρτύρων) as *martyrs*.

2192 S.D. Farmer has Nobility, Clergy, and Civil Order enter here with Verity; an entrance after l. 2213 is possible if, as seems likely, the *fryndes* of l. 2193 are the members of the audience (see l. 770 and note).

[Scene v (ll. 2193-2649)]

In this final scene the setting changes without warning from thirteenth- to sixteenth-century England. In his *Pammachius* Kirchmeyer employs a similar device with somewhat more skill: up through IV.iii the action is set in the reign of the Emperor Julian; but in IV.iv (ll. 3177 ff.) Dromo must awaken Satan, Pammachius, and their adherents from the stupor following "yesterday's" carousals ("Quam graviter queunt / Hesternam prorsus crapulam destertere!" [ll. 3195-96]) to report that the "new doctor" (l. 3203) Theophilus (i.e., Luther), with the assistance of Veritas and Paul, has begun to rouse the German people against papal doctrines.

Bale's Verity represents the Reformation generally; his Imperial

Majesty, the champion of political independence of the papacy, is obviously Henry VIII. Nobility, Clergy, Civil Order, and Sedition (in his undisguised condition) are the only characters held over from the previous scenes.

In terms of dramatic structure, this scene presents the final movement of the tripartite protagonist—a sudden "conversion" leading to a state of "regeneration." As in the traditional morality, conversion entails repentance, but without the doctrinal and ritualistic elements of the Catholic penitential system (see ll. 2306 ff., 2329 ff.).

2195 *Polydorus*. See Intro., pp. 29-30.

2198-99 John Leland was insane from 1546 until his death in 1552, and it is to his condition during these years that Bale is probably alluding. See Intro., p. 23, and Pafford and Greg, pp. xv-xvi.

2198 *out of thy slumbre awake*. Bale's anticipation of the following line proves that he was transcribing, perhaps from one of the lost leaves of the scribal copy.

2201-04 *Sigebertus*. See *Continuatio auctorium mortui maris*, ed. Louis Conrad Bethmann, in *Monumenta Germania historica: scriptores*, VI (Hannoverae, 1844), 466 (*sub anno* 1209), and 467 (*sub anno* 1214). This is the only continuation of Sigebert of Gemblours that Bale shows any sign of having known (see his reference to "Additiones Sigeberti" in the *Index*, p. 386).

Vincentius: evidently Vincent of Beauvais (see Intro., p. 29), whose *Speculum historiale* (Venice, 1494) is cited as an authority by Bale in the *Catalogus*, II, sig. B1^v. Other writers by this name certainly or probably known to Bale do not treat King John (see, e.g., the *Index*, p. 462, and the *Catalogus*, I, 300, for references to Vincent of Coventry, the first Franciscan at Cambridge). The *Narratio historica vicissitudinis, rerum quae in inclyto Britanniae regno acciderunt, anno Domini 1553* ([Wittenberg], 1553) by Peter Vincentius (or Vietz) and the same author's *Vera nobilitas* (Rostock, 1553) are also irrelevant.

Nauclerus. For John Nauclerus' brief comments on King John, see his *Memorabilium omnis aetatis et omnium gentium chronici commentarii*, 2 vols. in 1 (Tübingen, 1516), II, fol. 206 (*Generatio* xli). This seems to have been a popular work with early English reformers because of its harsh criticism of abuses among the Roman clergy; see, e.g., *The Works of James Pilkington, B.D., Lord Bishop of Durham*, ed. James Scholefield (Cambridge, Eng., 1842), p. 509.

Paulus Phrigio. See his summary treatment of John in his *Chronicorum regum regnorumque omnium catalogum* (Basle, 1534), pp. 460-463, admittedly drawn from Polydore Vergil.

Verity's other authorities are treated in the Intro., pp. 27-30, and in Appendix B.

2202 *with . . . take*. See l. 1560 and note.

2214-16 The charter by which John in 1215 granted the citizens of London the right to elect annually their own mayor (but not sheriffs) is printed in William Stubbs, *Select Charters and Other Illustrations of English Constitutional History, from the Earliest Times to the Reign of Edward the First*, 8th ed. (Oxford, 1900), pp. 314-315. According to Frederick Maurice Powicke, in *Cambridge Medieval History*, VI (Cambridge, 1929), 245, John's purpose in granting this concession was to placate the city in anticipation of the barons' uprising. Actually London had had a mayor from at least 1193 (see Roger of Hoveden's *Chronica*, ed. William Stubbs [Rolls Series 51], III, 212, and the "unique document" cited by J. H. Round, *The Commune of London and Other Studies* [Westminster, 1899], pp. 235-237); only the right to elect this official was granted in 1215.

Bale's source of information was undoubtedly one of the many "London Chronicles" or their imitations, which usually assign the creation of the office to the year 1208, and sometimes imply that the sheriffs were created along with the mayor. See, e.g., *The Great Chronicle of London*, ed. Arthur Hermann Thomas and I. D. Thornley (London, 1938), p. 4: the entry for 1208 concludes with the note that "Alle these men before writen were but Baillifs and wardeyns of the Cite of London," and the entry for the following year begins, "Here begynneth the names of the first Maires and Shreves of london." See also William Gregory's "Chronicle of London," in *The Historical Collections of a Citizen of London in the Fifteenth Century*, ed. James Gairdner (Westminster, 1876), p. 59; Fabyan, p. 318; Grafton, II, 115; John Rastell, *The Pastime of the People* (London, 1811), p. 177; and cf. Foxe (1570), I, 336, and Holinshed, II, 298.

2214 *premye*: a 'prize' or 'gift,' from the Latin *praemium*. *OED* cites only two occurrences of this word, both in Bale's works.

2217 According to the London Chronicles, the old wooden bridge was rebuilt in stone during John's reign; all those sources cited in the second paragraph of the note to ll. 2214-16 treat this event together with the London charter. See in addition *A Chronicle of London from 1089 to 1483* [ed. Sir Nicholas H. Nicolas and Edward Tyrrell] (London, 1827), p. 7. This last and *The Great Chronicle* have misleading marginal summaries implying that the bridge was first built during John's reign; cf. Foxe (1570), I, 336: "In the raigne of this kyng Iohn

... the bridge of London was first builded of stone: which before was of woode."

2220 The Jews were not expelled from England until 1290, long after John's death; see the statements of various monastic chroniclers in *Ann. mon.*, II, 409; III, 361-362, 467; IV, 326-327, 503; etc. Bale may have in mind one of the several reports of John's cruelty in extorting money from the Jews. Norgate, p. 137, repeats one of the more sensational of these. But it is possible that he was relying on the *Eulogium*, III, 96, which notes briefly that in 1210 many English Jews were expelled from the country after their goods had been confiscated.

2227-30 Eccles. x.20. Also quoted by John above, ll. 1404-07.

2231-32 The idea has not been discovered in Jerome's works.

2237-38 Cf. Prov. xvi.10 and ll. 1342-43.

2243-44 Prov. xxii.11.

2249-50 See Acts i.26.

2251-53 See Aristotle's *Historia animalium* ($605^b.11$): "In bee-hives are found creatures that do great damage to the combs; for instance, the grub that spins a web and ruins the honey-comb: it is called the 'cleros.'" (*The Works of Aristotle Translated into English*, ed. John Alexander Smith and W. D. Ross [Oxford, 1910], IV.)

2258 *mare*: interlined above *yche*, which has not been deleted. Neither *mare* 'more'(?) nor *yche* 'each'(?) makes very good sense; the meter of the line suggests that only one word should stand.

2259-60 Perhaps an allusion to Socrates' argument in the *Republic* I.343 *A*-347 *E* (cf. VI.502 *C*), or to the summary statement of it (as the first of "Plato's rules") in Cicero's *De officiis* I.xxv. The Ciceronian version is included in the influential moral treatise by William de Conches (ed. John Holmberg [Uppsala, 1929], p. 36), which Bale seems to have known. See his *Index*, p. 122.

2259 *thought alwayes that no*. Bale's correction has partly obscured the first two words of the b-reading.

2262 See Judges iii.12-30.

2263-64 See Ezra (I Esdras) 7 ff.

2268-70 See Mantuan's ninth eclogue, ll. 141 ff.

2273-74 See Chrysostom's homily on Priscilla and Aquila and his commentary on Isaiah (*Patrologia Graeca*, Vol. LI, col. 190 and Vol. LVI, col. 15). Chrysostom is speaking not of "friends" in the modern sense but of family or ancestry (cf. *OED, friend*, 3).

2279-80 Cf. Seneca's *Epistulae morales* LXXXIII.

2291-94 II Kings i.2-16 (Vulgate). See below, ll. 2366-86 and note.

2300 *hatefull*: interlined above *odyouse*, either as an alternative or a substitute; neither word has been deleted.

2301-02 The reference has not been explained.

2303 "Probably a reference to stained-glass windows showing the punishment accorded to evil kings at the Last Judgment" (Creeth).

2329 See l. 506 S.D. and note.

2350-57 Cf. Rom. xiii.1-2 and see l. 1178 and note.

2366-86 Imperial Majesty's speech seems to be closely modeled on a passage in Tyndale's *Obedience*, fol. 31ʳ·ᵛ. Tyndale first relates David's killing of the man who claimed to have slain Saul (II Kings i.2-16), his execution of Isboseth's murderers (II Kings iv.5-12), and Christ's judgment on paying tribute to Caesar (Matt. xxii.15-22), and then concludes as follows: "Here by seist thou yᵗ yᵉ kinge is in this worlde without lawe & maye at his lust doo right or wronge and shall geve acomptes / but to God only. A nother conclusion is this / that no person nether anye degre maye be exempte from this ordinaunce of God. Nether can the profession of monkes and freres or anye thinge that the Pope or Bisshoppes can laie for themselves / excepte them from the swerde of the Emperoure or kinges / yf they breake the lawes."

2398 *slypper*: related to the verb *slip*; hence 'shifty,' 'unreliable,' 'deceitful.' Cf. Bale's *Image of Both Churches*, in *Select Works of John Bale*, ed. Henry Christmas (Cambridge, Eng., 1849), p. 479: "Only are the false prophets received and taken of the foolish, fantastical, and slipper-witted sort." See also *Three Laws*, l. 175.

2417-18 See Matt. xvi.17.

2432 Something possibly erased after *and*.

2457 Evidently the opening lines of a song. In the manuscript these words are written beneath the musical staff here reproduced.

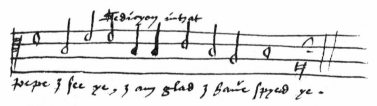

HM 3, folio 57. Upper section showing musical notation.

2470 *prate*: interlined above *saye*, which has not been deleted.

2499 Evidently Sedition, even without his historical disguise, is here thought of as a priest.

2500 The sense is that there is no confession which may properly conceal (*but ought to discouer*) treason.

2506 *Pasquyll. OED* (*pasquyl*, and cf. *pasquin*) cites an example of this word as applied to the author of satires or lampoons as early as 1533.

2508-09 *taught : laught.* See Wyld, *Studies in English Rhymes,* pp. 111-112, for similar rhymes from sixteenth-century poetry.

2514-15 These lines evidently refer to the uprising in the north of England in 1536. Pafford and Greg, p. xiv, argue that this couplet was included in the A-text and adopted by Bale in rewriting the lost leaves of the scribal manuscript, and that the following couplet, in which Sedition claims to have accomplished similar feats *sens that same tyme,* was added at the time of rewriting. Their purpose in proposing different dates of composition for the two couplets is to explain the apparent anachronism in referring to actions performed *now of late* and further actions performed *sens that same tyme.* It is clear, however, that the expression *now of late* has no very precise meaning and could have been used of events from the mid-1530's even as late as 1560. Cf. Bale's use of this and related expressions in ll. 930, 2285, 2580, 2626, 2670, and 2680.

2531 *sacramentaryes*: in sixteenth-century usage, a generic term for those who denied the doctrine of the Real Presence.

2532 Collier, Manly, and Farmer read the second half of this line with the following line.

2533 *proppe vp*: interlined above *helpe*, perhaps as an alternative; neither word has been deleted, but the meter requires only one.

2535 *marshall*: first *s* of b-reading touched up before being deleted.

2566 *paxe*: a piece of altar furniture; *osculatorium.* See William Maskell, *The Ancient Liturgy of the Church of England,* 3rd ed. (Oxford, 1882), pp. 170-173.

2607 *destytute*: "to make void, frustrate, defeat, disappoint" (*OED,* citing this example). The preterit form without *-ed* is unusual.

2616-17 Bale may have had in mind *Iliad* IV.129, V.185, VIII.311, or XX.430.

2626-31 The point of view here—with Imperial Majesty evidently unaware of Elizabeth's proclamation against the Anabaptists—is at odds with that of a later reference to the Anabaptists (see ll. 2680-81 and note). Of course insofar as Imperial Majesty represents Henry VIII, it is only proper that he not know of a proclamation issued thirteen years after his death, but it seems more likely that the two Anabaptist passages were composed at different times than that Bale was striving to avoid anachronism. See Intro., pp. 23-24.

2629 From February 1534 to June 1535 Münster existed as an Anabaptist community under the fanatic rule first of Jan Matthys and later of Jan Bockelson (John of Leyden).

2630 *begonne*: *o* smudged, perhaps altered from *u*.

[Epilogue (ll. 2650-91)]

The six rhyme-royal stanzas of the epilogue constitute a direct, non-dramatic address to the audience. The first three stanzas expound the exemplary value of the play; the last three offer a compliment to Elizabeth.

2659 Creeth puts a comma after *driftes* and glosses *traytery passes* as "treacherous devices." To make syntactical sense of the line, however, it is necessary to construe *traytery* as a noun (as in l. 1591), the object of *passes* 'surpasses,' 'exceeds.' The subject of *passes* is *driftes* 'schemes,' 'plots,' 'devices,' evidently thought of as a singular.

2680-81 These lines must have been written after September 22, 1560, the date of Elizabeth's proclamation threatening to imprison all Anabaptists who did not leave the country within twenty days. See *Calendar of State Papers, Domestic Series*, ed. Robert Lemon (London, 1856), p. 158, and *A Bibliography of Royal Proclamations of the Tudor and Stuart Sovereigns*, ed. Robert Steele (Oxford, 1910), I, 56 (No. 529). Similar proclamations had been issued by Henry, perhaps as early as 1530 (John Strype, *Memorials of . . . Archbishop Cranmer*, I [Oxford, 1848], 411-412), certainly in 1535 and 1538 (*Tudor Royal Proclamations*, ed. Paul L. Hughes and James F. Larkin, I [New Haven, 1964], Nos. 155, 186). But Imperial Majesty's earlier reference to the Anabaptists (ll. 2626-31) as a sect which should be but has not yet been suppressed proves that Bale, when writing this passage, thought of these proclamations as no longer in force; in fact they seem to have been revoked by Henry's proclamation of February 26, 1538/9 (Hughes and Larkin, No. 188).

2690 *hir*. Bale apparently began to write *the queens* before deciding on the present reading.

2691 Below this line is written *Pretium xx*^{s}, in an ink very similar to that used by Bale (cf. Pafford and Greg). The hand does not resemble any other that appears in the manuscript.

The two "playes" of the explicit is evidently a reference to the two-act structure introduced by Bale in preparing the B-text. For a different interpretation, see Intro., p. 22, n. 11.

APPENDIX A

(See Introduction, p. 69.)

S. Lang. I passe not on yt now þat ye are amendyd. (p *1[c], fol. 21)
Eng. Ser, yender is a clarke which ys condempnyd for treason.
    Þe sreyves wold fayne know what to do with hym this season.
K. John. For so moch as he hath falsefyed owr coyne,
A5   As he is worthy late hym with a halter ioyne.
    Card. What, styll agaynst þe chirch? Get me bocke, bell and candell,
    And as I am trew prist I shall yow yet better handell.
    Remember ye not how ye vsed Peter Pvnfret,   (p. *2, fol. 21ᵛ)
    A good symple man, and as they say, a prophet?
A10   *K. John.* I ded prove hym, ser, a verye supersticyose wreche.
    S. Lang. He prophesyed of yow, and therfor ye ded hym vp streche.
    Ded he any more than call yow a deuyll incarnate?
    K. John. Yes, he toke vppon hym my yeares to predestynate.
    Well, as for this man, be cawse þat he is a prist
A15   I geve hym to yow; do with hym what ye lyst.
    Card. Than forth and byd them to set hym at lyberte.
    Eng. I shall be full glad to do as ye commavnd me.
    Card. Ere I releace yow of the interdiccyon here,
    In þe whych yowr realme contynewed hath this vij yere,
A20   Ye shall make Ivlyane, yowr syster in law, this bonde,
    To geve hyr the thyrd parte of Ynglond and of ȝerlond.
    K. John. Oh, ye vndo me vpp, consyderyng my great paymentes.
    Eng. Ser, dyscomfort not, for God hath sett debaytementes.
    The woman ys ded; soch tydynges is hether browght.
                        Go owt Ynglond
                and dresse for Dyssymvlacyon.
A25   *K. John.* Oh lord, for me, wreche, what a myracle hast þou wrowght!
    Lyke as Dauid sayth, þou dost not leue þat servont
    That wyll trust in the or in thy blessed covenant.
    Card. Than I here releace yow of þe interdiccyons all,
    Straytly chargyng yow vppon danger þat may fall

A1 *Cf. 1804.*
A2-3 *Cf. 1807-08.*
A4-5 *Cf. 1871-72.*
A6-7 *Cf. 1875-76.*
A8-13 *Cf. 1883-89.*
A12 *Cf. 1908.*
A14-17 *Cf. 1910-15.*

A18-21 *Cf. 1941-44.*
A21 & of ȝerlond] *b;* & ȝerlond *A.*
A22-23 *Cf. 1949-50.*
A24-25 *Cf. 1953-54.*
A26-27 *Cf. 1957-58.*
A28-35 *Cf. 1967-74.*

A30 No more to meddle with þe chyrchis reformacyon,
   Nor kepe them from Rome for any appellacyon,
   By God and by all þe contentes in this boke.
  K. John. Ageynst holy churche I wyll nowther speke nor loke.
  S. Lang. Opyn the churche dorys and let þe belles be ronge,

A35 And throwgh owt þe realme se þat *Te Devm* be songe.
  Card. Go yowr wayes apace and see that yt be done.
  K. John. At yowr commaundement yt shall be performyde sone.

           Here go owt þe kyng.

  Card. By the messe, I lawght to se this clene convayance!
  He is now full glad as owr pype gothe to daunce.

A40 *S. Lang.* I promyse the suer; yet wyll I not leve hym soo.
  Card. Why, felow Sedycyon, with hym what wylte þou doo?
  S. Lang. Mary, feche yn Lewes, kyng Philyppes son in Fraunce,
   To fall vppon hym with his men and ordynaunce.
  I wyll not leve hym tell I bryng hym to his ende.

A45 *Card.* Well, God be with the. Do as shall lye in þi mend.

          Here þe cardynall go owt
           and dresse for Nobelyte.

  S. Lang. I mervell greatly wher Dyssymylacyon ys.
  Diss. I wyll cum anone yf thow tary whyll I pysse.

      [*Enter Dissimulation.*]

  S. Lang. I beshrow yowr hart! Wher haue ye ben so longe?
  Diss. In þe gardyn, man, þe herbysse and wedes amonge,

A50 And ther haue I gott þe poysson of a toode.
  I hope at þe last to worke sum myscheffe abroode.
  S. Lang. I was wonte sumtyme of þi secrett cownsell (p. *3, fol. 22)
   to be.
  Am I now a dayes becum a strangere to the?
  Diss. I wyll tell the all vndernethe *Benedicite,*

A55 What I mynd to do in cace þou wylt asoyle me.
  S. Lang. Thow shalt be assoylyd by the popys avctoryte.
  Diss. Shall I so in dede? Be þe messe, than, haue at the!
   Benedicite.
  S. Lang. Dominus. In nomine domini pape, amen.

A60 *Diss.* Syr, this is my mende: I wyll geve kyng Iohn this poyson
   And make hym suer that he shall neuer haue good foyson.
   And this mvst thow say to colure with the thyng,
   That he wold haue mad a loffe worthe xx shelyng.

A36-39 *Cf. 1982-85.*   A40-43 *Cf. 1998-2001.*
A36 & see that] *b*; & that *A.*   A44-65 *Cf. 2004-25.*

S. Lang. Nay, þat is soch a lye as esly maye be felt.

A65   *Diss.* Tushe, man, among folys yt shall neuer be owt smelt.

S. Lang. I am swer than þou wylt geve hym yt in a drynke.

Diss. Mary, þat I wyll, and þe ton halfe with hym swynke

    To corage hym to drynke the botome off.

S. Lang. Yf thow serve hym so þou shalt knavyshly with hym scoffe.

A70   Thyn owne carkas than ys lyke to suffer lasshes.

Diss. Tush! What thow I dye, man, þer shall rysse more of myn asshes.

    I am suer the prystes wyll pray for me so bytterlye

    That I shall not cum in hell nor in purgatory.

S. Lang. Nay, to kepe the from thens þou shalt haue .v. monkes

      synggyng

A75   In Swynshed abbey so long as þe world ys dwryng.

Diss. Whan the world ys done what helpe shall I haue than?

S. Lang. Than shyft for þi selfe so well as euer thow can.

Diss. Cockes sowle, he commyth here! Asoyle me þat I were gon then.

S. Lang. *Ego absolvo te in nomine domini pape, amen.*

                Here go owt Dissimylacyon and
                Stevyn Langton together, and
                kyng Iohn cum in [*with England*].

A80   *K. John.* No prince in þe world in soche captyvyte

    As I am this hower, and all for ryghtosnes.

    Agenst me I haue both the lordes and commynnalte,

    Bysshoppes and lawers, whych in ther cruell madnes

    Hathe browʒt in hyther þe french kynges fyrst son, Lewes.

A85   The chance vnto me ys not so dolorowsse,

    But my lyfe this howr ys moche more tedyowse.

    More of compassyon for shedyng of Christen blood

    Than anye thyng els, my crowne I gave vp lately

    To þe pope of Rome, whych hath no tyttle good

A90   Of ivrysdycion, but vsurpacyon onlye.

    And now to þe, lord, I wold resygne vpp gladlye

    Bothe my crowne and lyfe; for thyne owne ryght it ys,

    Yf yt wold please the, to take my sowle to þi blys.

Eng. Sur, dyscomfort not; in the honore of Christ Iesu

A66-73 *Cf. 2028-35.*   A82 both the lord*es*] *b*; both lord*es*
A74-75 *Cf. 2042-43.*   *A.*
A76-97 *Cf. 2046-67.*   A90 ivrysdycion] *ed.*; ivrysdyccon
                                       A.

A95 God wyll neuer fayle yow, entendyng not els but vertv.
 K.John. The anguysh of spyrytt so pangeth me euery wher
  That incessantlye I thyrst tyll I be ther.
 Diss. (syng this) Wassayle, wassayle, in snowe, frost (p. *4, fol. 22ᵛ)
  and hayle,
  Wassayle, wassayle, that moch dothe avayle,
A100 Wassayle, wassayle, that neuer wyll fayle.
 K.John. Who is that, Ynglond? I pray the stepe forth and se.
 Eng. He doth seme afarre of sum relygyose mann to be.
    [*Enter Dissimulation.*]
 Diss. Now Iesus preserve your worthy excelent grace,
  For dowtles ther is a very angelycke face.
A105 Now for sothe and God, I wold thynk my selfe in hevyn
  Yf I myght remayn with yow but yeres alevyn;
  I wold covyt here non other felycyte.
 K.John. A lovyng person thow shuldest seme for to be.
 Diss. I am as ientell a worme as euer yow dyd se.
A110 *K.John.* But what is thy name? I besych the hartyly, shew me.
 Diss. My name ys callyd monastycall devocyon.
  Here haue I browt yow a very helsum porsheon,
  For I hard yow say that ye were very drye.
 K.John. In dede I am thyrstye. I pray the, good monke, cum nygh.
A115 *Diss.* The dayes of yowr lyfe neuer felt yow such a cuppe,
  So good and holsum yf ye wold drynke yt vppe.
  Yt passyth mavmsey, capryke, tyrre or ypocras.
  Be my fayth, I trow suche a drynke neuer was.
 K.John. Begynne, gentyll monke; I praye þe drynk halfe to me.
A120 *Diss.* Yf ye wold drynke all yt ware the better for ye.
 K.John. Nay, thow shalt drynke halfe. Ther is no remedy.
 Diss. Good lucke to yow than. Haue at yt evyn harttely!
 K.John. God seynt the, good monke, with all my very hart.
        Drynke to þe kyng.
 Diss. Loo, I haue dronk yow halfe, now drynke yow owt that part.
A125 Where art thow, Sedycyon? I dye! I dye, man, I dye!
    [*Enter Sedition.*]
 Sed. Cum of apace, than, and gett þe to the farmary.

A95 entendyng] *b;* enbendyng *A.*＊ A123 S.D. kyng] *ed.;* kng *A.*
A98-110 *Cf.* 2086-2101.＊   A124 drynke yow owt that part] *b;*
A111-120 *Cf.* 2103-12.   drynke owt that *A.*
A121-122 *Cf.* 2116-17.   A126-130 *Cf.* 2123-27.
A123-125 *Cf.* 2119-21.

    I haue provyded for the, be swet saynt Powle,

    .v. monkes þat shall syng perpetualy for þi sowle,

    That I warant the thow shalt neuer cum in hell.

Here haue hym owt of the place.

A130   *Diss.* To send me to hevyn, I pray þe go ryng þe holy bell.

    K. John. My body sore grogeth; of þe collyck I am afrayed.

    Eng. Alas, sur, alas! I fere þat ye are betrayed.

    K. John. Why, where is the monke þat dranke with me here lately?

    Eng. He is poysond, ser, and lyeth a dyyng, suerly.

A135   *K. John.* What? Yt is not so, for he was with me here now.

    Eng. Dowȝtles yt is so trew as I haue told yow.

    K. John. Ther is no malyce to the malyce of þe clargy.

    Well, þe swete lord of hevyn on me and them haue marcy.

    For ryghtosnes sake they haue euer hated me.

A140   They cavsyd my londe to be excommynycate

    .   .   .   .

A131-136 *Cf. 2138-43.*   A137-140 *Cf. 2158-61.*

APPENDIX B

(See line 2202)

APPARENTLY Bale knew almost nothing about the works of Matthew
Paris until some years after the composition of the A-text of *King Johan*.
In the *Summarium* of 1548, his earliest published catalog of British
writers, he does include a brief notice of Paris' life together with two
titles ("Antiquitates fani Albani" and "Gesta Anglorum"), but all of
his information was admittedly drawn from Leland; even the apology
for his ignorance seems to have been borrowed from Leland.[1] The
earliest reference to Paris in the *Index*, drawn *"Ex Bostoni Buriensis
catalogo,"* is similarly vague and reveals the same lack of familiarity
with the works mentioned.[2] In the continuation of the *Catalogus*
(1559), however, Bale notes that one of the many works which he had
been forced to leave behind him when he fled Ireland six years earlier
was Matthew Paris' "ingens Chronicorum opus."[3] This is undoubtedly
the work cited by Bale in a letter to Archbishop Parker as "Chronica
Matthaei Parys"[4] and, again, in a later entry in the *Index* as a chronicle from the Conquest plus a continuation, nine books in all.[5] It would
seem, then, that Bale's study of Paris dates from the period of his Irish
residence, or at least not much before this period. In any case, there is
no doubt that he studied his copy of Paris closely and received it
favorably.

But which of Paris' works did Bale study? We now know that
Matthew Paris was only one of a series of chroniclers attached to the
monastery of St. Albans and that his best-known work, the *Chronica
majora*, is to a great extent a compilation from the work of his predecessors. In fact, only the portion of the *Chronica* covering the years
1236-1259 is exclusively his; for the reign of King John (1199-1216) it
is essentially the work of Roger of Wendover, corrected and occasionally augmented.[6] The *Historia Anglorum* (the so-called "Minor
Chronicle"), on the other hand, although sometimes considered a
redaction or abridgment of the *Chronica*, has the qualities of a more

[1] Fol. 143ᵛ. Cf. John Leland, *Commentarii de scriptoribus Britannicis*, ed. Anthony Hall (Oxonii, 1709), pp. 269-271.

[2] Page 289.

[3] II, 160.

[4] "A Letter from Bishop Bale to Archbishop Parker, Communicated by the Rev.
H. R. Luard," *Cambridge Antiquarian Communications*, III (1879), 172.

[5] Page 290.

[6] Paris, *Chronica*, VII, xii; Richard Vaughan, *Matthew Paris* (Cambridge, Eng.,
1958), Ch. ii.

or less independent treatise based on the materials in the earlier work.[7] Bale was very poorly informed as to the nature of these works, however, and consequently it is necessary to treat his citations and references with caution.

Bale's fullest account of Paris, that in the *Catalogus*, shows his acquaintance with two works: "Histories from the Conquest" in eight books, and "Continuations of the Histories" in one book. The first is described as covering events from the Conquest to 1251, the second as extending the original for about nine years (". . . continuationes nouem ferè annorum . . . annexuit") and adding certain "appendices addimentorum."[8]

In most respects Bale's description indicates that he is here dealing with the *Historia*. The *incipit* to the original "Histories," for example, is given as "De chronographia locuturi primo," which agrees substantially with the opening words of Paris' Prologue to the *Historia*: "De chronographia, id est temporum descriptione locuturi, primo. . . ."[9] According to the *Catalogus*, the second work, the "Continuations" from 1251, begins "Dominus rex fuit apud Vuinton." Fortunately there is a fuller *incipit* for this work in the *Index*: "Dominus rex fuit apud Wyntoniam ad natale, A.D. 1251, qui est annus regni."[10] Again Bale's description agrees with the *Historia*, which Paris originally brought to a close after completing his account of the year 1250, only to continue the work at a later date, beginning his continuation with a notice of the king's presence at Winchester during the Christmas season of 1251.[11] The continuation that Bale describes, however, extends to about 1260 ("nouem ferè annorum"), whereas the continuation of the *Historia* concludes at 1253. In this last particular, then, there is reason to doubt that Bale is in fact describing the *Historia*.

Actually, it appears that Bale was describing a manuscript which contained both the *Historia* and its continuation (1067-1253), as well as the final segment of the *Chronica* (1254-1259), and, failing to see the proper disposition of its parts, surmised that he was dealing with a single work whose composition had been interrupted with the narrative of events belonging to 1250. This manuscript was undoubtedly Brit. Mus. Royal MS. 14. C. vii, the only manuscript containing the complete *Historia* and the only one which preserves the 1254-1259 sec-

[7] Thomas Duffus Hardy, *Descriptive Catalogue* . . . , Rolls Series 26, III (London, 1871), 135; cf. Paris, *Historia*, I, xxii.

[8] I, 315.

[9] I, 3.

[10] Page 290.

[11] "Hic terminantur fratris Mathei Parisiensis, monachi Sancti Albani cronica" (III, 96).

tion of the *Chronica*.[12] Bale's familiarity with this particular version of Matthew Paris is suggested by his comment in the letter to Archbishop Parker mentioned above that the only manuscript of Paris with which he was acquainted had previously formed part of the "quenes majestyes lybrary,"[13] as well as a late entry in the *Index* which locates Paris' "History" (eight books) and "Continuations" (one book) in the royal library (*"Ex bibliotheca domini regis"*).[14]

Probably Bale knew no more of the *Chronica majora* than the 1254-1259 continuation in Royal MS. 14. C. vii. Several times he refers to a "Chronica maiora D. Albani" and its companion piece, the "Additamenta chronica," as among the works of Paris, but since he never provides *incipits* for these works, it is likely that he derived the titles from some earlier catalog, or even from references in the *Historia* itself.[15] In any case, when Bale cites Matthew Paris in connection with King John's reign, it is to the *Historia* rather than the *Chronica* that he is referring, as can be seen by comparing the following three passages from the *Catalogus* with their possible sources in Paris.

First of all, there are the accounts of certain unspecified spectacular events connected with John's birth and baptism:

Catalogus (I, 208):

Eodem anno [1166] (inquit Matthæus Parisius) Ioannes regis filius nascitur: de quo cum adhuc esset in utero matris, & cum baptizaretur, mira, sed relatu indigna prognostica euenisse referuntur.

Chronica (II, 234):

Eodem anno [1166] Alienor Anglorum regina peperit filium, et vocatus est Johannes.[16]

Historia (I, 340):

Anno sub eodem [1166] Alienora, Anglorum regina, peperit filium, et vocatus est Johannes. De quo, cum adhuc esset in ventre matris suae, et cum baptizaretur, mira sed relatu indigna pronostica evenisse referuntur.

---

[12] See George F. Warner and Julius P. Gilson, *Catalogue of Western Manuscripts in the Old Royal and King's Collections*, II (London, 1921), 135-136; see also Paris, *Historia*, I, xlviii-lii, and Vaughan, *Matthew Paris*, pp. 49-59.

[13] *Cambridge Antiquarian Communications*, III, 172.

[14] Page 290; see also *Historia*, I, xliv.

[15] He could have found such references in the *Historia*, I, 406; II, 387, 440; III, 6. Madden (*Historia*, I, xliii, n. 2) is quite certain that Bale never saw a copy of the *Chronica*; Poole (*Index*, p. 291, n. 7) is inclined to agree; cf. Davies, p. 212, who offers no support for his opinion that "Bale [in writing *King Johan*] got most of his facts from the *Chronica Majora* of Roger of Wendover and Matthew Paris."

[16] The entry as quoted is complete and was adopted by Paris from Roger of Wendover.

More revealing are the three accounts of a speech said to have been delivered by Archbishop Hubert on the occasion of John's coronation. The sermon puzzled many who were present, and the following quotations record Hubert's explanation of his behavior:

Catalogus (I, 239):

Et cum secretius fuisset interrogatus archiepiscopus, cur talem præmisset in eius coronatione sermonem: asserebat se certificatum fuisse coelesti oraculo, super multis quæ in ipso uentura sunt. . . . Hæc Matthæus Parisius, in 7 libro suorum chronicorum.

Chronica (II, 455):

Interrogatus autem postea archiepiscopus H[ubertus] quare hæc dixisset, respondit se præsaga mente conjecturare et quibusdam oraculis edoctum et certificatum fuisse, quod ipse Johannes regnum et coronam Angliæ foret aliquando corrupturus et in magnam confusionem præcipitaturus. Et ne haberet liberas habenas hoc faciendi, ipsum electione, non successione hæreditaria, sic tunc eligendum affirmavit.[17]

Historia (II, 81):

Postea vero interrogatus archiepiscopus secretius, quare talem præmiserit in coronatione sermonem, asserebat se certificatum fuisse cœlesti oraculo super multis, quæ de ipso rege fuerant ventura.

In regard to John's dealings with his nephew Arthur, all three accounts trace the events up through Arthur's imprisonment at Rouen and assert that his subsequent fate is unknown. Each one, however, records some speculation on the latter subject:

Catalogus (I, 248):

Matthaeus Parisius lib. 7. . . . Veruntamen ab aliquibus est dictum, quòd clàm euadere uolens, in Sequana submersus sit, nec postea inuentus: alijs affirmantibus, quòd præ cordis tristitia & rancore contabuerit. Franci uerò, quibus propter eorum odium non est adhibenda fides, asserunt ipsum præcepto regis Ioannis fuisse interemptum. Hæc addidi propter Polydorum Vergilium, qui . . . omnia mala in hunc bonum regem odiosissimè uertit.[18]

Chronica (II, 480):

. . . Arthurus subito evanuit, modo fere omnibus ignorato; utinam non ut fama refert invida.[19]

[17] This passage is not in Roger of Wendover.
[18] The reference to Polydore Vergil is, of course, Bale's addition.
[19] From *modo* on is Paris' addition; the remainder of the entry was taken from Roger of Wendover.

Historia (II, 95):

Verumtamen ab aliquibus dictum est, quod volens clam evadere, in Sequana submersus est, et sic periit non inventus; aliis affirmantibus, quod præ cordis rancore in accidiam decidens, contabuit in semetipso, et sic obiit. Franci vero, quibus propter hostilitatem plena fides non est adhibenda, asserunt ipsum manibus vel præcepto regis Johannis fuisse peremptum.

Although the *Historia* is in general less harsh than the *Chronica*, neither of Paris' histories is at all sympathetic toward King John. In the later work John is still depicted as a raging tyrant and a crafty hypocrite, even though some of the more devastating criticisms found in the *Chronica* are omitted.[20] The most favorable comment on John occurs in Paris' final summation, and even this is far from what Verity's citation would lead us to expect:

Cum autem regnasset rex Johannes annis xviii., mensibus v., dies autem iiii[or]., ab hac vita, post multas hujus seculi perturbationes et labores inutiles, in multa mentis amaritudine distractus transmigravit, nihil terrae, immo nec se ipsum, in pace possidens. Sperandum est autem et credendum confidenter, quod quædam bona opera, quae fecit in hac vita, allegabunt pro eo ante Summi Judicis tribunal.[21]

Nevertheless, it is easy to see why Bale was attracted to the work of Matthew Paris. Paris fearlessly attacked the depravity and immorality that prevailed among certain of the clergy—including the hierarchy, the pope, and on occasion prominent individuals at St. Albans.[22] It is

[20] See, e.g., *Historia*, II, 114: "Desævit itaque diatim cum incremento rex jam factus tirannus, non tantum in ecclesiasticas personas, sed etiam [in] suos naturales barones, milites, cives et burgenses, eosdem bonis suis multipliciter spoliando, zelotipando." Criticism in the same vein can also be found in III, 103 and 159. But the *Historia* omits the remarkable account (found only in the *Chronica*, II, 559-563) of John's plan to relinquish his kingdom to the emir of Morocco in exchange for the latter's protection. The story concludes with the following evaluation of John's character by Robert of London, one of the ambassadors sent to the emir: "Dixit igitur assertive, quod 'potius tirannus fuit quam rex, potius subversor quam gubernator, oppressor suorum et fautor alienorum, leo suis subjectis, agnus alienigenis et rebellibus; qui per desidiam suam Normanniæ ducatum et alias multas terras amiserat; et insuper Angliæ regnum amittere vel destruere sitiebat; pecuniæ extortor insatiabilis, possessionum suorum naturalium invasor et destructor; paucos vel potius nullos strenuos generavit, sed patrissantes. . . .'"

[21] *Historia*, II, 194. This is substantially unchanged from the *Chronica*, II, 668-669, except that the following verses, reported (though not endorsed) in the earlier work, are omitted: "Anglia sicut adhuc sordet fœtore Johannis, / Sordida fœdatur fœdante Johanne gehenna."

[22] See, e.g., *Historia*, II, 146-147, 154, 174.

for this reason that Bale valued the *Historia* so highly; as he told Archbishop Parker, "no chronycle paynteth out the bysshop of Rome in more lively colours, nor more lyvely declareth hys execrable procedynges, than it doth."[23] The sentiment (as well as the metaphor) appears again in the *Catalogus*, which includes a striking list of these "procedynges."[24] But the fact remains that Bale's citation of Matthew Paris in support of the historical thesis of *King Johan* is characteristically inappropriate.

[23] *Cambridge Antiquarian Communications*, III, 172-173.
[24] ". . . Romanorum pontificum auaritias, fraudes, mendacia, dolos, pompas, impudentias, tyrannides, blasphemias, & artes pessimas ita depinxit, ut nullus unquam Apelles melius" (I, 315).

APPENDIX C

(See note to line 2002)

In ADDITION to Collier's transcript of pages *1-*4 (see Introduction, p. 1), there is at the Huntington a second incomplete transcript of the *King Johan* manuscript. It is made up of eleven detached leaves, six of which contain the watermark "Simmons 1825," and presents a page-for-page copy of manuscript pages 26, 39-49, 52, all but the last fifteen lines of page 55, and pages 61-63. (Five leaves have writing on only one side.) The unknown transcriber's hand appears once in the manuscript itself: on page 42 (at l. 1844) he has added, in pencil, the accidentally omitted speech-prefix *Treason*.[1]

The quality of the transcription suggests the work of a somewhat careless amateur not altogether familiar with sixteenth-century handwriting. There is only one misreading (*charge* for *chaunce* in l. 1963), but there are numerous accidental omissions as well as seven blanks for words or letters which the transcriber was unable to decipher. None of these irregularities appears in Collier's Camden Society text.

In view of the transcriber's evident inability to read parts of his original, it is curious to find that he has recorded with no apparent difficulty the two words most seriously obscured by a blot near the top of page 46 (ll. 2004-05). For the first of these Collier was able to supply *yende*, but he left a blank in place of the other, adding a note on the blot and a conjectural *intende*. The transcriber, however, has copied *yende* and *myende* without comment. A close inspection of the manuscript places the first reading (*yende*) beyond any reasonable doubt and shows the transcriber's *myende* to be at least as plausible as Collier's *intende*. Under the circumstances it seems more than likely that the transcriber was himself responsible for the blot, having first copied the words in question and thus, ironically, preserving an authentic manuscript reading which he has almost put beyond recovery.

---

[1] Pafford and Greg are inclined to attribute this notation to Collier, but there can be no doubt that it is the transcriber's.

APPENDIX D

MANY of the technically "accidental" changes made by Bale in the scribal text reveal his interest in spelling—an interest also evident in the unusually consistent spelling in those passages entirely in his hand. This is not to say that Bale has altered scribal spellings with single-minded thoroughness. The scribal *ynglond*, for example, which occurs dozens of times (even excluding speech-prefixes), Bale has corrected in only eighteen instances, four times producing his own spelling *England*, twice simply changing *o* to *a*, and twelve times simply changing *y* to *E*. Nevertheless, it is clear that Bale has reviewed the scribal text with considerable attention to matters of spelling and that we have as a result a document of some linguistic interest. The following survey of orthographic alterations in the scribal text, although far from complete, will suggest some of the kinds of material for linguistic analysis that the manuscript affords.

VOWELS

1. There are some twenty-five examples of *-ond* altered to *-and*, as in *land* for *lond*, *stand* for *stond*, etc. All but a few are unmistakably authorial in origin. In Bale's writing the *-and* spelling is definitely the preferred one.

2. The negative prefix has been changed from *on-* to *vn-* in seven instances; the preposition *onto* has once been changed to *vnto*. Most of these alterations are certainly Bale's; his preferred spelling in the holograph section of the manuscript is *vn*.

3. Bale has occasionally added final *e* to a scribal form to indicate the length of a preceding vowel: e.g., *pryde, swyne, crowe, shewe, rewe* (twice), *made*, and (more unusually) *heate*. He has also added the final *e* in *cheryshe* (l. 170) and *confunde* (l. 491), evidently to emphasize the rhymes with *peryshe* and *grovnde*.

4. Bale has substituted *e* for *y* in some present indicative and past participle forms: e.g., *ableth* for *ablyth*, *cummeth* for *cummyth*, *exyled* for *exylyd*, *sacred* for *sacryd*. Other examples of authorial alteration of *y* to *e* appear in *ceremony* for *cerymony*, *lyneall* for *lynyall*, *exedyngly* for *exydyngly*, *breche* for *bryche*, and *desyre* for *dyssyre*.

5. There are seven instances of an original *be* 'by' altered to *by*. At least four of these are authorial; one (l. 800) was made by the scribe in revision. The *be* spelling may indicate an unstressed pronunciation.[1]

---

[1] See *OED, by*, and E. J. Dobson, *English Pronunciation, 1500-1700* (Oxford, 1957), II, 451.

The two changes of *mend* to *mynd*, both by Bale, may also reflect alternate pronunciations.

In a fair number of words an original *e* representing the vowel *ĭ* has been changed by Bale to *y*: e.g., *wedowe* to *wydowe*, *sleppe* to *slyppe* 'to slip,' *levynge* to *lyvynge*, *whech* to *whych* (twice), *rabel* to *rabyll*.

6. The majority of Bale's changes of scribal *e* to *a* occur in similar phonetic situations: e.g., *rayne* for *reyne* 'to reign,' *dysdayne* for *dysdeyne*, *saynt* for *seynt*, *playne* for *pleyne*, and perhaps *aganste* for *agenste* and *congregacyon* for *congregecyon*.[2]

7. Scribal *a* before *r* has been altered by Bale to *e* with some consistency: e.g., *answare* to *answere*, *harmytes* to *heremytes*, *clargy* to *clergy*.

CONSONANTS

1. Bale has frequently altered scribal forms to produce more or less "learned" spellings: e.g., *fawte* to *faulte*, *avance* to *advaunce*, *contemte* to *contempte*, *salme* to *psalme*. Perhaps the following changes (all by Bale) represent a similar obscuring of phonetic values: *owr* to *howr* 'hour,' *abyte* to *habyte*, *hole* to *whole*, *aborre* to *abhorre*, *goded* to *godhed*, *falsed* to *falshed*.

2. Bale's preference in the treatment of medial or initial [s] in some words of French origin is seen in the following *c* / *s* variants:

a) *c* altered to *s*: *falce* to *false* (four instances), *ypocracye* to *hypocrysye*, *cencerly* to *syncerly*, *cycell* to *Sycell* 'Sicily,' etc.

b) *s* altered to *c*: *sawse* to *sawce*, *prynse* to *prynce*, *presepptes* to *precepptes*, *syvyle* to *Cyvyle* (six instances), *sease* to *cease*, *serymonye* to *ceremonys* (two instances), etc.[3]

3. Bale has frequently doubled medial consonants, especially after *a*; the following examples illustrate the different phonetic situations in which the alteration occurs: *badde, canne, applye, dally, shappe* (rhymes with *happe*, altered from *hape*), *conquarre, pyggys, begynne, synne, somme* 'sum,' *sonne* 'son,' *ponnyshment, rottyn, grosse* 'to engross,' *thretten*.

Conversely, there are four cases in which a medial double consonant has been affected by deletion: *hosse* has been altered to *hose* 'stocking,' *losse* to *lose* 'to lose,' *talle* to *tale* 'a story,' and *pennalte* to *penalte*. All but the last of these changes definitely originate with Bale.

---

[2] The last of these is possibly a scribal correction.

[3] Cf. Bale's treatment of [ʃ] in words derived from the French: he has changed *sedysyon* to *sedycyon*, *condysyon* to *condycyon*, *marsyall* to *marcyall*, and *peryche* to *peryshe*. (The scribal spelling of the last of these is somewhat doubtful.)

4. Bale has three times modernized scribal *Davyth(s)* to *Davyd(s)* and frequently altered the scribal *heder* to *hyther* and *ferder* to *farther*.

Other of Bale's minor alterations—technically orthographic—include the expanding of scribal contractions, the deletion and addition of macrons (changing *-oun* to *-on* or *aun* to *an* and vice versa), the change of one form of a letter (such as *r*) to another, and the change of *y* to *i* (especially common in Latin words), and medial *v* to *u*. Some additional cases which might be considered orthographic (e.g., the frequent change of *nowther* to *noyther* or *neyther*) have been treated as substantive variants and included in the textual apparatus.